Why is Collective Bargaining Failing in South Africa?

First published in 2016

ISBN: 978-1-86922-629-9 (Printed)
ISBN: 978-1-86922-630-5 (ePDF)

Published by KR Publishing
P O Box 3954
Randburg
2125
Republic of South Africa

Tel: (011) 706-6009
Fax: (011) 706-1127
E-mail: orders@knowres.co.za
Website: www.kr.co.za

Printed and bound: HartWood Digital Printing, 243 Alexandra Avenue, Halfway House, Midrand
Typesetting, layout and design: Cia Joubert, cia@knowres.co.za
Cover design: Marlene de Villiers, marlene@knowres.co.za
Editing and proofreading: Valda Strauss, valda@global.co.za
Project management: Cia Joubert, cia@knowres.co.za

Why is Collective Bargaining Failing in South Africa?

A reflection on how to restore social dialogue in South Africa

Dr Geoffry Heald

kr
publishing

2016

Dedication

Glenn Smith of Connecticut won the 2015 Pulitzer Prize for Public Service Journalism. It is said of him, as it is of the journalistic profession, that he wrote the first draft of history.

I wish to dedicate this book to South Africa's intrepid journalists who too write the first draft of history.

I have enjoyed the privilege of learning from these talented voices during the course of writing this book. I have deep respect for their extraordinary intellectual, moral and physical courage in their pursuit of the truth. They offer deep wisdom about the reality of South African life, and their critique presents the hint of a better path into the future.

They often enter dangerous physical, intellectual and spiritual places to discover and tell the truth. We are deeply indebted to them. Their voices enter our conversations and their hard work is often used to make a better life for all.

The journalists whom I have cited include:

Chris Barron, *Business Times*
Stephen Bevan, *The Telegraph*
Stefaans Brummer, *Mail & Guardian*
Ilanit Chernick, *The Star*
Rod Cokayne, *The Star*
Anna Cox, *The Star*
Rebecca Davis, *Daily Maverick*
Deon de Lange, *Independent Newspapers*
Sibusiso Dludla, *Independent Newspapers*
Max du Preez, *Pretoria News*
Linda Ensor, *Business Day*
Sarah Evans, *Mail & Guardian*
Dineo Faku, *The Star Business Report*
Louise Ferreira, *Africa Check*
Ilse Fredericks, *The Star*
Paddy Harper, *City Press*
Ray Hartley, *Sunday Times*
Leanne Jansen, *The Star*
Luke Johnson, *Financial Times*
Michael Kahn, *Daily Maverick*
Wiseman Khuzwayo, *Sunday Times Business Report*

Mia Lindeque, *Eyewitness News*
Kgopi Mabotja, *Independent Newspapers*
Ntsakisi Magwanganyi, *Business Day*
Theto Mahlakoana, *The Star*
Solly Maphumulo, *The Sunday Independent*
Sipho Masondo, *City Press*
Craig McKune, *Mail & Guardian*
Vumani Mkhize, *Eyewitness News*
Siyabonga Mkhwanazi, *Saturday Star*
Sphumelele Mngoma, *News24 The Witness*
Phalane Motale, *Independent Online Business Report*
Amy Musgrave, *The Star*
Baldwin Ndaba, *Sunday Independent*
Phakamisa Ndzamela, *Business Day*
Bongani Nkosi, *Times Live*
Karabo Ngoepe, *Times Live*
Genevieve Quintal, *Times Live*
Khadija Patel, *Daily Maverick*
Carol Paton, *Business Day*
Sandiso Phaliso, *Independent On-Line News*
Verashni Pillay, *Mail & Guardian*
Piet Rampedi, *Sunday Times*
Athandiwe Saba, *City Press*
Sam Sole, *Mail & Guardian*
Ed Stoddard, *Reuters*
Lisa Steyn, *Mail & Guardian*
Steven Tau, *The Citizen*
Glynnis Underhill, *Mail & Guardian*
Paul Vecchiatto, *Mail & Guardian*
Francesca Villette, *The Star*
Mzlikazi Wa Afrika, *Sunday Times*
Adam Wakefield, *Times Live*
Govan Whittles, *Eyewitness News*

Finally, I wish to thank my excellent editors for their skill, patience and dedication. They include Jenny Croll, Ana Ferreira, Inés Ferreira and Cia Joubert. Wilhelm Crous offered wonderful support and was crucial to this project.

Contents

List of Figures

List of Tables

About the author

Dr Geoffry Heald is a senior lecturer in negotiation at the University of the Witwatersrand Graduate School of Business Administration (Wits Business School) in Johannesburg, South Africa. He has always been fascinated by the power of focused conversation and started his career in industrial relations negotiation with the emerging trade unions in the Eastern Cape during the various states of emergency in the 1980s. Geoffry negotiated out many recognition agreements with the emerging trade unions. These agreements shadow-danced the constitutional negotiations. It was in the Eastern Cape that he faced and learned about how to address deep-rooted conflict. He was invited to join Stellenbosch University Business School as a senior researcher and wrote a book for the Institute of Futures Research entitled: *The South African Trade Union Movement and its Possible Impact on Future Political Scenarios*. He subsequently conducted *An Analysis of the Viability of CODESA*, which correctly anticipated its breakdown.

Geoffry later joined Wits Business School and has become deeply engrossed in teaching commercial negotiation and deal making on both academic and executive education programmes. Geoffry has a PhD (Wits), LLM (Wits) and MBA (University of Stellenbosch). His doctorate was on *Learning Amongst Enemies: A Phenomenological Study of South Africa's Constitutional Negotiations from 1985-1998* and his LLM was on *South Africa's Voluntary Relinquishment of its Nuclear Arsenal and Accession to the Treaty on the Non-Proliferation of Nuclear Weapons in Terms of International Law*. In the course of the latter research he compared South Africa's nuclear relinquishment approach to the process that was chosen in Iraq in order to understand the extent to which the knowledge that was created on this matter was transferable to other countries.

Geoffry personally writes-up almost all the negotiation cases that he uses in teaching negotiation. Organisations typically approach Geoffry to share a negotiation challenge that requires a tailor-made solution. These deal-prototypes are designed to accurately simulate the actual negotiation scenarios and the decision-making that is required in real time to solve the problem. They are designed to elevate the performance of the negotiation teams to achieve the negotiation objective. These deal-prototypes enable negotiation teams to gain a deep understanding and mastery of the critical elements of their own transactions. Geoffry often uses a film crew to facilitate organisational memory and understanding of the deal.

Most recently, Geoffry has been working on creating an *African Negotiation Project* to be seated at the University of Witwatersrand in Johannesburg, South Africa. *The African Negotiation Project* entails creating a negotiation research, education, training, conferencing and consulting service for commercial, trade, legal, industrial relations and political negotiations across the continent of Africa. The *African Negotiation Project* will partner with other universities and business schools on the continent in order to build negotiation capacity, and provide advanced academic executive education and training to students and stakeholders across the continent.

Dr Geoffry Heald
Sketch by Adam Heald

Foreword by Liv Tørres, Nobel Peace Center

The right to organise and collective bargaining are fundamental human rights. Yet, collective bargaining is much more than a theoretical or legal concept. Collective bargaining, essentially, establishes a recognised system of jurisprudence with a set of agreed legitimate rules rather than arbitrary decision-making. It is a tool for interest justification as well as a platform for political development and mobilisation.

Millions of workers all over the world have improved their wages through collective bargaining. Millions of workers have seen reduced inequality due to collective bargaining. Millions of workers have seen their power increase vis-à-vis employers through the sheer strength of standing shoulder to shoulder with others when advancing their demands. And millions of workers have also learnt the power of decision-making, mandating and accountability through discussions and deliberations when deciding on demands and electing shop stewards to present them. Simultaneously, millions of employers have seen the value and strength of constructive collective bargaining in contributing to predictability in planning, to responsible business, to professional corporate endeavours and to increased productivity. And we have seen, amongst others from Tunisia, and reflected in the award of the 2015 Nobel Peace Prize, what immensely constructive political and societal value sound labour relations and negotiations hold for conflict resolution and peace in a broader perspective. Collective bargaining is immensely powerful when used correctly. When the players in the game understand the rules. Respect the game. And stick to the rules. But if those conditions are not met, it can also be a divisive and destructive device.

Historically, collective bargaining has deep roots in South Africa through the industrial bargaining council system. It has traditionally taken place at both plant level and industrial level. Through the years, millions of workers have improved their wages through the system. In the 80s, the bargaining system also provided important political impetus to the new trade union movement with several unions building up shop-floor power through demands for recognition agreements. Millions of black workers had their first meetings with democratic decision-making around bargaining at the workplace which, in turn, mobilised for broader political action. And at the central level, the networks and contacts built up by union and employer leaders on the basis of the bargaining system in turn provided a key basis for new institutions such as the National Economic Forum (NEF) and later the National Economic, Development and Labour Council (NEDLAC) et al, and also gave input into the political negotiations about a new democratic dispensation. Over the past decades, however, the collective bargaining system has changed considerably both in coverage, level, outreach and efficacy. Plant-level bargaining has been reduced. And bargaining no longer plays the same constructive role it used to play.

According to Geoffry Heald, the South African collective bargaining system requires a total overhaul. With long-lasting and staggering unemployment figures; world record levels of inequality; a struggling economy; and a huge need for education and training to adapt both individuals and country for the transition towards a more competitive global digitalised economy, the collective bargaining system is of crucial importance. With Heald´s solid background and vast experience in trade unionism, labour negotiations and conflict resolutions, he has unique insight and experience worth listening to.

Geoffry Heald's book on collective bargaining is an important book. The bargaining system is of critical importance in order to reduce inequality and create jobs. It is a key instrument in managing transitions and adapting to external shocks. And it is a crucial platform on which to build trade unionism and employers' associations democratically bottom-up. Yet, for the system of bargaining to work, South African employers and unions need level playing fields, trust and agreement about the rules of the game. Heald argues, however, that employers and unions have totally different understandings of the goals of the collective bargaining system. While employers perceive the purpose of the negotiation system as being to reach a fair deal on wages and working conditions, for unions the purpose is also to discover satisfiers for fundamental human needs. Collective bargaining is failing in South Africa because the mental models and worldviews that inform its practice are incongruent with the complexity and nature of the problems that it seeks to solve. In other words, both employers and unions are out of touch with reality, with each other and with what is happening in the townships and on the shop floor.

Heald calls for a major reshuffling of the whole legal, institutional and nature of collective bargaining. Whether we fully agree with his recipe or would like to add ingredients, his book should be read, his recommendations discussed and actions taken. Because establishing a sound system of dialogue and negotiations between the social partners is essential in order to turn South Africa around. It is urgent.

Liv Tørres, Nobel Peace Center
July 2016

Executive Summary

This book will be of interest to thought leaders, strategic planners, decision-makers, businessmen and -women, trade unionists, employees, investors, religious leaders, politicians, academics and students, as well as concerned South Africans from all walks of life who are seeking to make South Africa a better place in which to live. South Africa is in a very vulnerable position at the moment. Its currency is on the edge of junk bond status; according to Statistics South Africa, its structural unemployment among our youth is among the highest in the world; Bhorat and Tseng[1] confirm that it is the fifth highest industrial unrest-prone country in the world; De Visser and Powell[2] show that the country has an extremely high level and wide spread of service delivery and political conflicts; and the educational system is floundering, awash with school curricula that almost appear to be designed for the purpose of achieving youth unemployment. The accelerating encroachment of the Fourth Industrial Revolution, with its amplifying disruptive innovations that are digitally integrating technology with automation, means that those persons who are currently gainfully employed, cannot be assured that this presumption of job security will prevail into the future. It clearly would be futile to try and resist the coming automation of thousands of jobs. The central question is: how can we identify and mitigate the risks of these changes, over the longer term, by designing an educational system that places our youth on the right side of the Fourth Industrial Revolution?

Collective bargaining is conducted in a sclerotic and conflictive manner and it is imperative that new and pragmatic bottom-up ways of co-operation are discovered to reconcile the needs of the various parties. Employers will need to constantly retrain and update the knowledge and skill of their employees throughout their working lives because of the rapid obsolescence to which many jobs and careers will be subjected due to the digital revolution arising from increasing computerisation. Very large numbers of people will be compelled to follow a number of careers over the course of their lives because of the pending rapid obsolescence of a wide spectrum of current jobs.[3]

Collective bargaining is a very important mode of social dialogue. This book offers an extensive and considered critique of the current nature of collective bargaining in South Africa. Collective bargaining is failing because the parties to the process have not sought to seriously engage in a process of social dialogue that will lead to the discovery of satisfiers of fundamental human needs. Collective bargaining is failing in South Africa because the parties to the process have failed to seek ways of achieving inclusive social development and of balancing the requirements of a competitive economy, the imperative for employment creation and the achievement of an ecologically sustainable environment. This means that many of the inequalities in the labour market that were created by apartheid remain unaddressed. Had a meaningful social dialogue between business, trade unions and the state been conducted at a much deeper level of human interaction, and with a longer view, and had the parties agreed to let down their guards, co-operate and discard their obsolete conflictive and counter-productive modes of negotiation, they might have seriously and systematically started to develop a modus operandi to address the profound challenges that are confronting South Africa in the world of work. The parties to collective bargaining all know that they need desperately to co-operate, but their capacity to do so is severely constrained because of the normative ethos in which the process is conducted.

This book is intended to encourage the major stakeholders in the South African economy to undergo self-reflection and to consider whether the manner in which they are interacting with one another is contributing to the greater good or whether they are complicit in sustaining poverty, ignorance and polarisation.

Chapter 1, entitled 'Business as an Agency for Change in South Africa – the Contested Meaning and Purpose of Collective Bargaining', shows that collective bargaining is defined and understood differently by business, trade unions, employees and the state. These fundamental differences in the understanding of its meaning and purpose are the root cause of many of the breakdowns in collective bargaining. Employers and employees have different understandings of the meaning and purpose of collective bargaining. Employers regard the purpose of collective bargaining as being to reach a fair deal on wages and conditions of employment by means of the process of negotiation with a recognised and representative trade union. Employees' understandings of the meaning and purpose of collective bargaining are subtly different from those of employers. For the employee, the purpose of collective bargaining is to reach a fair deal on wages and conditions of employment *and* to discover satisfiers of fundamental human needs. The imperative to make use of the process of collective bargaining to discover satisfiers of fundamental human needs is usually unspoken, but the need to do so is evident in light of South Africa's high levels of violent unrest when collective bargaining breaks down.

Trade unions too have a subtly different understanding of the meaning and purpose of collective bargaining from the employees that they represent and from employers. For the trade unions the purpose of collective bargaining is to achieve a living wage. The employees' and trade unions' wage and conditions of employment aspirations may, or may not, correspond. Trade unions see the wage aspiration as both a practical and ideological issue. It is usually only when it is discovered, via the process of collective bargaining, that the business model cannot uphold the aspiration for an ideological living wage that employee expectations are dropped. Collective bargaining is also used by trade unionists to advance their own personal career ambitions at the expense of the needs of their members. Collective bargaining is used by trade unions to create pension and provident funds and institutional investment.

The collective bargaining process draws the trade unions into the centre of economic power in South Africa. The cumulative wage and conditions of employment agreements that are reached across South Africa by collective bargaining increases the leverage that trade unions have over the Tripartite Alliance. These wage agreements also strengthen the influence that the Tripartite Alliance has over business.

The state regards the trade union movement as a source of reliable voter support. Trade union membership is therefore regarded as a measurement of state legitimacy. For the state, the trade union movement is a source of assured political power implicitly based on the legitimacy accorded by virtue of its role in the redistribution of improved salaries, wages and terms and conditions of employment effected through the collective bargaining process. Collective bargaining is, for the state, an instrument of administrative law and it is used to apply a normative, regulatory and policy structure on the labour market. The state uses collective bargaining to extend centralised bargaining agreements to non-parties by decree.

Businesses have tended to have rather a narrow view of the role of the enterprise as an agency for change. They have historically regarded what happens beyond the factory gate in the lives of their employees as remaining outside of their managerial remit. This external environment in which the workers live has become increasingly complex and volatile over the years, and this complexity and volatility is flowing back into business, and therefore can no longer be ignored. Service delivery conflicts, xenophobic violence, political protest, consumer boycotts and other forms of civil disobedience that emanate from across the entire society are imposing themselves onto business with intensity. These divergent forms of protest are therefore increasingly becoming an aspect of collective bargaining. Mass retrenchments have a direct bearing on the level of crime and violence in the broader society and there is, no doubt, a systemic connection between the levels of violent crime that affect business and the decision to retrench employees.

The Solms-Delta case is presented as a positive example of how business can function as an agency for change. This case illustrates the preparedness of business leadership to have the courage to seek to discover satisfiers of fundamental human needs and the far-reaching benefits to all the stakeholders that arose from this approach. Human needs have a twofold nature. Human needs can be addressed as both causes of deprivation and as sources of potential.[4] Mark Solms applied this insight about human needs as both deprivation and as potential to a practical business model that is an exemplar of excellent industrial relations and an inspiring example of business as an agency for change in South Africa.

Chapter 2 investigates: Fundamental Human Needs as Both Deprivation and Potential. It uses research conducted by Max-Neef et al to provide a theoretical framework for persons who are involved in collective bargaining to discover satisfiers of fundamental human needs. Max-Neef and his colleagues categorised human needs, into two categories: existential needs and axiological needs. Existential needs are our needs of existence and include: Being, Having, Doing and Interacting. Axiological needs are needs of value and needs of value include: Subsistence, Protection, Affection, Understanding, Participation, Idleness, Creation, Identity and Freedom. The interaction between the existential needs and axiological needs leads to the discovery of satisfiers of human needs. These satisfiers of human needs are unique to a culture and rather analogous to a microclimate in the sense that each community discovers and is characterised by its own specific satisfiers. The satisfiers are therefore the product of the interaction between the existential and axiological needs and can be understood as the dependent variable. Max-Neef and his colleagues' research is of great potential value as it enables a structured and non-polarised exploration of transformation in South Africa.

In **Chapter 3**, entitled 'The Relevance of an Understanding of Normal and Deep-rooted Conflict to Collective Bargaining', it is asserted that collective bargaining is failing in South Africa because it is conducted without a practical and comprehensive theory of fundamental human needs that is sufficiently robust to meaningfully address the complex and harsh South African reality of mass unemployment and high politicisation.

This absence of a practical and comprehensive theory of human needs is accompanied by a similar absence of understanding and knowledge about the complex interrelationship between normal and deep-rooted conflict. Max-Neef and his colleagues (1989:26)[i] from the Dag Hammarskjöld Institute in Sweden developed a useful and far-sighted framework that might be employed to empower the parties to negotiation and their stakeholders to set about systematically discovering satisfiers of fundamental needs. In this way one might start to practically set about rolling back the elements of apartheid that remain in the labour market. Their frameworks help in clarifying the many intangible causes of deep-rooted conflict, which arise from needs such as deprivation, and also help in diagnosing needs as potential satisfiers of fundamental human needs, and thereby create an environment that is conducive to economic growth. There are many occasions when these satisfiers of fundamental human needs can be configured into a business model and monetised, and that might lead to the creation of material wealth. It follows that their theory of human needs can be used for both diagnosis and prognosis.

---

i   www.daghammasrkjold.se/wp-context/uploads/1989/05/89_1.pdf

The discovery of satisfiers of fundamental human needs should be understood in their interrelationship with normal and deep-rooted conflict. It is imperative to understand the nature of normal and deep-rooted conflicts that emerge during the process of collective bargaining, and how to address these different forms of conflict with appropriate levels of discretion. Many South Africans engage in collective bargaining without a deep and practical understanding of the nature of normal and deep-rooted conflict. It is argued that there is nothing as practical as a good theory. John Burton[5] viewed normal conflict as a distinctive type from deep-rooted conflict. Normal conflicts pertain to transitory desires and can be compromised. Deep-rooted conflict revolves around fundamental human needs that are enduring, cannot be compromised and will be pursued regardless of the consequences. In South Africa, it is imperative that we should seek to gain an understanding of what factors will trigger normal conflicts to escalate into deep-rooted conflict, and how we might de-escalate deep-rooted conflicts into processes that result in human development and growth. The application of dysfunctional satisfiers of human needs during the collective bargaining process often results in the escalation of normal conflict into intractable deep-rooted conflict.

In South Africa, as is the case with many countries around the world, there is a strong tendency to address matters simplistically and symptomatically rather than to address their root causes. This often results in very bad policy decisions being implemented that are contrary to the interests of all the key stakeholders in society. It was in order to avoid the pitfall of addressing symptoms instead of causes that Argyris (1990) developed the notions of single- and double-loop learning. Single-loop learning is learning that addresses the symptomatic problems. Double-loop learning seeks to discover solutions to the fundamental root causes of the underlying problems. Collective bargaining is typically conducted in South Africa as a single-loop learning process on deeply complex matters that require double-loop learning interventions if they are ever to be effectively addressed. The Brexit referendum in the United Kingdom that is leading to Great Britain's withdrawal from the European Union can be understood as being the imposition of a simplistic single-loop learning process on an intensely complex matter requiring the deepest wisdom and double-loop learning. De Visser and Powell[6] conducted research on the causes of service delivery conflicts in South Africa. It is interesting to note that many of the causes of these are also the selfsame triggers of strikes, and they both pertain to the failure to discover satisfiers of fundamental human needs. Collective bargaining is failing in South Africa because the mental models and worldviews that inform its practice are incongruent with the complexity and nature of the problems that it seeks to solve.

Chapter 4 explores 'The Disjuncture between Employment Creation and Collective Bargaining in the Fourth Industrial Revolution' by investigating the foreseeable impact that the Fourth Industrial Revolution might have on collective bargaining in South Africa. According to Schwab and Samans,[7] the Fourth Industrial Revolution, in which we are currently immersed, involves an integration of dramatic advances in integrated technologies including: automation, robotics, artificial intelligence, machine learning (which will anticipate the satisfaction of certain human needs), crowd platforms, cloud learning and information capacity, Massive Open Online Courses (MOOCs), drones, the internet of small things, 3D printing, clever software, crypto-currencies and block chain technology, genetics, artificial intelligence, self-healing materials with microvascular networks, nanotechnology, biotechnology and other forms of computerisation, including new innovative applications of web-based services "that are building up and amplifying each other… [and] blurring the lines between the physical, digital and biological spheres". The phrase "amplifying each other" is key because these changes are currently in a process of escalation, creating a perfect employment/unemployment storm, not only in South Africa, but across the globe as well. These integrated technologies and scientific advances are changing the entire nature of work and have rapidly and continuously led to the creation of new types of business models that are rendering many current business models and commercial legal arrangements entirely obsolete. When a business model fails because of disruptive innovation, the entire skills set upon which that obsolete business model is based usually becomes redundant as well. It follows that the trade unions' service offerings to its members, which are systemically connected to the business model, also become redundant. It further follows that collective bargaining needs to develop a feedback loop to 'talk to the business models' if the process is to be responsive to disruptive innovation. At present, the feedback loop between business models and collective bargaining is very crude and inflexible. The feedback loop is implicitly measured in business closures, retrenchments, redundancies, non-investments when the economy is going badly, and in start-ups, employment creation and investment when the economy is growing. The ideological narrative that is presented by trade unionists to explain the world of work is largely based on the critique of the many different forms of exploitation that accompanied the First and Second Industrial Revolutions which led to the mass production processes of the 19th and 20th centuries that was subsequently exported across the world. A new critique of the world of work that is fundamentally different from the critique of neo-liberalism will need to be devised to evaluate the lived experience of the Fourth Industrial Revolution. It is anticipated that it will emerge as the reality of the impact of the Fourth Industrial Revolution becomes increasingly evident to all.

The entire gamut of industrial relations and employment relations as we know them will have to be addressed completely afresh. This is not merely a South African issue. It is a global issue as well.

Most South Africans are steadily gaining access to multimedia through their ownership of cellular telephones and computers, and their access to other multimedia platforms. There has been a basic change in the way that we communicate and negotiate with one another over the past decade due to innovations in multimedia. Multimedia is now increasingly being used across the spectrum of activities that underpin collective bargaining. It will render traditional union mandating processes associated with town hall crowds and mass meetings increasingly redundant.

South Africa's key economic and development challenges will be to create massive labour market absorption into the new economy arising from the employment tsunami of the Fourth Industrial Revolution. The Fourth Industrial Revolution demands that the quality of conversation between trade unions and business is elevated during the process of collective bargaining in order to meaningfully address the ongoing challenges that are confronting the future of employment. It is imperative that high-quality co-operative communication between the parties becomes the norm.

Chapter 5 is devoted to an investigation of 'Strikes, Rolling Mass Action and Civil Conflicts as Indicators of South Africa's Unrest Proneness'. Are these various forms of conflict and protest actually so different that they can be deemed to be conflicts of a different species? Are they perhaps telling us the same story in different guises? The Western Cape farm workers' strike of 2012 defied the International Labour Office's (ILO) Laborsta Data Base's[8] definition of a worker and a strike. The employers in this case were the farmers who owned the farms where the strikes and unrest usually took place. The unemployed in this province engaged in a strike, and acted in solidarity with the employed against the owners of the farms. Many persons who could be defined as non-employees – the unemployed or the underemployed – participated in industrial action against the farmers. The farm workers and the unemployed also pursued grievances against the political authority of the state. The farm workers and unemployed were therefore striking against a non-employer (the state) as well. This pattern of the unemployed or non-employees acting in solidarity with the employed is common in South Africa. The term 'workers' is constrained and implies that a strike exists if there is an employment contract between employer and employee. This is a narrow definition. There are many cases in South Africa where non-employees have been intrinsic to strike action and the industrial action has not been directed against an employer, as is the case with sympathy strikes and conflicts.

Extraordinarily high levels of conflict of different types characterise the day-to-day lived experience of ordinary South Africans. There is a plethora of different forms of industrial, civil unrest, political and criminal conflict that combine into waves of protest, often having similar root causes. In South Africa, strikes are energised by the same dynamics that cause service delivery conflicts, political conflicts, student fee protests, Zama Zama conflicts, gang warfare and xenophobic violence. These other forms of social conflict are not discrete from strikes and have overlapping basic root causes, including the failure to discover satisfiers of fundamental human needs in terms of which many and different forms of poverty manifest themselves.

The Marikana Massacre is emblematic of many other conflicts in South Africa. Bell explains: "The first executions saw 10 persons killed.[9] A few days later on the 16 August 2012 a further 34 miners were shot, bringing the total number of deaths to 44 killed." Bell reflects that the Marikana Massacre "is merely the most brutal, and most obvious of thousands of unrest incidents around the country.[10] We have them almost on a daily basis. There are illegal marches, burning barricades and stoning of ANC councillors' residences."

The destructive attribution of blame to the other is characteristic of the hectoring culture in which collective bargaining is conducted in South Africa. Collective bargaining is failing in South Africa because it is locked into a win-lose retributive mental model characterised by mistrust and attempts to blame the negotiation counterparts. It is also failing because of a stakeholder conflict in worldviews that subscribe to a First and Second Industrial Revolution for diagnoses of the causes of labour conflict versus a Fourth Industrial Revolution diagnosis of the future of employment, and vice versa.

This hectoring culture of collective bargaining is seen in many other areas of society as well. The intensity of South Africa's proliferating socio-political conflicts is illustrated by the fact that the country underwent 3 000 protests over a period of 90 days in 2014.[11] An average of 30 political, industrial and service delivery conflicts took place per day and involved more than 1 000 000 (one million) people. This equates to approximately 4 000 000 (four million) people over the year.

Chapter 6, entitled 'Stakeholder Fragmentation and Collective Bargaining in South Africa – the Interaction of Pathologies of Conflict and Poverty', seeks to understand the emerging patterns of Stakeholder Fragmentation and Collective Bargaining in South Africa. It analyses these drivers of pathologies of conflict and poverty. Gordon, Roberts and Struwig[12] measured the trust that South Africans have in trade unions and other institutions including churches, the SABC, national government, traditional leaders, local government, trade unions and politicians. They found that there has been a precipitous decline of trust in the South African trade union movement by nationally representative samples of ordinary South Africans. These authors point out that "Trade unions in South Africa, many established during the political struggle for democracy, have long claimed to represent the entire working class and not just their own members." This claim is now palpably false. Gordon et al.[13] state that "Trade unions stood out among other institutions showing a significant fall in confidence. In 2011 43% of South Africans indicated that they trusted trade unions, falling to 29% in 2012." This chapter is approached as an environmental scan based on current media and literature that is subjected to a content analysis. It endeavours to offer a systems configuration of the causes of fragmentation between nine different stakeholder groupings and reveals their impact on the collective bargaining interface.

The nine themes that are explored in this stakeholder analysis are:

1. Corruption and Financial Incompetence – Unions v Employee Members and Employee Members v Financial Advisers – Stakeholders Without a Stake
2. South African Democratic Teachers Union (SADTU) v The Ministry of Basic Education
3. Disruptive Innovation in Protest Movements – University Student Protests #FeesMustFall
4. Interaction Between the Employed, the Unemployed and the Tripartite Alliance
5. Social Grants
6. Police
7. Unprotected Strikes, Vigilante Action, Xenophobic Attacks on Foreign Businesses and Nationals, and Zama Zamas
8. Loan Sharks as Predators on the Poor
9. The Incremental Erosion of the Social Compact in South Africa since 1994.

Xenophobic attacks on foreign nationals and the looting of their businesses is a form of economic vigilantism. Xenophobic attacks, unprotected strikes, vigilantism and illegal Zama Zama mining all involve taking the law into one's own hands, 'self-help' and a deliberate decision to disregard South Africa's constitutional framework. Similar root causes drive unprotected strikes, vigilante violence and Zama Zama mining in South Africa.

Chapter 7 explores the matter of 'Collective Bargaining on Dysfunctional Premises'. The rationale for extending collective bargaining agreements to non-parties is that it allocates terms and conditions of employment to the greatest number of people ostensibly for the greater good. This process of extension of agreements to non-parties has been conducted without any feedback loop with the underlying business models of the individual enterprises that are impacted by these edicts. Collective bargaining in South Africa is all too frequently conducted on flawed economic and financial assumptions. Johnson[14] points out that South Africa's unit labour costs increased exponentially between 2007 and 2013 by 60%. These centralised agreements are extended without consideration of productivity and this has contributed to the shrinkage of the contribution of the manufacturing sector from 23-24% in 1994 to 11.1% in 2014. This has resulted in large-scale retrenchments in small, medium and micro enterprises (SMME's). The wage levels that have been accorded from collective bargaining have often been completely unsustainable. This has rendered South Africa's manufacturing sector profoundly uncompetitive in international markets.

Osterwalder and Pigneur[15] show that business models are not simply interchangeable from one business to the next. Customer relationships in one business will take on different nuances and require different work from labour in the next, and the employment contracts will therefore differ. The channels and supply chains that are required to service the customer will be unique to the geography, technology and type of business. The cost structure of businesses in identical economic sectors will vary considerably, depending on taxation regimes, accounting practices, the mix of factors of production, market factors, availability of natural resources, cost of energy, regulatory regime and quality of labour, to mention but a few. For some businesses, labour is a critical resource that cannot be dispensed with; while for others in the same economic sector, it can be displaced by capital technology. The key activities that are required to support a business model therefore will vary according to how the value proposition is understood and implemented.

The presumption that all businesses in the same economic sector have the same business models is wrong and dangerous. Collective bargaining in South Africa has failed in many important cases to be sensitive to the differential spread and variety of business models. This means that collective bargaining, as it is conducted in South Africa, is unresponsive to the specificity of business models and it is not connected with an adaptive feedback loop to the business models. The collapse of the clothing, leather and furniture sectors in South Africa can be attributed in large part to this insensitivity and lack of responsiveness. The sensitivity and responsiveness of extending centralised collective bargaining agreements by ministerial decree to non-parties needs to be assessed in this light. Collective bargaining is thus failing because it is conducted without sensitivity to the requirements of the individual enterprise's business model. The foreseeable consequence is that the business will fail and the workers will be left unemployed. This inflexibility has a negative impact on economic growth and employment.

During the process of collective bargaining, in South Africa, the strategic outlook for the sector, enterprise, or business is typically presented *after* the receipt of the wage and conditions of service demands have been submitted and received from the trade union. The wage, salary and conditions of service demands are therefore not thoroughly grounded in economic and financial reality. We therefore follow the opposite negotiation sequence to that which is wisely chosen by the Germans.

In South Africa we thus enter into the collective bargaining process with the implicit presumption that wages, salaries and conditions of service are more important than the economic and financial conditions in the sector, enterprise or business. The business model that underpins the enterprise is almost ignored. The trade unions' lists of demands are usually not taken up by the business but they keep quiet about this for the moment because both parties have acquiesced to the collective bargaining sequence. The starting point for collective bargaining in South Africa is therefore a lack of consensus between business and labour on the financial, economic and strategic outlook for the enterprise. Furthermore, the wage demands and terms and conditions of employment requirements are spurious because they are not based on the business model. These fundamental and divergent presumptions about the process of collective bargaining result in inevitable conflict. The collective bargaining negotiations in South Africa traditionally begin with the trade union presenting claims that are not linked to the business model or the economic and financial strategic outlook for the sector, enterprise or business. When, during the course of collective bargaining, the hard reality of the actual constraints on the business model and economic and financial circumstances are finally realised by the workers as an inevitable truth, this realisation is often accompanied by deep disappointment and the evaporation of hope, leading to the declaration of disputes and needless cycles of conflict.

Schwab and Samans[16] noted that there is a powerful international trend across all industries towards flexible work and atypical employment. The Congress of South African Trade Unions (COSATU) (2012) rejects flexible work, atypical employment and labour brokers out of hand. It has sought to achieve a complete ban on labour brokers because they encourage the process of atypical employment which, in COSATU's view, results in exploitation. During November 2015, COSATU passed a resolution at its annual conference and announced a total ban on labour brokers. The Labour Relations Act and Basic Conditions of Employment Act were amended to provide additional security for temporary employees by legislating their permanency after a period of three months. These amendments to the Labour Relations Act were compliant with COSATU's search for a ban on labour broking and atypical employment. The purpose of the amendments was to both compel and impel employers to hire temporary employees and convert them into permanent employees after they had been employed by an enterprise for a period of three months, under the same terms and conditions of employment as those that had been previously accorded to those presently employed in a permanent capacity.[17]

Barron[18] cites the director of the Commission for Conciliation, Mediation and Arbitration (CCMA), Cameron Moranje, as asserting that retrenchments in business arising from the ban of temporary work in 2016 were being processed at a rate of

687 per day. This daily number of retrenchments approximates about 250 000 retrenchments per annum. The Labour Relations Act 66 of 1995 is predicated on the presumption of the emergence of inevitable conflict at the workplace. This is a dysfunctional premise that has embedded itself into almost all aspects of collective bargaining, and into much of the conduct of political and commercial negotiation as well. This legislated presumption of inevitable conflict creates a self-fulfilling prophecy of perpetual conflict. South African labour legislation, with its bias towards inevitable conflict, provides an assurance that matters that should ordinarily be addressed in a spirit of co-operation, collaboration and wise analytical problem solving are all too often approached divisively in a climate of conflict. Collective bargaining is failing because bigger-picture thinking about discovering solutions to fundamental human needs is actually discouraged by the energy-sapping pre-eminence of inevitable conflict.

The International Monetary Fund (IMF) and international rating agencies have noted with alarm the rigidity of the labour market and have called for far more flexibility from South African policy makers.[19] Collective bargaining in South Africa is inordinately conflictive and this conflict discourages foreign direct investment. The normative structure that guides collective bargaining in this country is the presumption of inevitable conflict. This creates a self-fulfilling prophecy of inevitable conflict, and rejects notions of co-operation, collaboration, joint problem solving and analytical problem solving. This severely dysfunctional process of collective bargaining is part of the legacy of apartheid where the once-successful methods of rolling mass action and conflict have become obsolete and their now inappropriate use is destroying new opportunities for growth and development. Old habits die hard.

The public sector has achieved the highest salaries and wages in the country which are now 43.6% higher than private sector earnings.[20] These public sector salaries are of course paid by private sector taxes and are granted without an effective feedback loop between the Independent Commission for the Remuneration of Public Officer Bearers and the public sector trade unions. Indeed one could argue that lobbying and advocacy have displaced collective bargaining as the principal means of reaching consensus on wages and terms and conditions of employment. Collective bargaining has therefore now failed in the sense that unjustifiable remuneration is paid to civil servants who are all too often grossly inefficient and ineffective, as testified by the never-ending service delivery conflicts that take place across South Africa on an almost daily basis.

Chapter 8 offers a series of conclusions and recommendations.

List of Abbreviations

AMCU	Association of Mineworkers and Construction Workers Union
ANA	Annual National Assessments (of school readiness)
ANC	African National Congress
BCEA	Basic Conditions of Employment Act 75 of 1997 as Amended by Basic Conditions of Employment Act, No 11 of 2002
BEE	Black Economic Empowerment
CBM	Consultative Business Movement
CCMA	Commission for Conciliation, Mediation and Arbitration
COSATU	Congress of South African Trade Unions
DA	Democratic Alliance
DEMAWUSA	Democratic Municipal and Allied Workers Union of South Africa
DSTV	Digital Satellite Television
FSB	Financial Services Board
GEAR	Growth, Employment and Redistribution
ILO	International Labour Office
IMF	International Monetary Fund
LRA	Labour Relations Act (LRA) Act 66 of 1995
MATUSA	Municipal and Allied Trade Union of South Africa
MOOCs	Massive Open Online Courses
NDP	National Development Plan
NEC	National Executive Committee
NEHAWU	National Education Health and Allied Workers Union
NUM	National Union of Mineworkers
NUMSA	National Union of Metal Workers of South Africa
PIC	Public Investment Corporation
POPCRU	Police and Prisons Civil Rights Union
RMI	Retail Motor Industries Organisation
SABC	South African Broadcasting Corporation
SACCAWU	South African Commercial, Catering and Allied Workers Union
SACP	South African Communist Party

SACTWU	Southern African Clothing and Textile Workers Union
SADTU	South African Democratic Teachers Union
SAMWU	South African Municipal Workers Union
SEIFSA	Steel and Engineering Industries Federation of South Africa
SME	Small and medium sized enterprises
SMME	Small, medium and micro enterprises
UDF	United Democratic Front
ZHC	Zero Hour Contracts
#FeesMustFall	Twitter description of the student protest movement started at the University of the Witwatersrand that had as its objective the cancellation of the annual increase in student fees
#RhodesMustFall	Twitter description of the student protest movement that started at the University of Cape Town that had as its objective the exorcising of colonial legacy

1

Business as an Agency for Change in South Africa – the Contested Meaning and Purpose of Collective Bargaining

For most South African employers the purpose of collective bargaining is to enter into negotiations, at agreed-upon time intervals, with a sufficiently representative and recognised trade union, on wages and terms and conditions of employment, with the objective of reaching a fair deal based on the employees' contribution to improving the productivity and profitability of the enterprise. The employer understands that the purpose of the collective bargaining process is to reach an agreement on the minimum wages and terms and conditions of employment that are offered at the enterprise *or* to reach an agreement on the actual wages and terms of conditions of employment, as the case might be. Employers, therefore, generally regard collective bargaining as pertaining to the negotiation process that seeks to achieve consensus on working conditions.

The employees' requirement and expectation of collective bargaining is that its purpose is to reach a fair deal on the minimum or actual wages and terms and conditions of employment, as the case might be, at an enterprise *that will lead to the satisfaction of fundamental human needs*. The employee therefore regards collective bargaining as having two purposes. The first purpose of collective bargaining is that it should create monetary value for the trade union members, and pertains to working conditions and wages and conditions of employment. This purpose, therefore, is congruent with the employers' understanding of the objective of collective bargaining. The employees' second purpose of collective bargaining goes further than negotiations to achieve consensus on wages and conditions of employment. The goal here is to engage in a negotiation process that seeks to achieve satisfiers of fundamental human needs, and therefore to improve living conditions. This latter employee aspiration is usually an unstated and implicit objective which always seeks a human development outcome. It is to extract oneself from being entrapped in a labour market that closely resembles that of apartheid.

The importance and, indeed, centrality of the *satisfaction of fundamental human needs* becomes evident when there are breakdowns in the collective bargaining process. The employees' developmental requirement and expectation of collective bargaining is most often understated or unstated. It is clear that the employer and employee definitions of the basic purpose of collective bargaining are different and do not align. The employer defines the purpose of collective bargaining in almost purely monetary terms that will lead to an agreement on working conditions. For the employee, collective bargaining involves both a monetary and a developmental purpose that will lead to the discovery of satisfiers of fundamental human needs as they pertain to working and living conditions. The employers' approach towards collective bargaining is thus predominantly quantitative, while the employees' approach is both quantitative *and* qualitative.

Employees often do not clearly express their fundamental human needs. This is unsurprising because very few people actually have clarity as to what their fundamental human needs are. They do understand their fundamental human needs intuitively, though, as an emotional truth. This emotional truth about their fundamental human needs often becomes evident when these needs are frustrated, or there are crises. When employees do eventually have occasion to express their fundamental human needs they are often vented with such emotional intensity that employers are overwhelmed by their fury. Employers therefore often choose to disregard these expressions of distress and frustration as falling completely outside of the remit of collective bargaining, thereby leaving these fundamental needs unaddressed and festering.

There is much practical evidence indicating that when a strike converts into a deep-rooted conflict, this deep-rooted conflict revolves around the failure to solve, or the process of ignoring, fundamental human needs. When the employers and trade unions ignore or fail to solve fundamental human needs, employees experience feelings of powerlessness. They often feel compelled to accept tremendous sacrifices at great human cost, and prepare themselves for a strike or showdown to compensate for these feelings of disempowerment.

Trade unions have a subtly different understanding of the meaning and purpose of collective bargaining from the employees whom they represent. For the trade unions, the purpose of collective bargaining is to achieve a living wage. For them the living wage is both a practical and ideological aspiration. It is usually only when it is discovered, via the process of collective bargaining, that the business model cannot uphold the aspiration for a living wage that expectations are dropped. Trade unionism is used as a career path for officials to gain employment and advance their careers in politics, state enterprises and business. Collective bargaining is therefore used by the trade unionists to advance their personal career ambitions. Employees are increasingly complaining that their trade union representatives' personal ambitions are often pursued at the expense of their needs. Collective bargaining is also used to create pension and provident funds and institutional investment.

The collective bargaining process draws the trade unions into the centre of economic power in South Africa. The accumulative wage and conditions of employment agreements that are reached across South Africa by collective bargaining increase the leverage that trade unions have over the Tripartite Alliance and business.

These wage agreements also increase the influence that the Tripartite Alliance has over business. The ANC regards the trade union movement as a source of reliable voter support. The trade union movement is therefore a source of assured political power, implicitly based on the legitimacy accorded by virtue of its role in the redistribution of improved salaries, wages and terms and conditions of employment that are based on the collective bargaining process. For the state, collective bargaining can be understood as an instrument of administrative law and it is used to apply a normative, regulatory and policy structure. The state uses collective bargaining to extend centralised bargaining agreements to non-parties by decree. Soko and Balchin[21] asserted that:

> The government's decision-making and labour market policies remain heavily influenced by the views of trade unions – particularly COSATU – and those of big business; to the detriment of medium sized and small businesses. The South African Minister of Labour has floundered and the African National Congress has said different things to different stakeholders, attempting to please everyone but doing little to chart a way forward out of the crisis. The government has publicly committed to implementing the National Development Plan (which means among other things, improving the social wage and growing jobs by cutting the cost and complexity of doing business) but has pushed through labour law amendments that will – in terms of its own impact policy assessment – have the opposite effect.

The state, together with the trade union movement, also uses the process of collective bargaining to define the normative, regulatory and policy structure of industrial relations in many ways. For example, severe legislative restrictions were applied to outsourcing of labour to labour brokers that granted business a period of three months to change the status of temporary employees into permanent employees. The government therefore uses collective bargaining as a mechanism to give life to the Constitution, the Labour Relations Act, the Basic Conditions of Employment Act, and all associated labour legislation as they pertain to the world of work. It will be shown that this process is often conducted in a crassly insensitive manner, resulting in damage to all the actors and a failure to achieve the intended objectives.

1.1 The Solms-Delta Wine Estate Case – Business as an Agency for Discovering Satisfiers of Fundamental Human Needs

The Solms-Delta wine farm in Franschoek in the Western Cape provides an excellent, but isolated, case of how an employer might successfully use business as a constructive agency for social change. Mark Solms founded the Solms-Delta wine estate and came to grips with the challenge of reaching an effective and sustainable covenant to find satisfiers of both minimum wages and fundamental human needs simultaneously. For him there was no artificial boundary between work, family and community. They formed an integrated whole. Solms found that the psychological relations that existed among labour and management at the farm when he purchased it were pathologically dysfunctional. When Mark Solms first engaged with his employees and sought to discover satisfiers of fundamental human needs, both the farm workers and also the local farmers in the community regarded his motives with deep suspicion. The local farmers thought that Solms' search for a sustainable covenant with labour was naïve at best, that it was financially ill-conceived, left field, courting ruin and created a dangerous precedent in employee relationships for the agricultural community as a whole.

The perception among the farm workers was similarly one of mistrust in the face of the centuries-old history of broken promises, abuse, disrespect and unfairness to which generation upon generation of farming relationships in the area have been subjected. The initially negative perception of Mark Solms' attempt to create an enabling environment and to discover satisfiers of fundamental human needs has since been completely reversed. He is now regarded as a path-breaker. There is complete buy-in from his workers, and considerable emulation from local farmers, who are now seeking to discover their own sustainable business models based on achieving satisfiers of fundamental needs themselves.

During the 2012 Western Cape farm strikes which covered much of the Boland with violence and conflict, the Solms-Delta wine estate remained peaceful in this midst of the mayhem. The reason for this harmony was because a great deal of hard work and wise consideration had been devoted over the years to ensuring that human relationships were sustainable, purposeful, harmonious and profitable. They therefore focused on simultaneously developing a viable business model and addressing the imperative to discover appropriate satisfiers of fundamental human needs. When Mark Solms purchased the farm in 2001 he was immediately struck by the apathy of the workers; their cynicism about any proactive gesture that was made, even when it was to their benefit; the pathological alcoholism and their general spirit of demotivation. Mark Solms is a world-renowned neuropsychologist. He diagnosed that the problem was a deep-seated trans-generational social psychological problem and that if it were not addressed at its root causes, it would threaten the viability of the wine estate. The moral hazard was a sufficient risk, with the potential to convert into a political risk that might possibly cause the business to fail. It is contended that this diagnosis is generally applicable to many businesses in South Africa. Solms proactively sought to mitigate the moral hazard–political risk. His first step was to commission an historian from the University of Cape Town to conduct a research project that involved studying all the relevant court records, public records and documents in the archives of Franschoek and the Cape over the previous few hundred years in order to achieve a deep understanding of the lived historical experience of farm labour. His premise was that this lived historical experience of the farm labourer would explain the present pathological relationships, and once these root causes of risk were understood, they could be systematically addressed and mitigated.

He found that the forefathers of many of the labourers who worked on the farm had been slaves. There was a public history of rape, abuse, floggings and betrayal that had become imprinted into their psyches over the centuries. He accordingly arranged that a museum of this private suffering would be created as part of their offerings to the public. Rather than conceal it, he decided to reveal to the world at large the truth of this suffering, as part of the narrative of their Solms-Delta wine of origin. This would ensure that there would be no hiding from history. This was also an astute business move because the story of the suffering of the labour became part of their marketing narrative that differentiated Solms-Delta from other wine estates in South Africa and around the world. Underhill[22] informed that upon purchasing the farm in 2001, Solms entered into a partnership with Richard Aster who owned a neighbouring farm. They used both of their farms as collateral to purchase a third farm for their workers. The employees' farm was called 'New Beginnings'. The three farms were placed into an estate to create Solms-Delta, and a trust was accordingly formed to regulate the agreement. Mark Solms, Richard Aster and the farm workers each were accorded a one-third share of the combined estate. They thus incurred a third share of the profits, and also carry the downside of risk in equal proportions. There were many teething problems that needed to be addressed when they decided to follow the path of discovering satisfiers of fundamental human needs. Underhill cited a farm worker employed at Solms-Delta as reflecting: "Alcoholism does not come from nowhere. It is part of the tragic history that we are still living with. Why would anyone want to obliterate their consciousness?"[23]

All the employees are now stakeholders and when there are problems these are quietly discussed. Underhill quotes this farm worker as reflecting that: "We decide what we want. Houses were built for us; we get medical aid, schooling for our children, a crèche, and DSTV. Salaries are an average of R100 a day and all workers have a giant share in the business. Drinking is no longer prevalent and there is a resident social worker to deal with problems. The farmers and the workers deal with problems by talking and solving problems in a relaxed way. There are multiple ways of trying to improve the quality of lives of people that work for you."[24]

The Solms-Delta case is an excellent example of the search for a viable grass-roots, bottom-up, Black Economic Empowerment (BEE) arrangement. It is a simple and obvious arrangement and is similar in its business model to an agricultural kibbutz in the Israeli tradition. This positive community orientation provides an invaluable developmental resource, and this structure leads to the satisfaction of fundamental human needs. The society was severely damaged by neglect, apartheid, slavery, non-investment and marginalisation over generations, and it is now being healed as a community. The manner in which societies fail to discover satisfiers of fundamental needs will determine the nature of their impoverishment. It is therefore imperative that negotiators should have a deep understanding of the historical precedents as these will shed light on current patterns of behaviour. It is significant that Mark Solms appointed a social worker in a leadership position. The social worker's task was clearly to assist in identifying these satisfiers of fundamental needs and translating them into reality by addressing them in a sensible way. Solms regarded these fundamental human needs as comprising both deprivation and potential, and on the basis of this insight, he developed a viable business model that synthesised both of these.

The Solms-Delta prototype of discovering satisfiers of fundamental human needs may be replicable and transferable. It could prove to be a viable model for negotiations between employers and labour in other areas of the agricultural sector. In addition, it might be adapted to education, apprenticeships, training, health, welfare, game parks, the military, fishing, the natural environment, arts and drama, to name but a few sectors of possible congeniality. Wise and far-sighted leadership will be essential if such interventions are to succeed. It would probably be more difficult to align the Solms-Delta prototype with business models in manufacturing, mining, retail, finance and enterprises that are on the cusp of the Fourth Industrial Revolution. But with creativity, and by dealing with each case on its own unique merits, it may be possible to achieve varying degrees of success.

2

Fundamental Human Needs as Both Deprivation and Potential, and Collective Bargaining

All too frequently collective bargaining is undertaken without the parties having a coherent theory of fundamental human needs. The Solms-Delta case illustrates that there is nothing as practical as a good theory. The method and theory in terms of which satisfiers were uncovered for the specific articulation of fundamental human needs at Solms-Delta is entirely congruent with the ground-breaking theory of Max-Neef et al.[25] from the Dag Hammarskjöld Institute. This theory has been widely applied in many countries around the world, including in Latin America, with the intention of satisfying fundamental human needs and of achieving human scale development.

Max-Neef et al.[26] characterise this uniquely dualistic nature of human needs thus:

> The very essence of human beings is expressed palpably through needs in their twofold character: as deprivation and as potential. Understood as much more than survival, needs bring out the constant tension between deprivation and potential, which is so peculiar to human beings. Needs, narrowly conceived as deprivation, are often restricted to that which is merely physiological and as such the sensation that something which is actually felt. However, to the degree that needs engage, motivate and mobilize people, they are a potential and eventually may become a resource. The need to participate is a potential for participation, just as the need for affection is the potential for affection.

The wise entrepreneur uses this basic insight to create innovative business models and to generate wealth.

Max-Neef et al.[27] provide a useful theory of fundamental human needs. Their research indicates that when satisfiers of fundamental needs are discovered in a scalable and structured form in a community and wisely implemented, this may provide the preconditions for economic growth and development. These authors assert that there is a generally held belief that human needs are infinite, change over historical periods, and differ deeply across national boundaries. They maintain that this presumption of the infinitude, temporal nature and variability of fundamental human needs is a wrong and unhelpful diagnosis. It has confused thinking and obstructed growth and development in situations where they are all too frequently desperately required.

Max-Neef et al.[28] reflected that fundamental human needs are: "Finite, constant over time, few and classifiable ... Fundamental human needs are the same in all cultures, and in all historical periods. What changes, over place, time and culture is the ways and means that these fundamental human needs are satisfied in a given society." The Solms-Delta case is useful because it illustrates that a unique scalable solution to satisfy fundamental human needs can be designed. It was linked to the historical memory of how racism destroyed the community and the solution was therefore to develop a healing community. The business model was indeed based on the narrative of those needs which were deprived over generations. The workers' voices were used to articulate satisfiers and this became the essence of the Solms-Delta business model. In this way, deprivation was converted into human potential. It is the satisfiers of these fundamental human needs, and not the fundamental needs themselves that are fluid and change over time and place. Therefore, while Max-Neef's fundamental human needs framework is stable over time it is the satisfiers of these fundamental needs that are fluid and unique to the specific historical context.

Max-Neef et al.[29] found that there is a basic difference between fundamental human needs and how these needs are satisfied. These fundamental human needs are satisfied by the creation of satisfiers. The discovery of satisfiers of fundamental human needs is a social process requiring leadership, supportive discussions, purpose and structure among those who are seeking them. It is a grass-roots process and is dependent on the specific geographical, socio-economic and political context in which the search is conducted, as well as the historical memory of the failure to discover satisfiers of fundamental human needs.

The discovery of satisfiers of fundamental human needs arises from structured, wise, informed conversations among representative groups of stakeholders. It is not a top-down process. It is a bottom-up process. These conversations can be guided by active listening and empathically placing yourself in the shoes of the other, and using this insight to offer constructive suggestions on how these fundamental needs might best be satisfied. The identification of satisfiers of fundamental human needs is therefore a co-operative and collaborative process that is very different from the conflictive premise on which collective bargaining is conducted in South Africa. It remains to be seen whether the parties extend the rules of engagement to include co-operation, collaboration and joint problem solving. Max-Neef and his fellow researchers (1989) placed human needs into a matrix that allowed them to clarify how human needs interact with one another, and how satisfiers are naturally discovered as a product of the interaction of fundamental human needs. This depiction of fundamental human needs is contained in Table 2.1 below entitled 'Matrix of Fundamental Needs and Satisfiers'.

The table places these human needs into a matrix depicting fundamental needs pertaining to human existence on the horizontal axis, and fundamental needs pertaining to human value and worth on the vertical axis. Max-Neef et al. term the fundamental needs relating to human existence Existential Needs. These are essential to our existence and are placed in a horizontal row across the top of the columns of the table. They are identified as: Being, Having, Doing and Interacting. The fundamental human needs pertaining to human value and worth are arranged along the vertical axis. These are referred to as Axiological Needs since the term 'axiology' refers to the notions of value and worth. These needs include: Subsistence, Protection, Affection, Understanding, Participation, Idleness, Creation, Identity and Freedom. The interaction between the needs for existence and the needs for value create the satisfiers of these fundamental human needs – satisfiers which will be unique to each community. Therefore, the Existential Needs and the Axiological Needs are the independent variables. Their interaction with one another reveals the satisfiers and these are the dependent variables. The satisfiers that will emerge are culturally specific and unique satisfiers, and arise from the interaction of the combined fundamental needs. Interestingly, Max-Neef et al. found that satisfiers of fundamental human needs are always pursued according to a specific local, geographical and cultural context. They are thus unique and have to be addressed on their own merits. These satisfiers are therefore analogous to a fingerprint of a culture.[30]

Table 2.1: Matrix of Fundamental Human Needs and Satisfiers

		EXISTENTIAL NEEDS			
		Being	Having	Doing	Interacting
AXIOLOGICAL NEEDS	Subsistence	1. Physical health, mental health, sense of humour, adaptability	2. Food, shelter, work	3. Feed, procreate, rest, work	4. Living environment, social setting
	Protection	5. Care, adaptability, autonomy, equilibrium, solidarity	6. Insurance systems, savings, social security, health systems, rights, family, work	7. Co-operate, prevent, plan, take care of, cure, help	8. Living space, social environment, dwelling
	Affection	9. Self-esteem, solidarity, respect, tolerance, generosity, receptiveness, passion, determination, sensuality, sense of humour	10. Friendships, family, partnerships, relationship with nature	11. Make love, caress, express emotions, share, take care of, cultivate, appreciate	12. Privacy, intimacy, home, spaces of togetherness
	Understanding	13. Critical conscience, receptiveness, curiosity, astonishment, discipline, intuition, rationality	14. Literature, teachers, method, educational policies, communication policies	15. Investigate, study, experiment, educate, analyse, medicate	16. Settings of formative interaction, schools, apprenticeships, universities, academies, groups, communities, family

		EXISTENTIAL NEEDS		
		Being	**Having**	**Doing**	**Interacting**
Participation		17. Adaptability, receptiveness, solidarity, willingness, determination, dedication, respect, passion, sense of humour	18. Rights, responsibilities, duties, privileges, work	19. Become affiliated, co-operate, propose, share, dissent, obey, interact, agree on, express opinions	20. Settings of participative interaction, associations, churches, communities, neighbourhoods, family
Idleness		21. Curiosity, receptiveness, imagination, recklessness, sense of humour, tranquillity, sensuality	22. Games, spectacles, clubs, parties, peace of mind	23. Daydream, brood, dream, recall old times, give way to fantasies, remember, relax, have fun, play	24. Privacy, intimacy, spaces of closeness, free time, surroundings, landscapes
Creation		25. Passion, determination, intuition, imagination, boldness, rationality, autonomy, inventiveness, curiosity	26. Abilities, skills, method, work	27. Work, invent, build, design, compose, interpret	28. Productive and feedback settings, workshops, cultural groups, audiences, spaces for expression, temporal freedom
Identity		29. Sense of belonging, consistency, differentiation, self-esteem, assertiveness	30. Symbols, language, religion, habits, customs, reference groups, sexuality, values, norms, historical memory, work	31. Commit oneself, integrate oneself, confront, decide on, get to know oneself, recognise oneself, grow	32. Social rhythms, everyday settings, settings which one belongs to, maturation stages
Freedom		33. Autonomy, self-esteem, determination, passion, assertiveness, open-mindedness, boldness, rebelliousness, tolerance	34. Equal rights	35. Dissent, choose, be different from, run risks, develop awareness, commit oneself, disobey	36. Temporal/spatial plasticity

Source: Max-Neef, M., Elizalde, A., Hopenhyn, M., Herrera, F., Zemelman, H., Jataba, J. and Weinstein, L (1989)[31]

Max-Neef et al. point out that each society adopts its own unique solutions to how it should best discover satisfiers of the same fundamental human needs. Some societies will be either more, or less successful than others in creating satisfiers of their own fundamental needs. Max-Neef et al. "go as far as to say that one of the aspects that defines a culture is its choice of satisfiers". The fundamental human needs are few and constant, while the discovery of satisfiers of these fundamental human needs is variable and will be contextually specific to a given community and society. For Max-Neef et al., food and shelter are not needs but satisfiers of the fundamental need for *subsistence*. As humans we all have a fundamental need to have the means for supporting life. Food and housing/shelter are in Max-Neef et al.'s terms, satisfiers of our fundamental subsistence need to continue with life. Similarly, education is not a need. *Understanding* is a need, and education is the satisfier of the need for *understanding*. The logic of Max-Neef et al. is that when we pursue an education, we do this to gain an understanding about a subject matter that will advance our lives. Understanding is the fundamental need that we pursue so that we can be employed, respected, earn a living, provide for our families, be stimulated and contribute meaningfully to the society in which we live. Education is therefore the satisfier of this need for understanding. Likewise, health care is not a need, but health care is a satisfier of the need for *protection*. You consult a doctor when your health is at risk. Your need is therefore for the protection of your health. The satisfier of this need for protection is, therefore, health care. The selfsame pattern of logic applies to all the fundamental needs and satisfiers in the matrix. This counter-intuitive inversion of traditional logic allows negotiators the opportunity to creatively identify many satisfiers of fundamental human needs.[32]

One of the first requests that the farm labourers at Solms-Delta made was for their newly constructed farmhouses to be furnished with a DSTV platform. The question that needs to be posed is: How could DSTV have any bearing on discovering satisfiers of fundamental human needs? The relationship of DSTV to satisfiers of fundamental human needs is illustrated by the fact that prior to Mark Solms' purchase of the farm, the farm labourers had extremely high rates of alcoholism. This alcoholism has since diminished significantly because of the discovery of many satisfiers of fundamental human needs in a stable community context. One can speculate that a possible contributor to the exceptionally high rates of alcoholism at Solms-Delta was boredom. The labourers' fundamental existential human needs of Interacting and Being in their relationship with the Axiological Needs of Creation, Idleness, Participation and Understanding were perverted by the 'dop-system' where the farm labourers were given wine in lieu of salary. Drunkenness has been used as a pseudo-satisfier of fundamental human needs in the Western Cape over the centuries. DSTV was a constructive and socially sustainable satisfier of these fundamental human needs and therefore displaced alcohol.

When we reflect on the relevance of fundamental needs and their satisfiers in the context of our South African society and how they fit in with working and living conditions, it becomes clear that there has simply not been a systemic and dedicated attempt by the major parties to address them. They have been all but ignored. This failure is reflected in the diverse forms of poverty that are evident across the land.

Little, if any, thought has been devoted to trying to understand how one might design a restorative collective bargaining process in South Africa, one that seriously seeks to discover satisfiers of fundamental human needs by using negotiation as a process that addresses these in a systematic and meaningful manner. The challenge is to invent appropriate negotiation rituals and processes that are credible to the key stakeholders and that do not remain entrapped in the prevailing pattern of collective bargaining which is mostly retributive and all too frequently de-humanising, due in part to its brutal history. The essential feature of the current approach towards collective bargaining is that it is inveigled in an undignified and dehumanising interactive cycle where 'good faith' is repeated like a mantra but is all too often characterised by its very absence. The business–union–government relationship is fraught and divisive.

Paulo Freire[33] refers to "humanization as being humankind's central problem ..." For him, humanisation is a pedagogical and restorative process of learning to understand and address, as best as one might, the needs and aspirations of the other, while de-humanisation is, in its essence, a retributive process which does not seek to understand, empathise, learn from, and address the needs of the other. In South Africa, empathy for the needs of one's negotiation counterpart is, all too often, ignorantly castigated as weakness. It is in the nature of empathy that a point of partial identification is discovered that enables relationships to make progress. Finland has one of the most successful educational systems in the world. Finland is not, by any means, a rich country. One of the basic reasons why the Finnish educational system is so successful is because their basic educational premise is that the most important resource in Finland is the human brain. This has enabled them to design an education system that has enabled their population to realise their own talent and creativity, and to discover satisfiers that address their fundamental human needs. South Africa could do well to emulate this approach.

Gainful employment offers satisfiers of an array of fundamental human needs including: Subsistence, Having, Doing, Identity and many more besides. These needs are omnipresent in all societies, and the perceived quality of a society is differentiated by how effectively these needs are satisfied. When they are generally not satisfied, as is the case with South Africa, that society will be plagued with poverty, inequality, addiction, social pathology, uncertainty, dissension, crime and conflict. Deep-rooted conflict involves the failure, or lack of inclination to seek to discover satisfiers of the fundamental human needs. When these fundamental human needs are not satisfied, members of society will suffer from various forms of impoverishment, and when this process is replicated, it quickly becomes a mass pathology.

2.1 Unrealistic Expectations of Collective Bargaining

Employees enter into collective bargaining in South Africa with expectations that are both high and unrealistic. Many accord it with the status of a panacea. This is because of the historically important contribution of the trade union movement towards bringing about the downfall of apartheid combined with the fact that the opportunities available for social dialogue on fundamental human needs are so few in South Africa. Employees expect that collective bargaining will naturally provide satisfiers of fundamental human needs, alleviate grinding poverty, ensure fair labour practices, and thereby contribute to a better life. The abrasiveness of collective bargaining creates insecurity, mistrust and inhibits vital unconditional learning. This popular employee expectation of collective bargaining as a generic fix-all instrument is rooted in the struggle mythology that saw mass mobilisation bring about the downfall of apartheid. This view of collective bargaining as a fix-all is doomed to fail. New solutions need to be discovered to address unique and novel challenges. Collective bargaining is failing because it is, by default, being used to discover solutions to deep-rooted conflicts that it is not structurally capable of addressing. Like many skills, collective bargaining can make matters better or worse, depending on the unique context in which these skills are applied. Needless to say, strikes and poor industrial relations characterise much of collective bargaining in South Africa and cause businesses to shut down and retrenchments to follow.

Business also regards collective bargaining as a panacea. It does this in a different manner from that of the trade unions. Companies bargain collectively upon the basis of an implicit business model framework which is not shared with the trade unions and employees, and is therefore not understood by or credible to them. The company's essential business model is not presented to the trade union as a shared and fundamental concern which pertains to the opportunities and threats that are confronting it. The employees' fundamental human needs are also not presented during the collective bargaining process and so the basic fears and concerns of all parties involved – business, trade unions and employees – remain unaddressed.

There are few effective formal and informal communication platforms in South Africa that enable communities to have conversations that seek to discover satisfiers on the matter of how to wisely address fundamental human needs. The absence of such platforms has resulted in collective bargaining negotiation fora becoming overloaded. It leads to a cacophony of voices that go mostly unheard. This offers a partial explanation of why South Africa has such exceptionally high levels of spontaneous political and civil conflict.

Businesses congregated together wisely and effectively during the period of South Africa's negotiated revolution to address crucial matters of common concern, including the explosive internecine violence that was terrorising the country at that time. They formed the Consultative Business Movement in order to create an essential ad hoc negotiation forum. During this transition, the Consultative Business Movement sought to come to grips with fundamental human needs in a manner that enabled the constitutional negotiations to be safely concluded. The Consultative Business Movement managed the implementation of the National Peace Accord, saving countless thousands of people's lives by so doing. A Consultative Business Movement is once again in need of reinvention to offer leadership and direction to South African business and the communities in which they operate. They need to seek to understand the crux of what is causing strikes, protests and violence, and thereby to learn how to address these phenomena in the wisest possible manner while enabling the discovery of satisfiers of these unmet needs.

3

The Relevance of an Understanding of Normal and Deep-rooted Conflict to Collective Bargaining

There is a deficit of professional knowledge and skill about how to address normal and deep-rooted conflict among the parties to collective bargaining in South Africa. This knowledge is particularly useful in understanding how normal conflicts might escalate into deep-rooted conflict, and how to de-escalate a deep-rooted conflict into a normal conflict and convert it into a development process. Unskilled, incompetent and unqualified persons are frequently appointed to engage in the collective bargaining process, with negative human consequences.

3.1 Normal Conflict

Burton[34] showed that normal conflicts are inherent in all human relationships. Normal conflicts often revolve around parties to negotiation holding different worldviews, ideas, priorities and considerations pertaining to what needs to be done. Normal conflicts, therefore, frequently challenge authority relationships in organisations. They are not perpetual conflicts or intractable conflicts and they thus do not seek to negate the discovery of satisfiers of fundamental human needs which often takes place under the scenario of deep-rooted conflict. Normal conflicts pertain to transitory desires which are important to the individual, but they are not about the fundamental values, needs, beliefs and the binding ethos of the group. Because normal conflicts are based on transitory desires, they are not enduring and tenacious conflicts as is the case with intractable deep-rooted conflict. Normal conflict agendas are relatively malleable and are therefore open to concessions and compromises without undermining fundamental human needs. Normal conflicts can be settled by legal interventions and adjudication.

Burton[35] shows that normal conflicts occur in all circumstances and in all organisations. He explains that human rivalry, ambition, authority relations and disagreements are paths of action that often drive normal conflicts. Normal conflicts might be triggered by perceived differences in status, different assessments of leadership capabilities, personal slights and rebuttals, conflicting judgments about expert competence, and judgments about the suitability of an individual for an important professional position. For Burton (1987), normal conflicts occur whenever people work and live together. When there is normal conflict about resources, scarcity is often the arbiter in how these resources should best be allocated between the parties. In these circumstances the parties would grudgingly accept the decision of allocation on the basis of reciprocity and self-evident scarcity, and then move on.

Discussion, conversation, negotiation, conciliation, mediation, lobbying, advocacy, arbitration, submission to a court decision, or a resolution from a board of governors are a few ways that normal conflicts can be addressed.

3.2 Deep-rooted Conflict

Deep-rooted conflict revolves around fundamental human needs. These fundamental needs were clearly articulated by Max-Neef et al.[36] in the previous chapter and include, inter alia, Being, Having, Doing and Interacting, and on the other hand, the needs of Subsistence, Protection, Affection, Understanding, Participation, Idleness, Creation, Identity and Freedom. When these fundamental human needs are suppressed or ignored, deep-rooted conflict will almost inevitably emerge. There may well be a latency period before its emergence, but emerge it will.

Deep-rooted conflict is conflict of a different and unique type and threshold from normal conflict. It is both logical and seemingly illogical. It is emotional and has an historical memory that may extend back through grudges and anger over centuries. Burton advised that deep-rooted conflict should be addressed according to separate protocols from normal conflict, and he composed a set of helpful, practical ground rules as to how this might be done. Deep-rooted conflicts are often deemed to be perpetual or intractable conflicts. When fundamental human needs drive a conflict, it cannot be compromised by court decisions no matter the legality. A deep-rooted conflict is often about intangible matters mythologised into symbolic values and connected to beliefs about human dignity and worthiness. It is therefore often imbued with religious belief that might sanctify the conflict, as is the case with a Holy War, by way of example. Fortunately, there has been wisdom and restraint among the religious leaders in South Africa and we do not have deep-rooted conflict on religion, although we do have robust and vociferous disagreement.

Failures in collective bargaining in South Africa can often be ascribed to misdiagnoses of deep-rooted conflict as being a normal conflict. The trivialisation of deep-rooted conflicts into normal conflict is experienced by negotiation counterparts as an act of gross condescension and is often, if not inevitably, escalatory. The Marikana Massacre was a deep-rooted conflict. The Lonmin management was at a loss as to how to address the strike because they did not have the knowledge and skill to address the matter. They therefore called in the police to resolve it. The Lonmin management team did not ask the basic question of whether the police had the knowledge, skill, capability and training to effectively address an escalating deep-rooted conflict. An elementary response to this question would have revealed that they did not. There was a derelict absence of knowledge about the social psychology of mass behaviour among the leadership. Both the police and Lonmin management addressed the conflict from the perspective of a mechanistic worldview. Forty-four people were consequently shot dead. When the negotiation leadership makes this type of misdiagnosis, their counterparts experience the misdiagnosis as being profoundly disrespectful and as trivialising their dignity and human worth. Unsurprisingly, this often triggers ever more cycles of violence. It is experienced as an act intended to humiliate the other. A failure to diagnose deep-rooted conflict and address this conflictive phenomenon on its own merits is therefore escalatory. The misdiagnosis of deep-rooted conflict and its incorrect ascription as a normal conflict are viewed as signifying an absence of empathy, gross indifference about the plight of the other, and as disrespectful, cynical and callous.

These behaviours are regarded as signifying contempt and are responded to with tit-for-tat contempt, causing the escalation of normal conflict into deep-rooted conflict. It is very difficult to heal relationships that are infused with contempt. Deep-rooted conflict might be suppressed for a while by violence, but it soon re-emerges and manifests itself in a different pattern. Apartheid is an example of deep-rooted conflict. The essential premise of apartheid was the denial of the other's humanity on the basis of race. This was a denial of fundamental human needs and it was inevitable that, in due course, it would be met with a violent uprising. Deep-rooted conflict involves the attempted suppression of these fundamental human needs. Ignoring them, or neglecting to address them, often triggers violence. Religious schisms almost always have the potential to escalate into deep-rooted conflict, and by definition, have all the ingredients of deep-rooted conflict. Kraybill[37] explained that deep-rooted conflict "is not based on transitory interests over land, money and natural resources. Rather deep-rooted conflict is tenacious because it revolves around basic human needs." These basic human needs are thus both tangible and intangible.

Heald[38] showed how, with imagination, creativity and respect, enemies could come to learn from one another during a negotiation process that is characterised by deep-rooted conflict. It is imperative that the leadership of these negotiation processes should develop an ethic of respect for one another, and the truth of their respective lived experiences. When this is undertaken with sincerity, goodwill and skill, it transforms a negative relationship into a mutually beneficial individuating relationship where the counterparts and their constituencies develop and grow from their relationship with one another. The dualistic nature of human needs as both deprivation and potential then starts to manifest. Burton[39] submitted that humans pursue their basic human needs in a deep-rooted conflict scenario regardless of the life-threatening consequences and risks that such action entails. Deep-rooted conflicts tend to erupt into emotional and violent displays. The needs that drive deep-rooted conflict cannot ultimately be subverted by human suffering, legal banishment (including imprisonment), torture, murder and death. The conflicts between Israelis and Palestinians, the Turks and the Kurds, Syria and Isis are but a few international examples of deep-rooted conflicts that are currently playing themselves out. The values and needs that underpin deep-rooted conflict are so powerful that people will sacrifice their lives in pursuit of them. Suicide bombings and martyrdom are symptomatic of the phenomena of deep-rooted conflict. Kraybill[40] concluded that: "The desire to be free, to rise to the fullest potential, to be respected and esteemed, and to secure these conditions for one's offspring is irrepressible. Ultimately it is stronger even than the individual instinct to survive." This finding is entirely congruent with the industrial conflicts that revolve around the failure to seek to discover satisfiers of fundamental human needs.

3.3 Dysfunctional Satisfiers of Fundamental Human Needs – Violators or Destructors as Triggers of Deep-rooted Conflict

Working and living conditions together form a continuum which can be equated with the quality of life. Those persons who are involved in collective bargaining need to seek to understand what elements comprise fundamental human needs. They also need to clarify how fundamental human needs differ from desires. Unless this basic principle is kept in mind, we navigate without a compass, and negotiate without a deeper understanding of why we are engaged in the process of collective bargaining in the first place. The failure to clarify the distinction between needs and desires causes many conflicts in collective bargaining. Needs are necessities and imperatives that arise from human existence while desires are wants that are transitory in the sense that they are not fundamental to life itself. Desires are perceived to be 'nice to have'. A negotiation process that is enacted to address serious fundamental human needs is bequeathed with gravitas. A negotiation process that is designed to address more transitory desires will not be accorded the same level of seriousness. When fundamental human needs are referred to as 'transitory desires' during negotiation this will be deemed by the negotiation counterparts as an escalatory and disrespectful human interaction, and deep-rooted conflict will often arise as a result.

Working and living conditions cannot be artificially disaggregated. Working conditions pertain specifically to the terms and conditions of work while living conditions pertain to the quality of health, education, service delivery and housing, and are closely associated with the satisfaction of fundamental human needs. Working conditions are therefore an integrated subset of living conditions. Industrial conflicts in South Africa often emerge around both. This leads to considerable complexity and a continuum between industrial conflicts, political conflicts, social protests, service delivery conflicts and other forms of civil and political dissent, including criminal violence. Max-Neef et al.[41] presented two dysfunctional categories of satisfiers that assist us in distinguishing fundamental human needs from desires. He and his fellow researchers coined the term 'Pseudo-Satisfiers' to describe "elements which stimulate a false sensation of satisfying a given need [that] may on occasion annul the need they were originally aimed at".

Examples of Pseudo-Satisfiers include a person who is obsessed with possessing status symbols and will undermine his or her fundamental need for Identity because the presenting persona that is placed before the public will be perceived to be more important than the self. Similar logic applies to the Pseudo-Satisfier desire to comply with fashion and fads that may also undermine the fundamental need of Identity. Prostitution is a Pseudo-Satisfier of the fundamental need for Affection. Max-Neef et al.[42] also offered a category of satisfiers called 'Inhibiting Satisfiers'. Inhibiting Satisfiers over-satisfy a specific need and simultaneously impede the satisfaction of other needs. Paternalism is an Inhibiting Satisfier that over-satisfies the need for Protection but impairs the satisfaction of Understanding, Participation, Freedom and Identity. Similarly, an over-protective family satisfies the need for Protection, but inhibits the satisfaction of Affection, Understanding, Participation, Leisure, Identity and Freedom.

Max-Neef et al.[43] identified various dysfunctional satisfiers of fundamental human needs. One such dysfunctional satisfier is termed a violator or destructor. Violators or destructors fester and lead directly to deep-rooted conflict. Max-Neef et al.[44] describe a violator or destructor thus: "A violator or destructor are satisfiers that have a paradoxical effect. Applied under the pretext of satisfying a given need, they not only annihilate the possibility of its satisfaction, they also render the satisfaction of other needs impossible. They seem to be especially related to the need for protection." Table 3.1 illustrates selected violators or destructors that resonate with the South African experience of the dysfunctional satisfiers of fundamental human needs.

Table 3.1: Dysfunctional Satisfiers of Fundamental Human Needs – Violators and Destructors

Supposed Satisfier	Need to be Supposedly Satisfied	Needs that have Impaired Satisfaction
Guns, arms, traditional and cultural weapons	Protection	Protection, Subsistence, Affection, Participation and Freedom
Migrant Labour from Mozambique, Zimbabwe, Lesotho etc.	Protection	Protection, Affection, Participation, Subsistence, Identity and Freedom
Gang Membership	Protection	Protection, Freedom, Being, Having, Interacting, Identity, Creation, Idleness, Participation, Understanding and Affection
Loan Sharks	Subsistence and Protection	Subsistence, Protection, Being, Having, Doing, Interacting, Understanding, Identity and Freedom
Vigilantes	Protection	Protection, Subsistence, Freedom, Identity, Participation, Understanding, Being, Having, Doing and Interacting
Unprotected Strikes	Subsistence and Protection	Subsistence, Protection, Being, Having, Doing, Interacting, Participation and Understanding
Social Grants	Subsistence	Subsistence, Being, Having, Doing, Interacting, Identity, Freedom, Creation, Participation, Understanding and Protection
Racism	Protection, Interacting, Subsistence, Freedom, Identity, Being, Having, Creation, Identity, Doing, Understanding, Affection	Protection, Interacting, Subsistence, Freedom, Identity, Being, Having, Creation, Identity, Doing, Understanding, Affection

3.4   Single- and Double-loop Learning

In a classic study, Argyris differentiated single-loop learning from double-loop learning.[45] The distinction between single- and double-loop learning provides a useful framework for understanding why collective bargaining in South Africa is failing. Single-loop learning is an analytical process that solves the presenting, or symptomatic problem, but fails to seek to understand and address the underlying causes of why the presenting problem existed in the first place. Double-loop learning poses deeper questions and seeks to understand why the problem exists in the first place. Double-loop learning therefore endeavours to discover the root causes and governing values that fuel a conflict. It involves a much more complex, nuanced and contextually relevant investigation than single-loop learning, seeking to understand the driving forces that cause the conflict configuration. Double-loop learning therefore discovers, identifies and understands culturally relevant satisfiers of the fundamental human needs that are driving a conflict while single-loop learning focuses on addressing the presenting agenda and symptoms in the most expedient manner possible.

In the event of a brewing conflict a single-loop learner would not endeavour to conduct a deeper analysis of what the root causes of this conflict might be. Neither would he or she seek to discover effective deeper and sustainable solutions to the tumult. It follows that a single-loop learner does not seek to gain a contextual understanding of the conflictive situation and accordingly remains ignorant of what to do when its driving forces change phase and it manifests as a deep-rooted conflict. This is referred to as learned ignorance. Max-Neef et al.[46] explain that learned ignorance and the fear of discovering the root cause of a problem are quite understandable. He and his team of researchers reflected:

> It is not easy to put aside theoretical and ideological constructions, along with the corresponding strategies for action, which have over the years been the basis of not only beliefs, explanations and hopes, but also of passions. But the fact is that the extent of this crisis seems to go far beyond our capacity to assimilate it fully, understand it and, hence internalize it. The crisis is not just economic, not just social, cultural or political. On the contrary it is a convergence of all these, which added together, become an entirety exceeding the sum of its parts.

When obliviousness to the contextual reality of a deep-rooted conflict is publicly displayed by a leader, and revealed in the media, the consequences are usually disgrace and shame. A recent case in point is that the Farlam Commission of Inquiry into the Marikana Massacre effectively found that Riah Phiyega, the National Police Commissioner of the South African Police Services, was incompetent in her leadership and fuelled the deep-rooted conflict. The Commission of Inquiry found that Riah Phiyega proffered simplistic and symptomatic single-loop learning solutions to complex deep-rooted conflict problems that require double-loop learning and a deep interrogation of the root causes and governing values that drove the conflict. This ignorance and incompetence caused a normal conflict to explode into a massacre. In this analysis, therefore, normal conflict can be addressed by single-loop learning, while deep-rooted conflict can be addressed by double-loop learning and, if appropriate, supplemented by elements of single-loop learning.

South African employers often seek to ignore the encroachment of complicated community conflicts into the workplace. The mental model can be stereotyped as: "What happens in the township – remains in the township." For the single-loop business manager, profitability, sales, growth and productivity are reality. Single-loop learning provides a neat and simplistic worldview for the employer to disassociate from the disturbing truth which exists in our poverty-stricken and conflict-ridden communities in which the majority of employees live.

Business leaders have retained a narrow view of the employment relationship and have tended to dismiss the socio-political reality of living conditions in impoverished communities and townships as falling outside of their managerial remit. They have tended, in general, to adhere to a single-loop learning model and have chosen to presume that the array of community conflicts that are taking place in South Africa are normal conflicts rather than deep-rooted. They have thus not sought to come to terms with the fundamental human needs that are driving these conflicts and to seriously address them as a stakeholder grouping. Business' failure to address fundamental human needs is untenable. It will inevitably lead to further polarisation and alienation that will, in due course, be visited on the entire community, including business itself. It is at this juncture that collective bargaining is failing.

Collective bargaining conflicts, service delivery protests, student unrest, xenophobic violence, vigilante action and gang wars are all fuelled by the same root cause of intractable poverty. The reluctance to engage in a double-loop learning process and to seek to discover satisfiers of fundamental human needs perpetuates the conflict.

Business should, and could, be an important and proactive agency for addressing social change in South Africa. After the transition to democracy, the parties to collective bargaining did not change the way that the process was conceived and conducted. They allowed it to remain ritualised in a single-loop learning process and did not seek to invoke a double-loop learning process in an effort to understand and address the governing values. An important opportunity to create social cohesion in post-apartheid South Africa was therefore wasted. In the meantime, the unattended conflict and associated goodwill fermented in the townships across the country.

There is a compulsion with single-loop learning and an avoidance of double-loop learning. This compulsion circumscribes reality by addressing deep-rooted conflicts as normal conflicts and thereby makes the conflicts ever more intractable. This approach creates a pressure-cooker effect. Deep-rooted conflict cannot be indefinitely suppressed and it will almost inevitably erupt in the fullness of time.

3.5 Negotiating on Tame Problems and Wicked Problems

Horst Rittel and Melvin Webber conducted ground-breaking research that explored the scientific basis for addressing intractable social problems.[47] They coined the term 'wicked problem' to describe problems that have two components namely: a technical and social element. This is particularly relevant to collective bargaining in South Africa because almost all the conflicts that arise from the process have both technical and social elements. Rittel and Webber[48] pointed out that traditional problem-solving approaches usually have a predominant focus on the technical elements of the problem. These technical elements are typically defined as 'the problem' and often ignore the social element involving the stakeholders who are addressing it. This is confusing because the social rather than the technical dimension of a problem is often the predominant problem. This means that the social element of a wicked problem requires particular attention if it is to be successfully addressed. The social element of a wicked problem results in the failure among stakeholders to create consensus as to the nature of the problem. The multiplicity of stakeholders and their views on how best to address the wicked problem therefore become the major problems in themselves. The social aspect of a wicked problem is manifested in the different opinions of the stakeholders. It is invariably more difficult to address than the technical aspect of the wicked problem because it constantly changes. Wicked problems do not have clear right or wrong answers. They have better or worse solutions. Tame problems have clear right or wrong answers. If one seeks to discover a right or wrong answer to a better or worse question, it is inevitable that the problem solver will get stuck. For this logic, Rittel and Webber[49] deduced that:

There is no definitive formulation of a wicked problem ... The information needed to understand the problem depends upon one's idea of solving it.

1.   Wicked problems have a no stopping rule.
2.   Solutions to wicked problems are not true-or-false, but good-or-bad.
3.   There is no immediate and no ultimate test of a solution to a wicked problem.
4.   Every solution to a wicked problem is a 'one-shot operation'; because there is no opportunity to learn by trial-and-error, every attempt counts significantly.

5. Wicked problems do not have enumerable (or an exhaustively describable) set of potential solutions, nor is there a well-described set of permissible options that may be incorporated into the plan.
6. Every wicked problem is essentially unique.
7. Every wicked problem can be considered to be a symptom of another problem.
8. The existence of a discrepancy representing a wicked problem can be explained in numerous ways. The choice of explanation determines the nature of the problem's resolution.
9. The planner has no right to be wrong.

A single-loop learning process therefore cannot solve wicked problems in collective bargaining and result in the discovery of satisfiers of fundamental human needs. A double-loop learning process is appropriate to addressing fundamental human needs. Similarly, a double-loop learning process can only address the discovery of satisfiers of fundamental human needs. These satisfiers of fundamental human needs are in themselves, by definition, solutions to wicked problems. Negotiations on minimum wages and terms and conditions of employment would be a tame problem if it excluded the corollary that the process is intended to seek to discover satisfiers of fundamental human needs. Collective bargaining in South Africa is therefore a wicked problem, all too often treated as a tame problem. Rittel and Webber's[50] research therefore is of assistance in understanding why normal conflict so frequently escalates into a deep-rooted conflict.

3.6 Negotiating to Discover Satisfiers of Fundamental Human Needs

De Visser and Powell[51] conducted research on the main causes of service delivery conflicts in South Africa. They identified 14 triggers that have regularly ignited service delivery conflicts. These causes are also frequent causes of strikes in South Africa. These triggers of service delivery conflicts have been subjected to a content analysis and been placed into Max-Neef et al.'s[52] framework of fundamental human needs in order to illustrate the configuration of triggers of service delivery conflicts in their relationship with the failure to discover satisfiers of fundamental human needs. It is evident from this content analysis that the causes of service delivery conflicts reside in the failure to seek satisfiers of fundamental human needs. The cause of this deep-rooted conflict can therefore be understood as a failure to engage in a double-loop learning process with the key parties to collective bargaining that will enable us to understand and address the root causes of these conflicts and discover satisfiers that will lead to their solution. These all fall into the category of deep-rooted conflict, and therefore cannot be solved by single-loop learning. Table 3.2 equates De Visser and Powell's designation of commonly articulated causes of service delivery conflicts with Max-Neef et al.'s (1989) fundamental human needs. The exploration of: the nature of normal conflict and deep-rooted conflict; single and double-loop learning; mechanistic and systems thinking; and tame and wicked problems are all perspectives that will assist the negotiators to diagnose and make prognoses about the mental models that will be required to make collective bargaining effective. De Visser and Powell's[53] causes of service delivery conflict are depicted in regular text while Max-Neef et al.'s (1989) fundamental human needs are depicted in bold italic text.

Table 3.2: A Content Correlation of De Visser and Powell's[54] Causes of Service Delivery Conflicts with Max-Neef et al.'s[55] Fundamental Human Needs

Causes of Service Delivery Conflict (De Visser and Powell)	Fundamental Human Needs that are Ignored Causing Service Delivery Conflicts (Max-Neef et al.)
Empty Promises	*Understanding, Creation, Affection, Interacting, Freedom and Doing*
Evictions and Forced Removals	*Subsistence, Having, Being, Interacting and Understanding*
Built Environment	*Subsistence, Participation, Interacting, Protection and Doing*
Ignored Grievances	*Understanding, Creation, Affection, Being and Interacting*
Poor Governance	*Understanding, Protection, Subsistence, Affection and Doing*
Infrastructure	*Subsistence, Participation, Interaction, Protection, Having and Doing*
Party Political Conflict	*Interacting, Participation, Identity and Protection*
Socio-economic Hardship	*Subsistence, Having, Interacting, Doing, Understanding and Freedom*
Corruption and Nepotism	*Interaction, Having, Protection, Understanding and Being*
Sanitation and Water	*Subsistence, Being, Interacting, Participation and Protection*
Water and Electricity	*Subsistence, Being, Interacting, Participation and Protection*
Poor Service Delivery	*Protection, Being, Interacting and Doing*
Land	*Participation, Interacting, Protection Doing, Subsistence and Having*
Housing	*Participation, Interacting, Protection Doing, Subsistence and Having*

De Visser and Powell's 14 triggers of service delivery conflict are alluded to in Table 3.2 above. An analysis of these causes reveals that there is some overlap, both within and across the categories. They have accordingly been clustered into nine groupings in order to avoid repetition. In the section below, these causes of service delivery conflict are correlated with triggers of industrial conflict and fundamental human needs. It is clear that common causes of service delivery conflict are also common causes of strikes and the failure of collective bargaining.

Empty Promises: The causes of service delivery conflict, together with the correlated fundamental human needs that are depicted in Table 3.2 are regular, and indeed, generic driving forces of strikes in South Africa. Industrial conflicts often arise from failed and *empty promises* that cause disillusionment and anger. Empty promises indicate insincerity and constitute a breach of contract. The result is damage to relationships and a conflict of expectations. The fundamental human needs that are transgressed by empty promises include: Understanding, Creation, Affection, Interacting, Freedom and Doing.

Poor Governance: *Poor governance* often triggers conflicts. One example of poor governance that has been noted is the plundering of employee pension and provident funds by union leadership and investment funds. The fundamental needs that are violated and give rise to strikes by poor governance include: Understanding, Protection, Subsistence, Affection and Doing.

Party Political Conflict: *Party political conflicts* conflate into industrial conflicts and often manifest in collective bargaining conflict as well. The fractionation of the Tripartite Alliance and the resultant inter-union rivalry and conflict has its origins in party political conflict. This results in the withering away of the social compact. The fundamental human needs that are transgressed by intra-party political conflict include: Interacting, Participation, Identity and Protection.

Corruption and Nepotism: Evidence of *corruption and nepotism* are regular causes of industrial conflict and result in alienation and polarisation of relationships. The fundamental human needs that are violated by corruption and nepotism include: Interaction, Having, Protection, Understanding and Being.

Socio-economic Hardship: Financial needs, debt and expectations of a better life translate directly into the lived experience of *socio-economic hardship.* Socio-economic hardship is often the root cause of industrial and community conflicts. (The role of loan sharks as predators on the poor is a case in point.) A failure to address unsatisfied fundamental human needs and to discover satisfiers often explodes into violence and deep-rooted conflict. Conflicts and grievances arise from the failure to address fundamental human needs in a systematic, serious, sincere and effective manner. A detailed understanding of needs and satisfiers would be helpful in avoiding unnecessary conflicts of all types. The fundamental human needs that are violated by socio-economic hardship include: Subsistence, Having, Interacting, Doing, Understanding and Freedom.

Evictions and Forced Removals: Housing insecurity is an important contributor to industrial conflict. The landlord–tenant relationship in South Africa is fraught with tensions and conflict that spill over into the world of work. It is noted that the same single-sex hostels with three-tier concrete beds that were used during the time of apartheid to house migrant labour on the mines are still used for accommodation. These hostels are consistently associated with bloody incidents of inter-group violence in the mining industry. *Evictions and forced removals* and the experience of homelessness cause intense existential insecurity and regularly spill over into industrial and deep-rooted conflict. The fundamental human needs that are transgressed by evictions and forced removals include: Subsistence, Having, Being, Interacting and Understanding.

Built Environment, Infrastructure, Land and Housing: One of the basic reasons why work is conducted is to gain shelter. Humans thus work to earn money to purchase *land*. Strikes often take place in the context of the need for decent housing in an aesthetic and functional *built environment*. The reality is that millions of South Africans live in shacks, in squatter camps, and in the most squalid of built environments. The fundamental human needs that are violated by the absence of an effective and aesthetic built environment, infrastructure, land and housing include: Subsistence, Participation, Interacting, Protection, Doing and Having.

Poor Service Delivery: *Poor service delivery* causes enormous human distress and results in industrial and deep-rooted conflict. The fundamental human needs that are violated by poor service delivery include the transgression of: Protection, Being, Interacting and Doing.

Sanitation, Electricity and Water: The absence of effective *sanitation and water*, as well as water and electricity, consistently inflame deep-rooted conflict. Shortages of potable water, together with the failure to secure sustainable sewerage removal and the absence of electricity, increase the chance of industrial unrest and often trigger the breakdown of collective bargaining. When *water and sanitation* services are absent, service delivery and strikes are ignited. The fundamental human needs that are violated by the absence of sanitation, electricity and water include: Subsistence, Being, Interacting, Participation and Protection.

4

The Disjuncture between Employment Creation and Collective Bargaining in the Fourth Industrial Revolution

Collective bargaining, as we currently understand and conduct it in South Africa, is being challenged by the integration of new digital technologies that are arising from the Fourth Industrial Revolution. These new digital technologies will shape almost all aspects of the future of employment. The prevailing worldview informing collective bargaining in South Africa has not addressed the potential impact of disruptive innovation of the Fourth Industrial Revolution. This is likely to result in the wide-scale obsolescence of many present business models. There has to date also been no systematic assessment of the knowledge and skills requirements that are necessary for South Africans to be employable in this new world of work.

The Fourth Industrial Revolution, according to Schwab and Samans[56] of the World Economic Forum, involves a completely new and dramatic alignment of automation, robotics, crypto-currencies, 3D printing, genetics, artificial intelligence, crowd platforms, cloud functionality, nanotechnology, self-healing materials with microvascular techniques, biotechnology and other forms of computerisation. These are seen to be "building up and amplifying each other ... [and] blurring the lines between the physical, digital and biological spheres". The phrase "amplifying each other" is key because these changes are currently in a process of escalation, creating a perfect employment storm, not only in South Africa, but across the globe as well. The Fourth Industrial Revolution will, in due course, introduce many new forms of employment, but it will also render a large number of current and familiar forms of employment, as we know them, redundant.

Two researchers from Oxford University, Frey and Osborne[57], identified 702 jobs on the probability of their obsolescence because of automation and computerisation. They found that many clerical and administrative positions would simply become redundant by virtue of labour-saving computer applications. These authors predict that "most workers in transportation, and logistics occupations, together with the bulk of office and support workers, production workers are at risk" of automation. *Scientific American* (2014) concurred with Frey and Osborne's[58] research, and estimated that 47 percent of all current American jobs would become eligible for automation over the next decade or so. It is reasonable to hypothesise that at least a similar proportion of South African jobs will become redundant across the same period of time because of disruptive innovation. The extent of redundant jobs that could be lost in South Africa might be much more because the overwhelming majority of employees in South Africa perform semi-skilled and unskilled work. These jobs are precisely those that are easiest to eliminate through automation and computerisation.

The Fourth Industrial Revolution takes mass production one major step further. It now involves *both* mass production *and* mass customisation. This means that individual tastes, needs and desires will be addressed by mass customisation. This is an enormous innovation on the system of mass production that was originally developed by Henry Ford in the 1920s. The innovation of robotics and 3D printing, and their integration with other new technologies, will improve and change both the structure and the nature of manufacturing, as we know it, in fundamental ways.

Basic economic theory holds that there are four factors of production that enable the production of goods and services. These four factors are: land, labour, capital and entrepreneurship. The Fourth Industrial Revolution is changing the definitions and the interrelationships of these four factors of production at their economic essence. Capital is described as a business's financial resources and includes goods that enable production. The capital goods that are being designed under the Fourth Industrial Revolution are now composed of a wave of integrated labour-substituting technologies including automation, robotics and artificial intelligence that are displacing labour. This means that certain businesses will only have three factors of production. The nature and status of labour as a factor of production is in a fundamental process of change. A case in point is that the traditional function of a fighter pilot, which has existed since about 1914, is now being supplanted by digital innovation incorporating algorithms and automation. Drones are pilotless aircraft and substitute the traditional labour of the pilot out of economic consideration. Similarly, our understanding of entrepreneurship as a factor of production is being redefined because it is being supplemented with artificial intelligence. Artificial intelligence will enable entrepreneurial decisions to be reached on the basis of complex algorithms that mitigate risk and enable expert choice.

4.1 Multimedia and Negotiation

Most South Africans are steadily gaining access to multimedia through their ownership of cellular telephones, computers and their access to other multimedia platforms. There has been a basic change over the past decade in the way that we communicate and negotiate with one another due to innovations in multimedia. Multimedia is now increasingly being used across the spectrum of activities that underpin collective bargaining, negotiation and our daily communication, in both our private and public lives. It will render traditional union mandating processes associated with town hall crowds and mass meetings increasingly redundant. Multimedia has the potential to democratise and also tyrannise the workplace, displacing traditional feedback and mass communication approaches. There are many occasions when it will be more efficient and effective to bargain collectively and negotiate via e-mail or Skype than to engage in face-to-face negotiation. A negotiator will have the added benefit of a permanent and accurate record of the entire negotiation process. Multimedia will save costs and encourage more precision in the communication and negotiation process. Negotiations using Skype, live-streaming or e-mail would tend to remove emotions and be more rational, efficient and cost-effective, than the current bombastic face-to-face verbal interchange that characterises collective bargaining. YouTube footage, live-streaming and cell phone filming can be used to build a vivid negotiation case, and exclude some unnecessary and tedious explanations. When mandates and claims of representivity need to be tested, accurate, lawful verifications and ballots can be readily conducted by SMS or e-mail, at great speed, and at little or no cost. This technology will, in due course, change the balance of power among the parties to collective bargaining and expose un-mandated, undemocratic and non-representative action and intent.

There will be a lesser need to stage mass meetings which would require sending out invitations and hiring transport and facilities. The negotiation counterparts now have access to an infinitely larger and more influential virtual crowd, both within South Africa and around the world, by live-streaming the collective bargaining process. The integration of multimedia into the negotiations increases the extent, richness and complexity of stakeholder engagement very significantly. Stakeholders who were previously on the periphery of negotiations will become increasingly central to these processes. Twitter can be used to build and influence a negotiation case, and can also be used to create community solidarity networks. A virtual crowd can be created to provide wisdom and direction to negotiators while they are actually engaged in the process. Multimedia can be creatively used to present an excellent visual and auditory negotiation case and reduce tedious text. The negotiations themselves can be filmed and recorded at a minimal cost and used evidentially if so required. Multimedia is increasingly being used as a fundamental technological and interactive aspect of negotiation and deal-making, including the collective bargaining process. Skype will change the nature of caucusing during collective bargaining, and one will be able to conduct multiple caucuses and interactive processes between the counterparts simultaneously. Travel, accommodation and downtime expenses will be dramatically reduced. One is now able to simultaneously negotiate in multiple locations, with multiple partners, across the city, country and globe. Multimedia is enabling the networking of large and diverse crowds of people, representing different stakeholder groupings. This access to hyper-efficient networks was most certainly not available during the time of the struggle to destroy apartheid. Multimedia has accelerated the tempo of revolutions and social change. This is evident in the Tunisian and Egyptian uprisings as well as in the #FeesMustFall movement at universities in South Africa during 2015 and 2016.

It is often forgotten that at the time of South Africa's political transition collective bargaining was reinvented to destroy apartheid. Innovative negotiation and legal processes were at that time combined with progammes of mass action to bring about the downfall of apartheid. The legal processes were enacted through the courts, and mass action was conducted, via interconnected networks of communities, on the ground. Those approaches were slow and cumbersome in comparison with the techniques and technologies that are available to influence mass behaviour today. The present technologies of the Fourth Industrial Revolution are exponentially more powerful than anything that was available at the time of South Africa's political transition. Since then, the World Wide Web, e-mail, Facebook, Twitter and SMSes have become part of daily life.

Collective bargaining in South Africa needs to be reinvented anew. There is no space for retaining a sentimental attachment to obsolete and static 20th-century negotiation approaches which are no longer appropriate in the face of 21st-century challenges. The ongoing application of these obsolete collective bargaining processes places South Africa in a time warp. The failure of individuals and groups to discover satisfiers of the fundamental human needs that are arising from the new world of work is setting South Africa back. Collective bargaining, as it is currently conducted in South Africa, has become an inefficient, ill-mannered, time-consuming, expensive and archaic ritual. It is detached from the modern world of work.

4.2   The First Industrial Revolution (1760 – 1850)

It is necessary that the reader be briefly reminded about the driving forces of prior industrial revolutions in world history in order to have a contextual understanding of how our current industrial revolution, the Fourth Industrial Revolution, aligns with its historical predecessors. These prior industrial revolutions have implications for the mental models that inform the conduct of collective bargaining in the 21st century in South Africa.

The First Industrial Revolution in England began in about 1760 and involved radical innovation in the production processes that were associated with the textile and clothing industry in England. Weaving was previously undertaken painstakingly by hand. Wool and textile frames were then invented and these inventions caused the redundancy of many jobs that had previously been done by hand. The First Industrial Revolution converted a venerable home craft of wool and textile weaving into an organised process of mass production. This was achieved by linking the textile-producing towns in England with systems of canals which then improved the entire supply chain and logistics of the newly formed clothing and textile industries. The First Industrial Revolution extended until about 1850. Towards the end of the First Industrial Revolution, coal and steam energy were used to power steam locomotives. Steam trains further revolutionised supply chains, logistics and mass transportation.

4.3 The Second Industrial Revolution (1850 – 1930)

Henry Ford introduced the factory assembly line and ushered in the process of mass production. The hallmark of the Second Industrial Revolution was that steam, gas, oil and hydroelectric power were used to create electrical power, and later resulted in the formation of the factory system of mass assembly-line production which reached its heyday in the 1920s. Thomas Edison's invention of the electric light bulb was, at that time, as disruptive an innovation as has been the invention of the microchip that has formed the foundation of the Fourth Industrial Revolution.

4.4 The Third Industrial Revolution (1985 – 2007)

Rifkin[59] coined the concept of the Third Industrial Revolution. His essential notion was that the internet and many renewable energy sources were intersecting to create an environmentally sustainable mass energy movement that would change the nature of energy creation, storage and supply. There is considerable conceptual overlap between the notions of the Third and Fourth Industrial Revolutions, and it is not very clear why they have been differentiated from each other. They both appear to be on the same continuum of disruptive innovation and systemic multi-disciplinary digital interconnectedness.

4.5 New Ideologies and New Luddites

From the perspective of understanding why collective bargaining is failing in South Africa, it is noted that the most important counter-protest movement to the First and Second Industrial Revolutions was the Luddite movement. The Luddite movement began in Nottingham in the heart of the new clothing and textile industry in 1811. The Luddites regarded the new technology of wool and textile frames, and other innovations which made production much more efficient, as being disruptive and threatening to the basic security of employment and their entire quality of life. The Luddite movement spread. Many new textile and clothing factories were attacked and destroyed. The Parliament in England passed legislation to make attacks on factories a capital offence. This resulted in executions. Many Luddites were expelled from England and sent by convict ship to colonise Australia.

Stiglitz[60] acknowledged that progress usually comes at a great human cost. This will almost certainly apply to the Fourth Industrial Revolution with its inclination to accelerate automation across the board. It is envisaged that new forms of ideology analogous to those that accompanied the Luddite movement will in due course manifest to represent contending narratives and impute meaning to the employment fall-out that will arise from the Fourth Industrial Revolution. These ideologies will seek to justify the behaviour of interest groups with respect to all matters relating to the nature of work in the Fourth Industrial Revolution. These Fourth Industrial Revolution narratives and putative ideologies will be significantly different from those associated with the First and Second Industrial Revolutions. This is because these are radically different revolutions involving completely different worldviews, technologies, work processes and times. The common denominator of all the industrial revolutions, from the perspective of labour, has led to high levels of human insecurity and distress that accompany the realisation that one's skills are redundant and the experience of being thrust unemployed into a hostile and unfamiliar world, without the skills or knowledge to gain a sustainable income. The individual experience of alienation and distress will be multiplied manifold and may become mass phenomena.

It is foreseen that new ideologies that are similar to but also different from those that inspired the Luddite movement will emerge in South Africa, and also across the globe, once the lived experience of new and unfamiliar forms of employment insecurity in the Fourth Industrial Revolution become manifest. The new ideologies will aim to capture the protests, voices and conflicts that will inexorably arise from the Fourth Industrial Revolution. These conflicts will revolve around the obsolescence of current skills and employment, as well as the collapse of familiar rules and contractual sources of security, including the continuity of employment. Anticipatory echoes of this are already audible in National Union of Metal Workers of South Africa's (NUMSA) formation of a United Front. Faku[61] explained that a new union federation would be formed in competition with COSATU and 3 000 delegates from 40 trade unions are scheduled to attend the founding conference on 30 April 2016. It is touted to include the NUMSA that has a membership of 365 000 workers and the Amalgamated Mineworkers and Construction Union. The membership of COSATU has become increasingly disaffected because of the failure to address "the needs of its members" and "corruption, unemployment, inequality and poverty". Zwelinzima Vavi has been identified as a possible leader of the new trade union federation.

The narrative of how trade unions affiliated to COSATU together with the ANC and the South African Communist Party (SACP) formed the Tripartite Alliance, and together with the United Democratic Front (UDF), used rolling mass action to bring about the collapse of apartheid, has become mythologised into folklore. According to Seekings,[62] it was the UDF that enabled the ANC to be re-integrated back into South Africa after its thirty-year banishment. The UDF's leadership constituted the chrysalis for the establishment of the post-apartheid ANC government.

In 2014, the National Union of Metal Workers Union (NUMSA), which was then COSATU's largest affiliated trade union, withdrew its support for the ANC on the basis of the latter's subscription to neo-liberal economic policies and the neglect of its worker constituency. NUMSA reached a decision to form a United Front that would be used as a catalyst to form a socialist labour movement. COSATU responded by expelling NUMSA, its largest affiliate. The United Front will challenge the current political leadership in the August 2016 municipal elections. The United Front would be directly competitive with COSATU. Should the United Front be born, it could come to constitute the germ of a new Luddite movement that would seek to oppose the disruptive innovation that will accompany the development of the Fourth Industrial Revolution.

Presumably the modus operandi of the United Front will be to seek to match that of its predecessor, the UDF. Rolling mass action was then used to induce regime change in the pursuit of the satisfaction of fundamental human needs, which was then defined as the abolition of apartheid. If this simplified assessment is indeed correct, then the nationwide industrial, political and service level protests that are occurring on a daily basis across the country would be channelled through the yet to be established structures of the putative United Front as a platform to oppose the Fourth Industrial Revolution.

This re-awakening of populism and the pursuit of a United Front arises, in part, from the failure of business leaders to effectively use the workplace relationship and collective bargaining to address the fundamental human needs that are perceived by employees to be at risk by virtue of the encroachment of the new world of work. There has been a vacuum in communicating about the future of employment to the masses by all key stakeholders.

New skills, trades, jobs, professions and careers will need to be designed from scratch. It will be difficult to plan for the future if flexible and atypical employment does not come with the assurance of regular and predictable sources of income. If this does not happen, we could move into an age of employment insecurity.

A partial explanation for the highly strike-prone and conflictive nature of South African society might be that the Fourth Industrial Revolution is tapping into the deepest subliminal insecurities of labour and contributes to an ethos of nihilism, anarchy and polarisation. These fears are not necessarily conscious, but multimedia, the internet, newspapers, television and day-to-day lived experience provide constant proof of the omnipresence of the digital revolution

4.6 Contending Mental Models

Collective bargaining, as it is currently conducted in South Africa, is based on the presumptions and mental models of mass production, and the labour-intensive, extractive mining system of the 19th and 20th centuries. The worldviews that explain the First and Second Industrial Revolution are based on mechanistic models of organisations, and these obsolete perspectives are ineffectively applied to our current world of work. Collective bargaining in South Africa is conducted from the perspective of a mechanistic mental model of organisation. Gharejadaghi and Ackoff[83] explained that organisations that are structured on the basis of a mechanistic mental model have the following characteristics:

> Work is reduced to machine-like behavior, and workers are treated as replaceable machine parts. Adherence by parts to rules and regulations is made an end in itself, either by rewarding compliance, or punishing non-compliance. By this means, human responses to stimuli are made to approximate mindless physical reactions. All members of the system, other than the one in ultimate authority, are deprived of all information except that which is required to do their jobs. Instructions from above are not explained or justified. A mechanistically conceived social system is inflexible. Therefore, as long as its input does not vary, its output will not vary. It thus can only operate in a static environment.

A mechanistic mental model is consequently a uni-minded system with the leader having exclusive access to power and knowledge. The boss is regarded as the single and all-knowing mind controlling the organisation. The workers are merely cogs in the wheel, and regarded as 'un-minded' components of the system. North Korea is a country that appears to fit into an extremely mechanistic worldview.

Employees are arranged into hierarchies, and the boss has ultimate power. This mechanistic model of organisation is matched by the structure of trade unions which are also hierarchically arranged. Trade union bosses frequently have the ultimate say regarding industrial action, union investments of their members' income and life savings in pension funds, and negotiation strategy. A basic presumption of the mechanistic worldview is that business and trade unions exist in separate silos in a sealed-off and stand-alone system. Therefore the business enterprise often subscribes to the view that what happens in the community outside of work is not their concern and does not exist. This mechanistic worldview is mirrored in the trade unions' approach towards the unemployed who are singularly excluded from their ambit of attention as an inconvenient truth. The mechanistic worldview is a convenient illusion because it implies that one can be exonerated from the duty of gaining contextual knowledge, thus negating the existence of a wider social responsibility. This worldview also enables a business to blank out the reality of its employees, living in a family, and community, with their own social life. It allows businesses to deem that living conditions in the townships are irrelevant to their own success or failure and enables employers to hold onto the delusion that there is no such thing as a wider community. The deafening silence in South Africa about our massive unemployment is a stark illustration of the disempowerment that accompanies this mechanistic model of organisation. This silence is but one example of the mechanistic model's unrepresentative voice.

Collective bargaining in South Africa is currently conducted in a manner that is oblivious to the fragility and potential for redundancy of current jobs and employment under the Fourth Industrial Revolution. It is alarming that the tacit presumption between business, trade unions and the state appears to be one of the permanence and stability of current jobs, trades, careers, professions and that employment as we know it will continue unimpeded into the future. Nothing could be further from the truth. It is because of the fact that a mechanistic mental model can only operate in a static environment that it is so vulnerable to disruptive innovation and the inherent systemic dynamism of the Fourth Industrial Revolution.

The systems mental model that underpins the Fourth Industrial Revolution assumes that an organisation is a multi-minded system. The parameters of a social system are knowledge, wisdom, choice, purpose, expertise, values and the capacity to invoke powerful networks. The systems concept of organisation is therefore entirely congruent with the knowledge economy. In a systems concept of organisation, planning is not so much about making plans but about changing minds. The inner world of work seeks to become aligned with the outer system, and vice versa. Max-Neef et al. (1989:19) contend that: "Human needs must be understood as a system, that is, all human needs are interrelated and interactive. With the sole exception of the need for subsistence, that is, to remain alive, no hierarchies exist within the system." Gharejadaghi and Ackoff[54] presented the essential dynamics of a social system thus: "The performance of a social system is not the sum of the independent performance of its parts. It is the product of their interactions. Therefore effective management of a social system requires management of the interactions of its parts, not their independent actions. Moreover, since a social system interacts with its environment, management of this interaction is also required for it to function effectively." The Fourth Industrial

Revolution will clearly impact on every social system in the world because of the connectedness between automation, robotics, crypto-currencies, 3D printing, genetics, artificial intelligence, crowd platforms, cloud functionality, nanotechnology, self-healing materials with microvascular techniques, biotechnology and other forms of computerisation, and digital technology.

Explanations about the human impact of the First and Second Industrial Revolutions are typically based on a mechanistic mental model of an organisation; while explanations for the Third and Fourth Industrial Revolutions will tend to be based on systems models of organisation. This creates a logical disjuncture in the collective bargaining process because, in the final analysis, the mechanistic and systems worldviews are oppositional. The mechanistic mental models provide a narrative that fits with the lived experience of the First and Second Industrial Revolutions, but it is seriously misaligned with systems thinking that underpins the Fourth Industrial Revolution, and vice versa. The mechanistic mental models cannot offer a coherent critique of the systems thinking which is inherent to the connectivity of the Fourth Industrial Revolution. The mechanistic mental model is essentially static and this stasis has become the hallmark of collective bargaining in South Africa. Collective bargaining has not yet evolved to address the enormous fluid and multidimensional challenges of the digital Fourth Industrial Revolution. Collective bargaining is indeed a product of the assembly line, Fordism and mass production; and many of its premises therefore no longer hold. Similarly, the Fourth Industrial Revolution has yet to be experienced and understood.

The evolution of the First and Second Industrial Revolutions was accompanied by the development of trade unions, employer associations, labour law, basic conditions of employment and the suffragette movement, resulting in women being given the right to vote, equal rights, public health legislation and many other improvements in working and living conditions besides. The challenge that is presented by the Fourth Industrial Revolution is for collective bargaining to be reinvented once again and to continue with this tradition, albeit in a very different form and under very different circumstances.

4.7   The Future of Employment under Collective Bargaining

The future of employment and the extent and quality of the labour market absorption of potential employees into the economy is clearly South Africa's single most important economic, social and political challenge. It is all too often forgotten that the failure to create employment is not only an economic problem; it is also, in its essence, a human tragedy.

Max-Neef et al.[65] explain the psychological trauma that an unemployed person suffers in the quest for employment against insurmountable odds of achieving employability:

> It is known that a person suffering from extended unemployment goes through an emotional roller-coaster experience which involves at least four phases: (a) shock (b) optimism (c) pessimism (d) fatalism. The last stage represents the transition from frustration to stagnation, and from there, to the final stage of apathy, where the person reaches his/her lowest level of self-esteem. It is quite evident that extended unemployment will disarrange a person's fundamental needs at a primary level. Due to subsistence problems, the person will feel increasingly unprotected, crisis in the family and guilt may destroy affections, lack of participation will give way to feelings of isolation and marginalization, and declining self-esteem may generate an identity crisis. Extended unemployment generates both individual and social pathologies.

This pathological collapse in self-esteem that arises from structural unemployment characterises the psychological state of millions of unemployed South Africans. Given the present circumstances of generalised economic crisis, it is fundamentally incorrect to designate these as only affecting individuals. South Africa has collective pathologies associated with unemployment that can, and might at any moment, explode into political violence. The Fourth Industrial Revolution makes this problem much more serious than it ever was before. This is because the potentially redundant jobs cover all economic sectors and almost all levels of skill. Many of these jobs and professions are under immediate threat of obsolescence.

Schwab and Samans[66] cite the apocryphal story of a current Grade 1 scholar entering school in 2016. This student will, on completion of schooling, discover that 65% of all currently available and identifiable jobs will have disappeared and become redundant. This Grade 1 scholar on completing school will, in all probability, be employed in a job or occupation that does not exist today.

Zero Hour Contracts (ZHCs) are flexible employment contracts that arise from the Fourth Industrial Revolution, and do not offer employees any guarantee of the number of hours that they will work. These ZHCs are increasingly becoming a familiar feature of employment across the world. Huws and Joyce[67] conducted important research that is congruent with that offered by Schwab and Samans,[68] cited above, on the nature, extent and types of crowd employment in the United Kingdom. Their sample consisted of adults between the ages of 15 and 75 years. They found that 8 million people in the UK are engaged in crowd employment of different types. Crowd employment is a new mode of employment that will have both positive and negative implications for the quality of work and the quality of life. Contracts of the zero hour type are flexible, exclude medical aid, life insurance and pension coverage and can be terminated at any time for any reason. The full implications are not yet clearly understood because they have not yet manifested definitively. 21% of Huws and Joyce's (2016) sample indicated that they intended to gain work via crowd platforms including Upwork, Uber, Handy, Freelancer, Clickworker, Peopleperhour, Taskrabitt, Mybuilder and Mop.

Huws and Joyce[69] opined that flexible and atypical forms of employment are clearly changing working and living conditions at a fundamental level. The employment contracts between a crowd employer and employee will be individual contracts that fall outside of the space of collective bargaining. Toohey, Sottos, Lewis, Moore and White[70] provided an interesting illustration of how maintenance engineering will be affected by this new digital technology. These scholars found that:

> Self-healing polymers composed of microencapsulated healing agents, exhibit remarkable mechanical performance, and regenerative ability, but are limited to autonomic repair of a single event, in a given location. Self-healing is triggered by crack-induced rupture of embedded capsules; thus, once a localized region is depleted of healing agent, further repair is precluded. Re-mendable polymers can achieve multiple healing cycles, but require external intervention in the form of heat treatment and applied pressure.

They therefore found that many materials would be manufactured that will be able to autonomously repair after repeated damaging events by inserting three-dimensional vascular networks into them. This innovation will enable polymers, steels, glass and concrete to be infused with a vascular network that results in self-repair in a manner that is analogous to tissue repair in the human body. The implications of Toohey, Sottos, Lewis, Moore and White's[71] research on the future of maintenance work are startling. Maintenance, as it is presently known, will change fundamentally in those areas where self-repair is possible. Self-healing metals are being created that will, for example, render certain types of panel beating jobs (say for hail damage) unnecessary because the metal, with its newly inserted vascular system, can now be designed to ensure that dents will pop out and self-heal. The same applies to painting tasks; the repair of cement and repairs to glass that is cracked; and many other materials besides, that can now, with currently available technology, be designed to self-repair. Collective bargaining will fail because the materials that are used in the engineering project will be able to self-maintain and therefore intelligent capital will increasingly substitute labour as a factor of production. Fewer people, employed via crowd sourcing, will be members of unions and thus the need for a union will fall away. The unions themselves will gradually disappear. Frey and Osborne[72] also observed that algorithms for big data are currently being used to automate very complex professional careers.

Schwab and Samans[73] observed that:

> An additional dimension to consider is the general trend towards flexible work, identified by our respondents as one of the biggest drivers of transformation of business models in many industries, and therefore also one of the topmost concerns at the national level ... Telecommuting, co-working spaces, virtual teams, freelancing and online talent platforms are all on the rise, transcending the physical boundaries of the office or factory floor, and redefining the boundary between one's job and private life in the process. Modern forms of workers' organizations like digital freelance unions and updated labour market regulation are starting to emerge to complement these new organizational models. The challenge for employers, individuals and governments alike, is going to be to work out ways and means, to ensure that the changing nature of work benefits everyone.

Labour-alternative innovations will be led and managed by highly skilled persons who are knowledgeable about robotics, computer automation and 3D printing, and other interconnected technologies. These new technologies will cost much less than labour and can work 24 hours a day over indefinite periods of time without illness, with exactly calibrated levels of precision, and with constant efficiency and quality. Crypto-currencies, block chain technology and crowd funding will disrupt employment in the financial sector. Disruptive innovation is expected to invoke the greatest change in the nature of banking since the first loan was made in Germany in the fifteenth century.

4.8 The Way Forward

Disruptive innovation is changing all aspects of employment and indeed, of the nature of work. Industrial conflict accelerates mechanisation and computerisation. It is therefore fuelling a switch from mechanistic mental models to systems mental models. South African society needs urgent education and training to give it direction to address the new world of work. This is a fundamental and difficult challenge because no one clearly understands what the new nature of employment and career requirements will be. Disruptive innovation is not restricted to unskilled employment, and will extend into highly skilled work and the professions over the next several years as well. All aspects of the economy will be affected by this development, including manufacturing, mining, education, finance, retail, entertainment, trade, agriculture, education, energy and health to name but a few.

Both management and union negotiation teams have naturally focused on the 'here and now' of wage negotiations because it is a practical and important next step in improving the day-to-day working conditions of employees. They have systemically failed to foresee the bigger picture of the radical changes that are taking place in the basic nature of employment in the Fourth Industrial Revolution. It appears that this critical information has not been conveyed to the employees and communities in which they operate. They have also failed to invoke a viable public process that will ensure employment creation in the digital age. Business and labour, as negotiation counterparts, have therefore generally failed to create effective feedback loops that enable employees to understand, cope with, and fully appreciate the consequences of disruptive innovation for the fundamental nature of employment. The negotiation counterparts have also failed to create a feedback loop between the imperative to discover satisfiers of fundamental human needs and how these might be integrated into the collective bargaining process. It would be far wiser to predicate collective bargaining on a feedback loop that is based on a systems worldview of the intense fragility and potential redundancy of jobs, employment and the accelerating obsolescence and half-lives of most business models, as well as the availability of new jobs, new careers and new business models in the digital age. Collective bargaining is failing because, in its present form, it is treating the symptoms and not the root causes of the conflict between employees and employers, which is that both parties are caught up in a radical change process that is revolutionising the nature of work and business.

The consequences of the Fourth Industrial Revolution have been manifesting with ever-greater intensity over the past few years, and are projected to accelerate exponentially into the future. If the changing nature of employment is not seriously and systematically addressed, South Africa's already critical youth unemployment problems could become intractable and lead to profound and endemic political unrest and violence. Much investment will need to be devoted to re-skilling and re-educating employees, whose skill-sets have become obsolete. The re-training, re-skilling and re-education of employees across the whole employment life span will clearly become a major educational and skills requirement in South Africa.

Frey and Osborne's[74] research is important to parents, children, employees, employers, teachers, professors, public leaders, politicians, religious leaders, communities, the media and all members of society. This should be disseminated as widely as possible in order to provide an informed basis for serious discussion and decision-making that might ensure that our future generations are indeed employable in the Fourth Industrial Revolution. This broad process of computerisation is therefore both a new technological *and* social movement and they combine into the Fourth Industrial Revolution.

The Fourth Industrial Revolution is similar to the preceding industrial revolutions in the sense that it is analogous to a socio-economic and political tidal wave. It will cause radical disruption to the world of work. Human ingenuity will, in due course, no doubt adapt to it, make meaning out of and derive benefit from it, leading to much greater levels of employment. South Africans should urgently do all that is in their power to be on the right side of change and to adapt as quickly as possible to this revolution because the quicker and deeper the adaptation, the less will be the pain that is experienced by choosing education, careers and work that lead to the dead-end of employment obsolescence.

Trade unions, in their present form in South Africa, will find it extremely difficult to act as collective bargaining agents for employees on crowd platforms. This means that they would have to oversee and negotiate upon thousands, if not millions of individual employment contracts. Trade unions will thus have to develop innovative electronic applications if they are to become effective participants in the Fourth Industrial Revolution.

Trade unions evolved to address the human challenges that resulted from mass production. They currently do not have the experience or expertise to contiguously address the challenges of *both* mass customisation and mass production. It is already clear that the electronic contracting processes associated with crowd platforms individualises relationships at the expense of the collective. It changes the dynamics of human interaction in the context of the world of work. Crowd platforms and the Fourth Industrial Revolution are therefore projected to not only render traditional business models obsolete, they will also make the traditional mode of trade unionism, including collective bargaining as it is currently conducted, redundant.

5

Strikes, Rolling Mass Action and Civil Conflicts as Indicators of South Africa's Unrest Proneness

The International Labour Office (ILO) is the United Nations' global labour authority. It defines a labour dispute in their Laborsta Data Base[75] as "a state of disagreement over a particular issue, or group of issues, over which there is conflict between workers and employers, or about which grievance is expressed, by workers or employers, or about which workers or employers support other workers or employers in their demands or grievances." This definition is applied to labour disputes across the world, including those that take place in South Africa.

For the ILO, a strike can only be arranged by one or more groups of workers who are expressing grievances against their employers. A lockout can be understood as a management strike by employers against workers who might use this device to enforce terms and conditions of employment on employees who oppose them. Therefore the unemployed cannot engage in a strike with a non-employer.

5.1 Strikes by the Unemployed against Non-employers

The Western Cape farm workers' strike of 2012 defied the ILO Laborsta Data Base's[76] definition of a worker and a strike. The unemployed engaged in a strike and acted in solidarity with the employed against the owners of the farms. Many persons who could be defined as non-employees, the unemployed or the underemployed, participated in industrial action against the farmers. The employers in this case were the farmers who owned the farms where the strikes and unrest usually took place. The farm workers and the unemployed also pursued grievances against the political authority of the state. The farm workers and unemployed were therefore striking against a non-employer (the state) as well. The term 'workers' is constrained and implies that a strike exists only if there is an employment contract between employer and employee. This is a narrow definition. There are many cases in South Africa where non-employees have been intrinsic to strike action, and the industrial action has not been directed against an employer as is the case with sympathy stay-aways. Kahn and Bernickow (2013) of the Commission for Conciliation, Mediation, and Arbitration (CCMA) observed, interestingly, that in South Africa:

Labour disputes are rarely confined to workers or the workplace. This can be seen in the fact that, day after day, the entire community of Stofland, De Doorns' informal settlement, came out in support of the workers' demands and added their own demands – related to their personal needs for better housing, better sanitation, access to work, and an end to inequality … Stofland residents joined striking De Doorns' workers in protesting, not just against low wages, but of the consequences of having to get by on those wages.

This experience is congruent with De Visser and Powell's[77] previously discussed research on the causes of service delivery protests. The farm workers' strike therefore became conflated with a service delivery conflict. Both of these conflicts were very complicated and did not fall into the ILO's definitions of either a strike or a dispute because in each instance the respective communities were involved in the conflict regardless of whether they were employees, employers or not. Unemployed members of the Western Cape community, who were not employed as farm workers, were actually party to the collective bargaining process and subsequent disputes and strikes. Wilderman[78] reports that:

> The large-scale protest began in De Doorns in early November, 2012 and by early December had spread to well over twenty towns across the Western Cape, involving tens of thousands of workers, unemployed, youth, and other members of the poor in the rural areas. The exact nature and size of the protests varied from town to town, but generally the activities of the protestors involved marches, blocking of roads, and, importantly, a refusal to go to work; in many cases, the protests also involved some destruction of property as well as confrontations with the police that involved tear gas, rubber bullets, and arrests.

5.2 The Temporal Aspect of a Strike – Temporary Work Stoppages and Intergenerational Conflicts

For the ILO, "A strike is a temporary work stoppage, effected by one or more groups of workers, with a view of enforcing or resisting demands, or expressing grievances, or supporting other workers in their demands, or grievances" (2013:1). The term 'temporary work stoppage' refers to the temporal component of their definition of a strike. It implies that a strike, in order to be a strike, should only take place over a short period of time.

In South Africa, strikes, and their repercussions, often play themselves out and simmer as low-intensity conflict over long periods of time and may even continue in a systemic cycle for years, even generations. Social conflict is often intergenerational and the

ILO's temporal definition excludes an understanding of poverty cycles that may take place over centuries and which are root causes of social conflict. The Solms-Delta case that was previously discussed involved centuries of abusive employment relationships in the Cape winelands, and part of its solution came from an acknowledgement of this historical and temporal legacy. A legal entity, including a trust, was created that sought to ensure that the historical memory of the farm labourers' oppression would be preserved for future generations and would not be repeated.

The Lonmin 2012 strike also demonstrated that there are practical limitations to the applicability of the temporal aspect of the ILO's definition of a strike as a 'temporary work stoppage' to the reality of industrial conflict in South Africa. Lonmin's 2015 decision to retrench 5 000 miners arose from the strike action that took place three years previously. The prior strike, which took place in 2012, strengthened the consideration mine managers were already giving to the automation of the mines. The decision to automate arose from the global trend of disruptive technological innovation that is already enabling the mechanisation of work previously done by labour. The ensuing conflict could therefore be ascribed to a disagreement about how capital could innovatively displace labour as a factor of production. The decision to substitute labour with capital straddled a period of about three years from 2012 to 2015, and has implications for all aspects of future employment relationships at Lonmin. While it might not have appeared that there was any conflict in the interceding years, the decision to automate and computerise had been taken. Lonmin's decision to retrench, therefore, can be directly attributed to the Fourth Industrial Revolution. The retrenchments can be ascribed to the disruptive innovation and changing business models that are arising from computerisation. Those miners who were earmarked to be retrenched might be expected to construe Lonmin's retrenchment decision as a retributive lockout in retaliation for the prior strike of 2012. This conflict itself can be expected to fester over time, and perhaps even for years to come. The employees' narrative explaining their retrenchment can be expected to revolve around their exploitation under the Second Industrial Revolution while the Lonmin management team's narrative justifying the retrenchment would be based on the new and efficient forms of employment, including robotics, that are taking place in the Fourth Industrial Revolution, confirming that the negotiation counterparts are worlds apart.

This case also demonstrates that a temporary work stoppage may lead to a long-term and insidious conflict over years and even over generations.

5.3 The Degree of Strike Proneness in South Africa

Bhorat and Tseng analysed South Africa's strike data in terms of the International Labour Office's definition of strike action.[79] They used the ILO's (2013) definition confining a strike to temporary conflicts between employers and employees, and asserted that the pervasive perception that South Africa's collective bargaining process is inordinately conflictive and strike prone is not substantiated by the ILO's data. They confirmed that South Africa has the fifth highest strike indicators in the world, contending that:

> South Africa's long-term strike rate ranks fifth in the world with 206 days lost per 1 000 workers ... [and] the results of these comparisons show that strike action, and the implied costs in terms of work days lost per strikers' working days, are common in any democratic society with a functional industrial relations environment where workers and employers are free to negotiate the terms of labour costs. Even in terms of strike intensity, South Africa's experience is no different from that taking place in both developed and developing countries in the long run.

These statistics, alone, cannot be used to impute or refute the assertion that South Africa has either a functional or dysfunctional industrial relations system. The quantitative data on its own cannot offer a qualitative judgment of South Africa's unrest proneness; it requires supplementation with appropriate contextual and qualitative information that offers a more complete and rounded picture. This would include a qualitative analysis of the prevalence of how other forms of conflict are manifesting and conflating in other parts of the society, and their interrelationship with industrial unrest. The integration of qualitative and quantitative data would enable one to gain a more holistic appreciation of South Africa's unrest proneness and its associated political risk.

Their conclusion about the normality of strikes in South Africa was reached on the basis of the ILO's confined definition of a labour dispute. The ILO's disaggregation of the strike data, based upon their legal-economic definitions of strikes and disputes, risks blurring a clear contextual understanding of the nature and extent of socio-political and industrial conflict in South Africa.

The data that is collected on strikes needs to be of such a quality that it can discern between the different forms of underlying conflict that arise in South Africa. This will enable the construction of a theory base which will enable the creation of practical frameworks for effective and differentiated conflict intervention approaches using appropriate methodologies and experts to address the different typologies of conflict. This will help us understand and address these different forms of conflict much more effectively and design contextually-specific negotiation solutions. Strike data should seek to differentiate normal conflicts from deep-rooted conflicts because they require both different negotiation competencies and levels of experience, knowledge and wisdom to address them. Different levels of political and economic risk also accompany normal and deep-rooted conflict. Normal conflicts bear a low political risk while deep-rooted conflicts carry a high accompanying political risk. This information could be used both diagnostically and for the purposes of prognoses.

It is necessary for businessmen and -women, trade unionists, the state and, indeed, all actors to develop a deeper understanding of the complexity of the systemic interrelationship of social conflicts taking place in South Africa and their impact on society in general. It is essential that professional competence and skill be developed in addressing these conflicts. It is necessary that leaders should gain knowledge of conflict and understand whether a normal conflict might escalate into a deep-rooted conflict and what steps should be taken to prevent such an escalation from occurring. Conversely, the leaders need to acquire the knowledge and skill to convert a deep-rooted conflict into developmental and growth processes. This will require appropriate education. The parties to collective bargaining have a data analytics need. They require qualitative and quantitative information that can be distilled into data that will provide a clear understanding of the factors that are driving conflict in South Africa and how they might be most wisely addressed.

Collective bargaining provides an important legislated platform for negotiations and social dialogue between trade unions, employers and the state, as they relate to working conditions. These improved wages and conditions of employment that arise from the collective bargaining are deemed to indicate an improvement in living standards.

5.4 The Marikana Massacre – a Fractal of Other Conflicts in South Africa

Bell[80] confirmed that the breakdown in collective bargaining, and the ensuing Marikana Massacre, involved two deadly incidents of deep-rooted conflict. The first involved the execution, by the police, of 10 miners at Lonmin. The subsequent incident involved the police shooting 34 striking miners. The Marikana Massacre has no recent international equivalent and represents an abysmal low in collective bargaining in South Africa. It is an example of the extreme escalation from normal conflict into deep-rooted conflict, arising from a breakdown in negotiation and the failure to discover satisfiers of fundamental human needs in a wise and peaceful way. The conflict at Marikana required that all the leaders possessed a deep understanding of the contextual factors that were driving the schism, including culture, history, religious beliefs, ethics, economics, psychology, politics, medicine and knowledge of the built environment. Simplistic and reactive single-loop learning processes were imposed on a situation that required deep and double-loop learning. Wicked problems were treated as tame problems and fundamental human needs were trivialised. Bell[81] explained: "The first executions saw 10 persons killed. A few days later on the 16 August 2012 a further 34 miners were shot, bringing the total number of deaths to 44."

Bell[82] reflected that the Marikana Massacre "is merely the most brutal, and most obvious of thousands of unrest incidents around the country. We have them almost on a daily basis. There are illegal marches, burning barricades and stoning of ANC councillors' residences." We cannot impute stable collective bargaining and industrial relations in South Africa in the midst of this socio-political and economic tumult.

The five-month strike that took place in the platinum mines during 2014 was not 'a temporary work stoppage'. It was a fundamental schism in industrial relations. This, according to Stoddard,[83] was the longest and most disruptive strike in South African history.

The knock-on effects of strikes can continue for years after the confrontation. About 22 000 mining jobs could be lost in the aftermath of this wave of strike action in the mining industry. This illustrates the power of technology, robotics and computerisation. It is clearly simply a matter of time before advanced robotics can be used to displace labour on a vast scale and perform onerous, physical and dangerous jobs in the mining industry.

5.5 Attribution of Blame to the Other

Lindeque[84] reported that Mr Piet Motasa, the president of the National Union of Mineworkers (NUM), alleged that the proposed retrenchments of 22 000 miners that was referred to above was simply a political ploy by big business that was intended to alienate voters from supporting the ANC in the 2016 municipal elections. Motasa's utterances trivialised a very real and deep-rooted problem about the future of employment in the mining industry. The basic question that remained unasked is: How on earth could the mining industry retrench 22 000 miners and continue to satisfy the demand of world markets for the supplies of platinum, gold and other commodities that they seek? Little concern is displayed for the factors that are driving unemployment, underemployment and the future of employment in South Africa. Instead these issues are used as ammunition in a game of tit-for-tat.

According to Lindeque,[85] NUM interpreted the intended retrenchments in the mining industry as simply a stratagem by business to impute responsibility to the ANC for these mass lay-offs. This diagnosis reflects a Second Industrial Revolution diagnosis of a Fourth Industrial Revolution configuration. The fact of the matter is that, in due course, there will be mass lay-offs in mines, not only in South Africa but also across all mining countries in the world because automation and advanced robotics that can perform the key underground jobs at the expense of labour are already being manufactured. This has already happened in the automotive industry and is clearly spreading into the mining industry as well.

Lindeque[86] cited the NUM president Piet Motasa thus: "Before each and every election we have had in the country, they are preceded by retrenchments." It is Motasa's assertion that business is engaging in a conspiracy to use collective bargaining as a tool to influence the political process in South Africa. This commentary represents a fundamental absence of trust between the key stakeholders in the collective bargaining process. Implicit in Motasa's comments is the notion that employees and their communities will perceive the retrenchment as an act of revenge for engaging in the prior strikes. Motasa's accusation suggests that collective bargaining is failing in South Africa because it is being undermined by a win-lose retributive mental model characterised by mistrust and attempts to blame the negotiation counterparts. One can also deduce that it is failing because of a conflict in worldviews that subscribe to a First and Second Industrial Revolution for diagnosing the causes of labour conflict versus Fourth Industrial Revolution diagnosis of the future of employment, and vice versa.

Similarly, Helen Zille, who was at the time of the farm workers' strike the Democratic Alliance's leader, asserted that this conflict was carefully fomented by the ANC in order to politically destabilise the Western Cape. Zille[87] alleged that at the time of the farm workers' strike: "I was tipped off about an ANC strategy to 'bring Marikana to the farms of the Western Cape' – a phrase used repeatedly by the ANC, and particularly by Tony Ehrenreich, who combines a role as COSATU provincial secretary and the ANC caucus leader in the City of Cape Town." Three people lost their lives during this conflict and homesteads, vineyards and orchards were burnt to ashes.

Zille alleged that the ANC's stratagem was purposefully and cynically escalatory. It sought to encourage the Western Cape farm workers' strike to manifest as a peasant revolt in order to distract attention from their responsibility for the Marikana Massacre, conveying the impression that 'we are all in the same boat' in order to impute normality into this tragedy. Collective bargaining is therefore failing because the external environment outside of business is so highly politically charged that it is being distracted from its purpose.

5.6 Rolling Mass Action

The Marikana Massacre took place on 10 August 2012 and the Western Cape farm workers' strike began on 27 August 2012. These two conflicts involved different economic sectors and took place approximately 1 500 kilometres apart in different provinces in South Africa. They have a temporal connection and similar root causes relating to the failure to search for and discover satisfiers to address fundamental human needs. They are configurations of the same broader South African social system. Both communities have suffered from desperate poverty over prolonged periods. They both included mostly unskilled and semi-skilled employees with very low levels of education and training. In both cases, the strikes resulted in the employees experiencing severe trauma, alienation, insecurity and polarisation. The Western Cape farm workers' strike ended in January 2013. As is the case with Marikana, its socio-political ramifications are still evident three years later. The causal factors are similar to those that have been described as existing at the time that Mark Solms purchased the Solms-Delta wine estate, and he too was confronted by the reality of these deeply destructive historical relationships. The Western Cape farm workers' strike starkly illustrates the complexity of collective bargaining in South Africa.

Du Preez[88] compared the quality and types of conflicts that were levelled against apartheid and led by COSATU and the UDF during the 1980s with the quality and types of conflicts that have been occurring in South Africa in recent years. He noted that a pattern of increased intensity and varieties of industrial and civil conflicts has emerged over the past decade. He asserted that the levels of strike action, social protest, civil disobedience and service delivery protests were now equivalent, in both quality and quantity, to the levels of protests that were enacted to bring about the downfall of apartheid in the 1980s and early 1990s, during the period of rolling mass action. Du Preez[89] declares that: "the last time that South Africa experienced this level of daily protest was when the UDF and COSATU's un-governability campaigns and rolling mass action of the late 1980s were aimed at bringing the apartheid government to its knees". It is contended that the root causes of these conflicts reside in the failure of the main social partners to find satisfiers of fundamental human needs. This has engendered a profound collective sense of existential and axiological insecurity. This fear and foreboding is further compounded by the perceived fragility and tenuousness of employment in the Fourth Industrial Revolution. This employment insecurity is enhanced by daily evidence and experience of retrenchments, dismissals, massive unemployment and underemployment, which are driven by computerisation. These are accompanied by toxic forms of poverty, including the failure of the national educational system to offer a curriculum design for employability. It is therefore a crisis of both meaning and being.

The intensity of these conflating socio-political conflicts is further illustrated by the fact that South Africa underwent 3 000 protests over a period of 90 days in 2014. An average of 30 political, industrial and service delivery conflicts took place per day, and involved more than 1 000 000 (one million) people. This equates to approximately 4 000 000 (four million) people over the year. In 2014, another strike took place, lasting five months, on the platinum mines in South Africa. This was the longest strike in South African history. These additional conflicts and protests therefore should be added to the ILO's Laborsta Data Base (2013) on strikes in South Africa, which signify the fifth highest strike proneness in the world, with 206 days lost per 1 000 workers. 3 000 conflicts over 90 days equates to approximately 12 000 protests in the year 2014. Over a period of 40 days, there were 40 violent conflicts. This equates to approximately 365 violent conflicts taking place in South Africa over the year. Patel[90] provided similar data about the rolling mass action, validating Du Preez's exposition. Patel[91] noted that Gauteng's Police Commissioner, Mzwandile Petros, had confirmed that the Gauteng Province, which is South Africa's (and Africa's) economic heartland, had experienced 560 protests over a period of 40 days and that 40 of these protests had been violent.

The research that was conducted by Max-Neef et al., and De Visser and Powell[92] show that these different forms of conflict about fundamental human needs cannot be artificially disaggregated if the picture is to be fully understood.

One must be cautious about separating industrial conflicts that arise from the failure in collective bargaining from the current wave of rolling mass action in the broader community. The latter includes solidarity strike action from non-employees, the unemployed, and the underemployed and is ignited by the failure to address fundamental human needs.

It is reiterated that the behavioural patterns that are exhibited in strike action are driven by the selfsame fundamental human needs that precipitate service delivery protests, vigilante action, xenophobic violence, Zama Zama mining operations, taxi violence and other forms of community-based conflict in South Africa.

It is easy to become blinded by the enormity of these conflicts, to become disheartened, and to presume that one cannot change the situation. The challenge is to confront and negate the root causes of deep-rooted conflict, as a concerted national project, by seeking to identify and implement satisfiers of fundamental human needs. Excellent leaders and ample state resources should be deployed to address the problem of the future of employment with the seriousness that the matter deserves. Max-Neef et al.'s (1989) notion that fundamental human needs have a dualistic character of both a deprivation and a potential provides an important challenge. How can human deprivation be converted into human potential?

6

Stakeholder Fragmentation and Collective Bargaining in South Africa – the Interaction of Pathologies of Conflict and Poverty

It is unhelpful to disaggregate industrial unrest from other forms of political and civil conflict. This distorts and obfuscates an understanding of the bigger picture which sees these multiple conflicts as coalescing into a unifying stream. The influence of collective bargaining on the worldviews of stakeholders in their interaction with other stakeholders is very strong. The rules of engagement in South African industrial relations are generally conflictive and competitive, and frequently reduce to a zero-sum game of tit-for-tat. The one party's loss is seen as the other's gain. These rules of engagement have now penetrated into many areas of society and characterise the interrelationship of stakeholders that were formally allies of the South African trade union movement. These hostile and conflictive rules of engagement are now inducing a far-reaching and seemingly unstoppable fragmentation of former stakeholder alliances. The driving force behind this fragmentation is the failure by the parties to seek to discover sustainable satisfiers of fundamental needs. Fundamental human needs are not addressed in their dualistic nature, as both deprivation and potential. Instead the parties tend to approach fundamental human needs in a bipolar and indeed binary manner. Deprivation is allocated to the other, and potential is accorded to oneself. This worldview is unsustainable and is causing the destruction of stakeholders who have a crucial role to play in creating a stable South Africa.

South Africa's social compact is fragmenting into a multiplicity of subsidiary and interconnected stakeholders that are conflicting with one another and causing different and distinctive forms of poverty. These conflicts between the subsidiary stakeholders have developed lives of their own. They consume a great deal of negative energy and prevent ordinary South Africans from engaging in constructive activities that enable the pursuit of growth, development and discovering satisfiers of fundamental human needs. These socio-political conflicts become ritualised and form repetitive patterns of negative and dysfunctional behaviour which become extremely difficult to break once they are established. They are obviously an important obstruction to investor confidence and muddy perceptions of South Africa's creditworthiness.

Insofar as these socio-political conflicts form predictable patterns, they can be managed if the root causes driving them are wisely addressed. This analysis seeks to offer insight into the configuration patterns of stakeholder fragmentation which is resulting in the emergence of a multiplicity of new stakeholders, all with different visions, purpose, resources and modus operandi of their own. Very few of these stakeholders have offered constructive solutions to providing satisfiers of fundamental human needs, or offered any solutions that will address the root causes of unemployment, underemployment and the challenges of the future of employment in the Fourth Industrial Revolution. There is an urgent need to discover ways in which this negativity can be converted into positivity.

Each stakeholder that is identified in this discussion presented with its own distinctive form of poverty and potential. These different forms of poverty configure with other forms of poverty, leading to social and pathological forms of impoverishment that hold the majority of South Africans in bondage. The South African state is in crisis with respect to economic growth, human development and the discovery of satisfiers of fundamental human needs, which together manifest in potentially catastrophic structural unemployment.

Collective bargaining is failing because it is not contributing to economic growth, employment creation, human development and the discovery of satisfiers of fundamental human needs. This analysis supports Max-Neef et al.'s (1989: 21) finding that traditional concepts of poverty are econometric where poverty is defined as an income that falls below a certain level. This economically-based definition of conflict is problematic because it is simplistic and inhibits the search for strategies that will counteract the many different forms of poverty that are known to exist. Max-Neef et al. assert that:[93]

> Any fundamental human need that is not satisfied reveals a poverty, some examples are poverty of subsistence (due to insufficient income, food, shelter, etc.), of protection (due to bad health system, violence, arms race, etc.), of affection (due to authoritarianism, oppression, exploitative relations with natural environment, etc.), of understanding (due to poor quality of education), of participation (due to marginalization and discrimination of women, children and minorities), of identity (due to imposition of alien values upon local and regional cultures, forced migration, political exile, etc.). But poverties are not only poverties. Much more than that, each generates pathologies.

Stakeholders are in dynamic interaction with one another. They have their own objectives, power, will, resources, purpose and values. They may be oppositional or allied to any or all of the other stakeholders at any one point in time. They act as a system such that a change in the behaviour of one stakeholder will have a knock-on effect and change relationships with other stakeholders. Changing stakeholder allegiances have revealed themselves in the collective bargaining process in fluctuating patterns of conflict, competition, collaboration and co-operation. These changing patterns of stakeholder fragmentation will be shown to provide compelling insight into why collective bargaining is failing in South Africa.

A synoptic environmental scan of stakeholder fragmentation of the parties to collective bargaining in South Africa was conducted to better understand how this pattern is configuring. Max-Neef et al.[94] asserted that: "If we wish to define and assess an environment in the light of human needs, it is not sufficient to understand the opportunities that exist for groups or individuals to actualize their needs. It is necessary to analyse to what extent the environment represses, tolerates or stimulates opportunities. How accessible, creative or flexible is the environment? The most important question is: *how far people are able to influence the structures that affect their opportunities.*"

This environmental scan will touch on all of these questions. It was subjected to a content analysis in order to clarify the patterns of stakeholder fragmentation. The content analysis was, in turn, disaggregated into nine broad areas of stakeholder conflict that are indicative of the failure of collective bargaining in South Africa. These nine broad areas of stakeholder conflict were identified on the basis of their interrelationship with, and the light that they shed on the question: Why is collective bargaining failing in South Africa?

These nine themes are:

1. Corruption and Financial Incompetence – Unions v Employee Members and Employee Members v Financial Advisers – Stakeholders Without a Stake;
2. South African Democratic Teachers Union (SADTU) v The Ministry of Basic Education;
3. Disruptive Innovation in Protest Movements – University Student Protests #FeesMustFall;
4. Interaction Between the Employed, the Unemployed and the Tripartite Alliance;
5. Social Grants;
6. Police;
7. Unprotected Strikes, Vigilante Action, Xenophobic Attacks on Foreign Businesses and Nationals, and Zama Zamas;
8. Loan Sharks as Predators on the Poor;
9. The Incremental Erosion of the Social Compact in South Africa since 1994.

6.1 Corruption and Financial Incompetence – Unions v Members and Members v Financial Advisers – Stakeholders without a Stake

6.1.1 COSATU's Kopana Ke Matla Employee Benefit Arm's Licence Rescinded for Money Laundering (2013)

A spate of thefts of employee pension fund deposits, fraud and money laundering has destroyed trust between employees, unions, financial advisers, provident funds and pension funds. This is an ominous trend that could foreseeably cause the destruction of COSATU, and therefore also of the Tripartite Alliance. COSATU is an institution that is based on trust. The trade union leadership, together with their pension fund advisers have, in the four cases that are cited, contributed to the systematic decimation of their members' life savings. These life savings were stolen and squandered by criminality, greed and abject financial incompetence. It is part of a much greater pattern of comrades stealing from comrades. Whittles[95] confirmed that a 2013 Financial Services Board (FSB) report revealed that COSATU had admitted that it had permitted R123 million in employee pension fund monies to be irregularly transferred through its Kopana Ke Matla employee benefit investment arm. The directors of Kopana Ke Matla were implicated in money laundering. Whittles put it thus: "Its directors were implicated in alleged money laundering and irregular payments of up to R50 million." Whittles additionally averred that: "The FSB report also questioned why payments were made from the investment arm to the benefit of the fund, and why directors were paid up to R50 million, despite doing almost no work. COSATU's deputy general secretary, Bheki Ntshalintshali, says the transfer of 4 000 workers' pension money to the federation's employee benefit fund was *wrong and indefensible*."[96] The Financial Service Board found that these employee pension and provident fund monies were at grave risk. The Kopana Ke Matla employee benefit investment fund's operating licence was accordingly rescinded in 2013. The directors of Kopano Ke Matla did not have the money to invest. Neither did they have the financial acumen to invest funds on behalf of their members in spite of being appointed by the trade union elite to exercise this responsibility.

The fund management was thus illegal and without good governance, needlessly costing impoverished trade union members their humble life savings. Millions of rands of employee savings were placed at catastrophic financial risk by the trade union leadership. The provident and pension funds were negotiated into existence with financial services companies via the process of collective bargaining and now are at grave risk of being bankrupted because of criminality and incompetence.

The crime is that of the theft of the employees' future. In this instance collective bargaining is failing because the trade union leadership and those with whom they interacted within the financial services sector did not abide by the available regulatory frameworks that would have securely preserved the trade union pension and provident fund contributions for their members. This was particularly painful because culpability lay with trusted advisers, comrades, fellow trade unionists and hitherto friends. Given South Africa's history, it is understandable that there are often low levels of trust between employer and employee. The crime of pension fund theft is an attack by trade union leaders on employees who are their members and whom they purportedly represent. This conduct constitutes betrayal and abuse of trusted relationships and is corrosive of confidence and solidarity. The trade union movement should be an instrument for achieving the greater good for its members. Instead of pursuing this with courage, wisdom and integrity, COSATU's Kopana Ka Matla stole from their own.

6.2 Southern African Clothing and Textile Workers Union's (SACTWU's) Canyon Springs Investments – misappropriated R100 million from Clothing Workers' Pension Fund (2012)

A similar depressing pension fund money-laundering fraud scheme to that committed by Kopana Ke Matla was allegedly conjured up by the leadership of SACTWU to defraud its own members of R100 million of their own pension fund money. Ndzamela[97] reported that a commission of inquiry found that the Public Investment Corporation (PIC), which is South Africa's largest institutional investor, was irregularly paid employee pension fund monies that were "misappropriated from Southern African Clothing and Textile Workers' Union (SACTWU) pensioners". Vecchiatto[98] claimed that the Democratic Alliance (DA) had alleged that the SACTWU leadership had closed ranks to protect those trade unionists who perpetrated this crime from prosecution arising from the misappropriation of R100 million worth of worker pension funds. Vecchiatto[99] also alleged that: "Canyon Springs Investments stole R100 million from SACTWU pension funds ... The PIC now faces a claim of R11 million despite apparently not being aware that the money had been stolen." The consequence of this is profound mistrust between members and their trade unions and the destruction of the rationale for conducting collective bargaining in the first place.

6.2.1 South African Commercial, Catering and Allied Workers Union (SACCAWU) Investment Company Litigate against SACCAWU for Stealing Pension Fund Money from Members (2012)

Musgrave identified a similar trend of financial malfeasance with respect to the plundering of the SACCAWU National Provident Fund. She pointed out that SACCAWU had "170 000 members in the retail and associated sectors". She indicated that the FSB placed SACCAWU's National Provident Fund under curatorship in 2002. Since then SACCAWU Investment Holdings has been litigating against SACCAWU for having stolen employee pension fund monies and SACCAWU has been in a constant state of financial crisis.[100]

According to Ndaba,[101] this crisis is so serious that "SACCAWU – one of COSATU's biggest affiliated unions in the food and retail industry is struggling financially and unable to pay staff salaries on time ... Last year the Department of Labour wrote two letters to the union threatening to terminate their registration as a registered trade union for failing to submit audited statements in 2012 and 2013 to the Labour Department in compliance with the Labour Relations Act." The pension and provident funds fraud that has been inflicted upon SACCAWU has caused the union to fragment into curatorship. Collective bargaining has failed because the institutional security that SACCAWU offered its members has been destroyed by acts of fraud conducted by its leaders.

6.2.2 South African Municipal Workers Union (SAMWU's) Leadership Presided Over the Loss of R120 Million of Employee Pension Fund Money – Corruption Causes SAMWU to Split into Three Different Trade Unions (2012)

A similar pattern of money laundering, fraud and theft of employee provident and pension funds is alleged to pertain to SAMWU. There are differing calculations of the quantum of money stolen from SAMWU's pension funds. Maphumulo[102] informed that certain members of SAMWU's leadership elite stole the amount of R178 million from municipal workers. Maphumulo indicated that the Hawks had charged the SAMWU leadership with theft, fraud and money laundering. Those who were charged included the senior leadership of SAMWU, deputy general secretary Moses Miya, legal adviser Surprise Minisi and financial administrator Zukiswa Ntsiko. They were charged in October 2015 at the Specialised Commercial Crimes Court in Johannesburg. Pillay[103] concurred with Maphumulo's[104] findings, but he calculated that the amount allegedly stolen by SAMWU's leadership was a lesser sum of R120 million of its cash reserves. The money that was stolen was thieved from the workers' provident and pension fund subscriptions. There is consequently uncertainty about the exact amount of life savings that have been stolen, but the fact is that it is a very large quantity.

Pillay reported that the union's annual financial report in 2012 signified that cash reserves were R177 million. These cash reserves have since been depleted by theft and fraud from R177 million to R50 million by February 2014.[105]

Meyer found that this pattern of malfeasance at SAMWU had resulted in violent threats to burn down the Oudtshoorn Municipality after members of the trade union discovered that their pension fund and medical aid deductions had been diverted by SAMWU from the salaries contained on the employee payroll. SAMWU had not paid their pension funds and medical aid across to the custodians, as was its fiduciary duty. The discovery of this criminality caused outrage among workers.[106]

Corruption caused SAMWU to fragment into three separate trade unions. According to Evans, the first breakaway from SAMWU took place on 27 March 2015.[107] The new trade union was called the Municipal and Allied Trade Union of South Africa (MATUSA). A second trade union arose from a split with SAMWU, called the Democratic Municipal and Allied Workers Union of South Africa (DEMAWUSA), and it formed almost contiguously.

This environmental scan and content analysis of the plundering of employee pension and provident monies reveals that the union leadership, together with their financial advisers and investment companies, have repetitively connived to steal the pension and provident funds of their members, which are their life savings. These frauds of employee pension and provident funds now form a clear and pathological pattern. It is deeply concerning that the pattern has been allowed to perpetuate itself in spite of the clear evidence of its manifestation. It would appear that the union leadership, in all the cases of financial malfeasance that have been cited, have either been active participants in the theft, fraud and money laundering, or have lacked the necessary basic financial acumen to offer responsible fiduciary leadership with other people's money. The Financial Services Board has consistently reported that the unions' financial advisers are themselves incompetent, and do not have the financial acumen, knowledge, skills and experience to manage these funds. This pattern of financial malfeasance and incompetence by the union leadership is unconscionable. It means that the employees' life savings in the form of pension and provident fund contributions are potentially at grave risk. It is evident that a cadre of self-seeking business trade unionists have emerged in recent years and that this is undermining the leadership and trust that is vested in the movement as a whole. Paton pointed out that COSATU commissioned research by the National Labour and Economic Development Institute (NALEDI) to evaluate workers' perceptions of trade unions in 2012 and found that there was growing distrust in the trade union movement with one in three union members believing that there was corruption among the leadership and one in seven expressing the view that they had experienced it.[108]

This criminality and incompetence in managing employee pension and provident funds, if not counteracted, will surely cause collective bargaining to fail and COSATU to collapse. These frauds could cause the disintegration of COSATU and those affected and affiliated trade unions. The split of SAMWU because of the fraud into three unions illustrates this point. High-profile and regular criminal prosecutions are essential to act as a deterrent to pension fund theft. It sabotages worker participation in institutional investment and prohibits employees from developing their own investment and savings portfolios. It appears that the prime predator on the workers' pension and provident funds savings are those persons and financial organisations that are entrusted with trade union fund management. Besides being criminal acts, such conduct reveals extraordinary callousness and cynicism. The case of *Durr v ABSA Bank Ltd and Another [1997] 3 All SA 1 (A)* is instructive. This judgment confirmed that banks have a vicarious liability for poor investment advice offered by their brokers to their clients. This judgment also set out a test for the minimum standards of skill that are required to be a financial adviser. The failure to heed such advice will result in increased fragmentation of the trade union movement and is causing collective bargaining to fail.

6.3 South African Democratic Teachers Union (SADTU) v The Ministry of Basic Education – Conflict between SADTU and ANC Government; Alienation of Parents, Children and the Community at Large

6.3.1 SADTU and the Malaise in Basic Education

Harper & Masondo, who are reporters for *City Press*, revealed *prima facie* evidence that members of SADTU's leadership were illegally trading teaching jobs in public schools across the country.[109] *City Press* reported that headmaster posts were transacted for approximately R30 000 each, whilst teachers posts were sold for about R6 000.

A little after the jobs for cash scandal arose, SADTU refused to conduct the Annual National Assessments on school readiness for children under their care. Schwab & Sala-i-Martin[110] confirmed that the quality of South African basic school education in mathematics and science was ranked as being the worst in the world, out of a sample of 140 countries. Basic education is therefore affected by a a dual problem of criminality and an abject lack of teacher professionalism. According to Nkosi,[111] "One of the reasons that was proffered by SADTU was that the Minister of Basic Education Angie Motshekga had embarked on an attack on collective bargaining and lack of proper consultation." Nkosi cited the general secretary of SADTU as issuing a statement confirming that: "The NEC had no option but to adopt a programme of action on all issues affecting the conditions of employment, including directing all members of SADTU not to administer the ANA until such time that the department stops imposing policies that are not meant to improve the working relationship, but create an environment that will compromise education and labour peace."[112]

SADTU as a trade union appears to have a primary focus on careerism. It seems to be little concerned about establishing a credible and competent professional teaching association to serve the complex and vast educational needs of the children under its care. Its primary employment preoccupation appears to be about advancing its members' employment contracts. Careerism appears to have eclipsed professionalism within SADTU. It is argued that this has created a serious malaise in Basic Education in South Africa and places the employability of youth at grave risk. This careerism is manifested in a conflictive, litigious and industrial union approach towards collective bargaining. This collective bargaining modus operandi destroys trust and displaces professionalism.

The allegations of fraud shocked Angie Motshekga the Minister of Basic Education. She accordingly instructed Professor John Volmink to appoint a Task Team to establish the veracity of this supposed malfeasance.

Volmink and his team's findings are contained in the *Report of the Ministerial Task Team Appointed by Minister Angie Motshekga to investigate the Selling of Posts of Educators by Members of Teachers Unions and Departmental Officials in Provincial Education Departments* (2016). This Report shall henceforth be referred to as the 'Jobs for Sale Report' (2016) for the purposes of brevity. The Task Team confirmed that there was indeed truth in the *City Press* allegations that were reported by Harper & Masondo (2014). It found that a pernicious practice of trading jobs for financial gain was widespread and had indeed taken place across the country in Basic Education. The 'Jobs for Sale Report' provided compelling indications that collective bargaining in Basic Education was in complete disarray. It is proposed that this situation would probably be reflected to a lesser or great extent across all public sector trade unions.

Masondo (2016) informed that SADTU was one of COSATU's largest trade union affiliates and had organised about 260 000 members across South Africa. Most of SADTU's members are teachers who are employed by the state, and teach at government schools. Other large public sector trade unions are the National Education, Health and Allied Workers Union (NEHAWU) which has about 235 000 members and the Police and Prisons Civil Rights Union (POPCRU) which has approximately 150 000 paid-up members. Masondo[113] asserted that SADTU had obtained almost complete control of the education departments in six of South Africa's nine provinces. SADTU had achieved hegemony by its use of a variety of interrelated strategies which appear to have converted SADTU into an informal closed shop.

The 'Jobs for Sale Report' (2016:119) only served to substantiate Masondo's[114] allegations. It found that Basic Education was under the hegemony of SADTU in the following six provinces: "Gauteng, KwaZulu-Natal, North West, Limpopo, Mpumalanga, and the Eastern Cape. The Department of Basic Education has retained semblances of managerial and administrative control in three of South Africa's nine Provinces. These are the Free State, the Western Cape and the Northern Cape. In all other Provinces, SADTU is in de facto control."

The 'Jobs for Sale Report' (2016:133) asserted furthermore that: "Teacher unions have captured significant areas of the education system. This ranges from the most senior levels, to new teachers in public schools ... The effect of this is to contribute to the Department's inability to control and develop an effective educational system." In a Court Judgment between *South Africa's Democratic Teachers' Union (SADTU) v Minister of Education and Others ((J5396/00) [2001] ZALC 144* (12 September 2001) it was confirmed in paragraph 4 that SADTU members are educators and fall under the ambit of the Employment of Educators Act No 76 of 1998 as Amended. It was further confirmed in paragraph 5 that SADTU and the Employer are party to the Education Labour Relations Council because it is in this forum that collective bargaining on wages and terms and conditions of employment take place. It is obvious why the trading of jobs does not take place in the Education Labour Relations Council. The employer parties to the Education Labour Relations Council include the Minister of Education and the leadership of education in South Africa's nine provinces.

The 'Jobs for Sale Report' showed that collective bargaining with the employer parties was by-passed. Those who were circumscribed included the Minister of Education and the educational leadership in South Africa's nine provinces. Collective bargaining was therefore profoundly undermined in Basic Education because the employer party appears to have connived in the dissipation of the authority of the department.

The 'Jobs for Sale Report' (2016:122) collaborated Masondo's allegation that there was a pervasive practice of criminal trading of teaching jobs. The Task Team discovered that: "transformation (was used) as a pretext for gaining control of schools and offices ..."

In spite of being a teachers' union, SADTU elected to follow a conflictive, strike-inclined and litigious industrial model of trade unionism. This has estranged it from its pursuit of teaching professionalism. It is presumed that this modus operandi was an effective organising tactic that legitimated the notion that the teachers were being exploited by the management of Basic Education. During the course of 2015 primary school teachers refused to conduct school readiness tests on school children. SADTU's refusal to conduct school readiness tests was effectively a strike with long-term negative consequences for school children. This standoff vividly illustrated the conflict between civic duty and the greater good versus cynical self-interest. In SADTU's case, cynical careerism and self-interest seem to have prevailed over civic duty. It revealed an underlying ethic of dismissiveness about the professional responsibility that teachers should uphold towards the children entrusted to their care. The impression, in the public's eye, was that the purpose of collective bargaining for SADTU was to create a normative and policy structure that was calculated to exempt teachers from a duty of care towards the scholars whose learning and absorption into the labour market were entrusted to them. This entrustment arose from the basic professional obligation of a teacher to act in the best interests of his/her students who are minors. The teachers' primary duty of ensuring that the scholars whose education is entrusted to them are ready for school was ignored. This meant that some scholars might enter school ready to fail. No scientific study of their school readiness was conducted. The question of whether these scholars will be employable in the South African economy when they leave school appeared to have been the least of SADTU's concerns. SADTU placed South Africa's catastrophic youth unemployment and labour market absorption problems secondary to their flawed collective bargaining position. The SADTU leadership and the teachers who followed their direction did not assist the scholars to discover satisfiers of their fundamental human needs. The teachers' refusal to co-operate in conducting these school readiness tests translated into their failure to offer solutions to the chronic problem of youth unemployment and appropriate curriculum design in the Fourth Industrial Revolution. Their collective bargaining approach appeared to be an attempt to abrogate teachers from having a duty of responsibility towards the children's parents as well.

SADTU publicly defied the authority of the government and the instructions of the Minister of Basic Education by declining to conduct certain school readiness tests involving the assessment of the numeracy and literacy of young children. This clash within the Tripartite Alliance, and among its key stakeholders, alienated parents, a new generation of children and the community at large.

It is noted that parents across South Africa have thus far not used the schools' governing bodies to inter-mediate on behalf of their children. The purpose of such inter-mediation would be to insist that SADTU forgo its industrial trade unionism modus operandi and conduct itself as a professional teaching association. Parents can be expected to start contesting SADTU's presumption of leadership of Basic Education across South Africa as the practical implications of the Fourth Industrial Revolution become increasingly evident and take hold.

Jansen, Villette and Fredericks (2015) asserted that: "The education of more than 8 million children [has] been brought into disarray because SADTU has refused to permit its teachers to assess the literacy and numeracy levels of Grades 1 – 6 scholars in terms of the Annual National Assessment." They explained that: "The General Secretary of SADTU Mugwana Mululeke and assistant Nkosana Dolopi accused the Department of Basic Education of waging a well-orchestrated *low-level war* against education unions and of continuously failing to improve teachers' working conditions." The conflict between Basic Education Minister, Angie Motshekga, and the unions has raised alarm about the government's ability to enforce policy and deliver stable industrial relations among trade unions that are affiliated to the Tripartite Alliance. It appears that the union leadership at SADTU is using the union movement to promote its own careers at the expense of the scholars who are entrusted to its care by their parents. The scholars, their families, and the communities in which they operate are treated with disregard.

This analysis re-asserted the validity of the critical question that was posed earlier on in this analysis. This question was: 'How far are people able to influence the structures that affect their opportunities?' The 'structure' in this instance can be defined as the capacity of SADTU in its present legal and operational framework to enable a world-class basic educational system that will allow South African children to reach their full potential in the world of work. It is contended that SADTU's present legal and operational framework is wholly unsuited to this task and is a clear example of why collective bargaining is failing in the public sector. It should be converted into a professional teachers' association as soon as possible.

At this point, the reader is referred back to the allegations of Mr Piet Motasa (the president of the NUM) that the mining companies engaged in retrenchments to destabilise the ANC's relationship with its voters and Helen Zille's allegation that the Western Cape farm workers' strike was encouraged by the ANC to destabilise that province because they do not lead that province. It is difficult to distinguish truth from falsehood but Mululeke's and Dolopi's accusations were expressed in conflictive language that is emblematic of why collective bargaining is failing in South Africa. They indicated serious underlying levels of deep-rooted conflict afflicting the collective bargaining process in this country. The phrase *low-level war* that was used by Mululeke and Dolopi was illuminating. It revealed that the basic ethos of the collective bargaining interaction between SADTU and the Ministry of Basic Education was conflictive and viewed as a win-lose game in circumstances that demanded nuanced collaboration and co-operation. These worldviews were mechanistic and revealed little scope for double-loop learning and challenge of ritualistic stereotypes and conduct, as well as an inability of the leadership to address wicked problems and discover sustainable solutions. The win-lose rules of engagement chosen by SADTU were simply wrong, and that is why collective bargaining is failing. This is probably indicative of poor and cynical union leadership that is unconcerned about the challenges facing Basic Education. SADTU is alienating public opinion because it is itself perceived to be disparaging about discovering satisfiers of the fundamental human needs of the school children under its care.

The foreseeable consequences of this chauvinism can only be to the detriment of the greater good. In this example, we have a clear zero-sum negotiation process where teachers are granted a short-term parochial benefit at the expense of the school children. It is an untenable situation. SADTU's starting point was to prohibit the youth from getting out of the starting blocks by disallowing the Annual National Assessment which would have enabled the scholars, in due course, to be absorbed into the labour market. Prospective employers constitute another stakeholder grouping who would regard SADTU's conduct as being unconscionable.

Gordon, Roberts and Struwig[115] measured the trust that South Africans have in trade unions and other institutions, including churches, the SABC, national government, traditional leaders, local government and politicians. They found that there has been a precipitous decline of trust in the South African trade union movement by nationally representative samples of ordinary South Africans. Gordon et al.[116] pointed out that: "Trade unions in South Africa, many established during the political struggle for democracy, have long claimed to represent the entire working class and not just their own members." This claim is now palpably false. They also mentioned that: "Trade unions stood out among other institutions showing a significant fall in confidence." Gordon et al.[117] pointed out that in 2011 43% of South Africans indicated that they trusted trade unions. The measures of confidence fell to 29% in 2012. By comparison, trust in churches, which are regarded as custodians of human rights, had a confidence level of 77%. The theft of worker pension funds by trade union leaders that was alluded to earlier and the dismissiveness that the teacher trade union SADTU has displayed towards school readiness and the ethos of teaching are indicative of a general trend of selfish behaviour that is alienating the general population's trust and confidence in the trade union movement. Gordon et al.[118] further showed that persons who had historically supported trade unions and included black and coloured employees from working-class backgrounds had become alienated and mistrustful of them. They asserted that the development of active mistrust should be a cause for deep internal reflection by the trade unions. They therefore deduced that: "Trade unions need to intensify their engagement with working class communities in order to build greater levels of public confidence. Without such confidence it is unlikely that the organised labour movement will be able to achieve its mandate of working class prosperity and greater economic equality."

6.3.2 Fear as a Control Technique

The 'Jobs for Sale Report' (2016:121-122) noted the extraordinarily aggressive, litigious and threatening negotiation approach and modus operandi that characterised the conduct of SADTU. The Ministerial Task Team appointed by Angie Motshekga asserted that: "The absence of home-grown traditions in the Department as an entity is echoed in the way that SADTU has adopted an industrial model based on serving workers in factories and the mines. SADTU ought to be an occupational union such as that for nurses. Furthermore, it must be asked why the relationship between the Department and the Unions has to be so adversarial when their common cause is the transformation of education of the young."

SADTU's response to the *prima facie* evidence of teaching jobs being transacted for cash was to accuse *City Press* of "having a big agenda of destroying the organization and its leaders. If not we believe the newspaper is being used to liquidate the organization." The language usage by SADTU spokesperson Nomarashiya Caluza appeared paranoid and aggressive. The truth of the matter was that alleged criminal activity was identified by *City Press* and Minister Motshekga had rightly called for an investigation to test the veracity of these allegations. Various of these allegations were proven. Caluza's response was to use language that invoked images of liquidation. The language usage appears to have been intended to intimidate both the Minister from performing her duty and the newspaper from presenting a vital matter of public interest before the eyes of South African readers. Collective bargaining therefore failed because the regulatory framework on which it was based was being undermined by threats and intimidation.

During August 2010 SADTU members engaged in a strike against Northdale Schools in KwaZulu-Natal. Mngoma[119] reported that the SADTU picketers were exceptionally aggressive towards non-striking teachers at these schools.

He averred that: "Shambok-wielding pickets allegedly drove teachers out of a number of Northdale Schools yesterday … These people are supposed to be professionals and I don't know how they can behave like that. There was a convoy of about 40-50 cars and they were moving from school to school. The teacher said the women teachers at their school were frightened and some were crying although there was no violence. The strikers told us that 'today we are talking, but tomorrow they won't be talking'. They would not leave before they saw us go." SADTU in this instance was denying a basic trade union right. It was effectively undermining the principles of the freedom of association and the consequent right not to associate. It denied its own members the freedom to disassociate from an industrial conflict that they did not support, under the threat of physical violence. SADTU clearly brooked no dissent from its members and did not hesitate to use violence to induce conformity. These threats to the non-striking teachers' physical being revealed an ethos of lawlessness. Fear and intimidation appear to have been used by the union to induce compliance.

Similarly, Masondo[120] reported that the secretary of SADTU, Mugwena Maluleke, embarked on an attack on the Basic Education Minister, Angie Motshekga, in retaliation to her call for an investigation into the corrupt sale of jobs in the Basic Education Department. Mugwena Maluleke claimed that: "Motshekga had colluded with right wingers to destroy the union ... and had targeted investigators to target the union." This commentary resonated with the paranoid statement by Caluza that the *City Press* newspaper was being used to liquidate them that was alluded to above.

Mugwena Maluleke asserted furthermore: "The report, even though I haven't seen it, is based on preconceived ideas. I don't want to prejudge the outcome of the report, but I know it will implicate us because of the fraught relationship that we have with her." In this citation above, Maluleke made an extraordinary unscholarly admission. He pronounced judgment on a report that he had not even read. There are many other examples of SADTU's unwaveringly conflictive and aggressive approach – too numerous to mention. Teachers should be treated as respected professionals if they are to offer their best to students and the communities in which they operate. Lawyers, engineers, nurses, doctors, and architects are examples of professions that have staff associations that pursue the greater good.

The 'Jobs for Sale Report' (2016:125), in considering the aggressiveness and rhetoric of the trade union, stated:

> The question has to be asked why has SADTU, for example, adopted a form of union which is based on an adversarial industrial model? Why, it must be asked, does the Department of Basic Education have to be regarded as a capitalist exploiter of labour, who are regarded as a capitalist exploiter of the working class? Teachers are not members of the working class. How can Departmental Managers (Union Members deployed there) be the enemy? Are the apparent differences between union members and managers real or illusory? There is distinct element of the absurd in the sorry situation in which the quality of South African schooling is demonstrably abysmal.

It is contended that SADTU has adopted these behavioural patterns purposively to engrain a sense of victimhood and create an imaginary enemy of the departmental managers. Divisiveness would appear to be used as a technique to induce compliance and fear amongst union members.

6.3.3 Cadre Deployment as an Informal Closed Shop and Control Technique

SADTU's constitution reveals that it does not have the legal status of a closed shop agreement with the Ministry of Basic Education. But, the union does appear to have operated as an informal closed shop with respect to its modus operandi and its conduct pertaining to cadre deployment. A closed shop agreement is a collective agreement between an employer and a trade union of a special type. This type of agreement insists that all employees of a particular category, for example schoolteachers, should be members of the trade union in question and subordinate themselves to the trade union's policies, affiliations and objectives. It is quite evident from the previous discussion about **Fear as a Control Technique** that an individual teacher's decision not to become a member of SADTU may be accompanied by severe professional and personal consequences, including threats of violence. A study of Professor Volmink and the Task Team's on 'Jobs for Sale Report' (2016) reveals that SADTU's policies, affiliations and objectives have profound and long-term implications for the quality of the professional lived experience of teachers who are employed in the field of Basic Education in South Africa. These policies, affiliations and objectives also have a profound impact on the quality of life and potential of scholars to create a positive future for themselves.

In exploring the question of whether SADTU follows the modus operandi of an informal closed shop agreement it is noted that there are two types of closed shop agreements. The first form of closed shop agreement is termed a pre-entry closed shop agreement. The second type of closed shop agreement is referred to as a post-entry closed shop. A pre-entry closed shop agreement prohibits an employer from employing an employee if he or she has declined to become a member of the relevant trade union from the moment that the employment contract is concluded. The reader is reminded that the 'Jobs for Sale Report' (2016) established that SADTU has complete control over all aspects of education in six of South Africa's nine provinces. Therefore, one has to deduce that the real employer in these provinces was not Basic Education. It was SADTU. From this is becomes evident that SADTU will only employ and support the employment of compliant persons who they can be sure will agree with the union's modus operandi. Although there is no formal closed shop agreement in place between the Ministry of Basic Education and SADTU, SADTU's informal modus operandi bares strong similarities to a pre-entry closed shop agreement. It is highly unlikely that a teacher will be employed, no matter how excellent that teacher might be, if he or she does not acquiesce to SADTU's policies, affiliations and objectives.

A post-entry closed shop agreement differs from a pre-entry closed shop agreement inasmuch as the prospective employee is obliged to join the trade union within a specified period of time after employment has commenced.

A newly appointed teacher employed in Basic Education will soon realise that there is much informal pressure to join SADTU. On balance the collective influence of SADTU will tend to overwhelm the teacher's individual rights.

Mantouvalou[121] explained that closed shop agreements require a delicate reconciliation of individual rights and collective rights if they are to be just and lawful. In countries like South Africa, with enormously high levels of unemployment, poverty and inequality, it is difficult to balance these rights. A closed shop agreement in this type of scenario may readily give rise to trade union racketeering, as is evidenced by the 'Jobs for Sale Report' fraud.

SADTU's modus operandi and inveiglement in cadre deployment, and its pervasive control over the decision-making process in all matters concerning Basic Education in South Africa make it nonsensical for a prospective teacher not to join the trade union.

It is contended that the aforementioned logic provides a coherent narrative as to why SADTU has total control of Basic Education in six of South Africa's nine provinces and a membership of 260 000 persons. The starting point, according to the 'Jobs for Sale Report', was that it effectively had almost complete control of all appointments.

The 'Jobs for Sale Report' (2016:119) averred that SADTU achieved its extraordinary domination over the Basic Education Department by following a combination of coercive strategies which included the following:

- Using its historical narrative of comprising an important sector of the liberation movement;
- By being an industrial and adversarial trade union;
- By means of its incorporation of office-based educators as members;
- Its use of a repertoire of strategies to coerce teachers, principals, officials and others to accede to its demands;
- By using teacher militancy to pressure members to be unionists first, and professionals second;
- By practising cadre deployment to ensure that high percentages of managers, decision-makers and others with power and influence in education are placed in well-paid positions where they can prioritise the Union's interests;
- By using undue influence at different stages of the appointments process to ensure that its candidates are appointed;

- By holding out the possibility for its prominent members to receive the opportunity of achieving high office in the Department, Parliament and the Cabinet;
- By blocking Department activities and programmes; and
- Using its membership of COSATU to influence the members of the Tripartite Alliance.

The SADTU leadership enacted all of these strategies contiguously. These have together resulted in the organisation of the union following the lines of a pre-entry closed shop agreement. It has resulted in an extraordinary process of undue influence, compliance and conformity. The 'Jobs for Sale Report' (2016: 121) therefore asserted that Basic Education had accordingly had its ranks populated by cadre deployment who were "Union loyalists first and administrators second. This situation has allowed the unions to use undue influence to the extent that the Department of Basic Education has lost control of two thirds of the country."

6.3.4 A Convenient Political Bargain as a Control Technique

Kahn[122] asserted that SADTU's policy of cadre deployment should not be viewed in isolation. It was in his view the operational element of a political bargain. He contended that a reciprocal and symbiotic relationship existed between the ANC and SADTU where the one benefited the other. The symbiosis resided in SADTU providing an operational framework for securing a platform of votes for the ANC. In exchange the ANC allegedly turned a blind eye to the malfeasance of SADTU, and paid the Basic Education budget. That appears to be his picture of the nature of the deal between SADTU and the ANC. The fact that Basic Education in South Africa is the worst in the world insofar as mathematics and science are concerned is deemed to be an acceptable compromise.

Kahn[123] explained that: "the collective beneficiary of this power play is the ruling party, because SADTU members use the schools as organisational bases whence they operate as party agents. Schools are ubiquitous, being spread across the country, they possess useful telecoms and other equipment, and are well suited to the purpose of political organization. SADTU shop stewards and officials act as party commissars who deliver votes at election time. The ANC thus needs SADTU as much as SADTU needs the ANC. The commissars in KZN have displaced the traditional purveyors of votes, the *Indunas*. This has been a source of intense friction since the founding of SADTU, with SADTU shop stewards often in conflict with the displaced Indunas. Modernity collides with tradition. The SACP controls the SADTU leadership."

The question that parents of minor children will need to pose to themselves and their families is: *"Is SADTU's aggressive industrial union hegemony going to create a teaching ethos in South Africa that will educate our children for unemployment?"*

SADTU's approach to education is therefore controlled by its political objectives. It appears to be generally indifferent towards education. The prime duty of the teacher under this informal closed shop arrangement is to be a compliant and dutiful member of SADTU. SADTU members are expected to strike, picket and obey union policy, no matter that it might be harmful to the education of the children. Adherence to the instructions of the shop steward commissars is the golden rule.

Bantu education was used by the apartheid apparatchiks as an instrument of racial deprivation. Unfortunately SADTU education does not appear to be very much better. SADTU is a trade union that appears to be suffering from an identity crisis. As a trade union, its values, mission and vision seem strangely narcissistic, litigious, aggressive, self-serving and narrowly materialistic. Their conflictive expressions of purpose seem all too often to cynically ignore the needs of their key stakeholders including the scholars, parents and the communities in which they operate.

SADTU deports itself as an aggressive industrial trade union and 'vanguard of the working class'. This is ironical, and indeed rather ridiculous, because its members are teachers and firmly ensconced in the middle class. It is a middle-class trade union that seems to play the exploited victim role of the industrial proletariat, from a bygone era.

South African teachers should be organised into professional staff associations if they are to address the profound learning needs of our young children. If this is done wisely the scholars will have a greater probability of being absorbed into the labour market when they leave school.

SADTU's aggressive and conflictive behaviour sets a normative standard of mediocrity, for scholars and parents to witness. Finland is the country that arguably has the best basic education system in the world. South African educationalists would do well to emulate the Finnish example of teaching professionalism. It is contended that SADTU's constitution is incompatible with the requirements of a professional teaching association, and therefore needs to be re-written. The outcome of this identity crisis is a perpetual poverty cycle.

The fact that the World Economic Forum found South Africa's basic education's ranking as being the worst in the world is arguably a breach of the Bill of Rights and Constitution of South Africa. SADTU's militancy and self-centeredness would appear to negate the promise on Education contained in section 29 of the Bill of Rights of the Constitution. Section 29 reads: "Everyone has the right to a basic education, including adult basic education, and to further education which the state, through reasonable measures, must make progressively available and accessible." SADTU's modus operandi inclines this provision of the Constitution to be unmet.

SADTU would also appear to act in regular breach of section 28 1 (d) and (e) of the Bill of Rights which pertains to protecting the rights of children. Section 28 1 (e) of the Bill of Rights assures that citizens have the right: "to be protected from exploitative labour practices" read with 28 1 (d) "to be protected from maltreatment, neglect, abuse or degradation." The violent picketing in front of children, for example, negates the teaching contract and covenant between teacher and scholar. The *Report of the Ministerial Task Team Appointed by Minister Angie Motshekga to Investigate Allegations into the Selling of Posts of Educators by Members of Teachers Unions and Departmental Officials in Provincial Educational Departments* provides ample evidence together with useful diagnoses and prognosis of why basic education in South Africa is failing. This leads in turn to the failure of collective bargaining and labour market absorption.

Section 23 (5) of the Bill of Rights reads: "Every trade union, employers organization and employer has the right to engage in collective bargaining. *National legislation may recognize union security arrangements contained in collective agreements. To the extent that legislation may limit a right in this chapter, the limitation must comply with section 36 (1).*"

It is contended that a class action suit might be taken before the Constitutional Court in order to decide:

a. *Is SADTU's modus operandi and structure contrary to the Bill of Rights?*
b. *Should SADTU be permitted to continue to be structured and operate as a militant industrial trade union in a learning and teaching environment?*
c. *Should the government intervene to regulate its constitution and change it into a professional teachers' association?*
d. *Should teachers be accorded professional status?*
e. *How can the quality of basic education in South Africa be improved to take our children out of the poverty cycle?*
f. *Is SADTU's modus operandi compatible with the learning requirements of South Africa which is aspired to become an advanced industrial economy?*

6.4 Disruptive Innovation in Protest Movements – University Student Protests #FeesMustFall[ii]

Collective bargaining and the acquisition of a tertiary education in South Africa are intrinsically connected by the nuclear family. A university education opens up the prospect that the student will be able to create an exciting career path that breaks away from the current deeply entrenched poverty cycle in South Africa. Impoverished families invest everything they have to enable their children to gain a tertiary education. Parents are typically reliant on the collective bargaining process to create the necessary minimum wage increases that will enable their life savings to be invested in the tertiary education of their progeny. This makes the crime of the decimation of employee pension and provident funds by trade union leaders even more heinous. The parents regularly sacrifice all their pension and provident fund savings to ensure that their children might gain a tertiary education. Many children of working-class parents come to university hungry and severely under-resourced. Some students do not have accommodation or access to transport and therefore are compelled to find empty rooms on the campus in which they can sleep. Their shelter includes empty classrooms, seminar rooms and toilets where they conduct their ablutions.

6.4.1 Student Accommodation was the Trigger for the #FeesMustFall Campaign

On the afternoon of Wednesday, 14 October 2015, a small group of students staged a protest at the entrance to the University of the Witwatersrand's Business School. This protest was arranged to challenge a decision that had been reached by the university's management to demolish student accommodation on the Parktown campus and to upgrade these premises in order to improve the quality of management education that is offered here. The student protesters were vociferous in their display and called upon Professor Habib, the Vice Chancellor of the University of the Witwatersrand, to respond to their demands that there should be a stay on the demolition of the students' accommodation, and to personally address them as a protesting collectivity. The group of student protesters kept Professor Habib waiting for a long period of time. They were engrossed in singing, toyi-toying and speech making. The protesters subsequently withdrew the invitation that they had originally extended to the Vice Chancellor to address them, without notice or explanation. In the beginning, the protest consisted only of a small number of students. It was a loud and audacious protest, but it was not yet evident that the conflict might morph and escalate into a deep-rooted conflict, and that the agenda would change from a protest about accommodation to a conflict about the intended increase in university fees, and

---

ii   The writer was witness to the of protest at the University of the Witwatersrand's Wits
      Business School

then to a conflict about other grievances, all of which revolved around the search for satisfiers of fundamental human needs.

It was clear though, by the nature of the invective and protest, that the selfsame fundamental human needs that drive industrial conflict, service delivery protests and the multiplicity of other forms of political unrest that are experienced in South Africa, lay beneath this conflict. The students blocked the entrances and exits to Wits Business School and prohibited those persons who were not protesting from leaving the property, thus violating their freedom of association.

6.4.2 Morphing of the Conflict into Changing Configurations

On Thursday, 16 October 2015, the protest morphed into the nationwide student conflict referred to as the #FeesMustFall movement. The students demanded that the university's budgeted 10.5% fee increase for 2016 should be cancelled. Their negotiation stretch goal was a zero per cent increase in university fees for 2016. In response to the student protests, Minister of Higher Education Dr Blade Nzimande's first negotiation ploy was to announce that the student fees would be dropped to an across the board 6% increase for 2016. The students ignored Nzimande's concession. On 21 October 2015, large numbers of students from, inter alia, the University of Cape Town, University of Western Cape, Stellenbosch University and the Cape Provincial University of Technology stormed Parliament while the then Minister of Finance, Mr Nhlanhla Nene, was delivering his mid-term budget for South Africa. (Mr Jacob Zuma subsequently dismissed the highly respected Mr Nene from his post as Minister of Finance on tenuous grounds, unrelated to this incident, causing an international economic crisis in South Africa.) Intensive student protest action was simultaneously erupting across the entire country. There were protests at the Nelson Mandela Metropolitan University, Walter Sisulu University, Rhodes University, University of Fort Hare, University of KwaZulu-Natal, University of the Free State, University of Johannesburg, University of Pretoria, University of the North West, Tshwane University of Technology and the University of Limpopo.

6.4.3 The Prognosis for a Stakeholder Alliance between Students and the Unemployed

On 23 October 2015 thousands of students marched upon the Union Buildings in Pretoria. Mr Zuma gave a speech and announced that the scheduled increase in fees of 10.5% for 2016 would be cancelled. The students' negotiation stretch goal was achieved. This announcement was met with an escalation in violent protest that degenerated into clashes between various student factions, university authorities, the general public and the police. It is probable that the generalised and unspecified conflicts arose from the students coming to the realisation that a host of other frustrated fundamental human needs could be addressed by further conflict and escalation.

Full-time students live an existential experience that is not that dissimilar from being unemployed. Their studies are conducted with the positive intention of becoming gainfully employed upon graduation. A natural empathy is bound to emerge between students and the unemployed, and a stakeholder alliance could conceivably develop between students and the unemployed, which might be co-ordinated by Twitter, Facebook and other multimedia platforms. If this change in stakeholder allegiance from dormancy to activism were to transpire, it would result in a fundamental change in South Africa's socio-political landscape. Students and the unemployed actually share the same concerns about being absorbed into the South African labour market. The difference is that the students are optimistic while the unemployed are fatalistic and pessimistic about their employment prospects. What students and the unemployed share is their mutual fear and insecurity about their entry into the labour market, and their prospects for gainful employment. These sets of concerns are far too complex and subtle to be addressed by the blunt instrument of collective bargaining which is largely conducted as a single-loop learning process. Collective bargaining will therefore not be a useful mechanism for addressing the intricate and complex matters that impact on the governing values that are influencing employability and labour market absorption.

The challenges for qualified students to gain employment are significant at the moment, but not overwhelming because of the present generally positive fit between curricula, degree and employability. This fit between curricula, degree and student employability is anticipated to become highly contested as the Fourth Industrial Revolution encroaches with fury. The future of employment for certain highly qualified students will become increasingly problematic as the Fourth Industrial Revolution takes hold because of the obsolescence of diverse career paths and the curricula on which they are based.

According to Ngoepe, Quintal and Wakefield[124] almost all the students who attended the #FeesMustFall protest meeting did so in an admirable spirit of peace. They pointed out that a group of *agent provocateurs* were in attendance and that these persons engaged in acts of provocation, stone throwing, arson and other acts of vandalism, intimidation and violence. The definition of the conflict underpinning the #FeesMustFall campaign was in a state of constant flux and continuously morphed as the situation played itself out and the students interacted with different realities. The #FeesMustFall campaign began as a protest against intended building alterations at the University of the Witwatersrand Business School that would displace student accommodation on the campus. The plans to modernise the teaching facilities necessitated the demolition of student accommodation on this particular property. The root cause of this initial conflict was that the intended demolition of their student accommodation undermined the fundamental needs of Subsistence and Having. After a day or two, the students placed the accommodation dispute with the university into abeyance. They then redefined the conflict as a protest against the intended 2016 fee increases and referred to it as the #FeesMustFall campaign.

The conflict was at that time based on the fundamental human needs of Understanding, Being, Having, Doing and Interacting. The conflict then changed phase and escalated from a normal conflict into a deep-rooted conflict, and it mutated into a national movement. The #FeesMustFall campaign captured the imagination of students across the country and was taken up at all the major universities in South Africa. It was at that time accorded the Twitter designation of the #FeesMustFall campaign and became the most interactive Twitter campaign in South Africa. The students were successful in achieving their primary objective of the #FeesMustFall campaign and this resulted in a fees freeze for 2016.

The conflict then morphed into a solidarity dispute supporting the termination of all outsourced contracts with support staff at South African universities. These outsourced contracts were largely with labour brokers, some of whom were good employers and others who were poor employers. The fundamental human needs that underpinned this conflict on outsourcing were Subsistence, Protection, Understanding, Participation, Identity and Freedom in conjunction with Interacting, Being, Having and Doing. The students called for the cancellation of outsourcing of the labour contracts of the universities' support staff to labour brokers and for these persons to be employed by the state on a permanent basis. The universities acquiesced to this demand without an adequate exploration of its financial and practical sustainability. They also do not appear to have clarified whether the in-sourcing of this labour to the universities will be sustainable from the perspective of employability. It is contended that this matter will prove to be impractical and unsustainable on both the financial and employability questions and that many of those persons who were switched to permanent employment by the universities will in due course be retrenched and made redundant. The first step will be that there will be a consolidated attempt to not replace them when they retire or resign. These employees generally have low levels of education and skill, and are intensely vulnerable to disruptive innovation that might substitute their labour for capital. This conflict against outsourced contracts could be seen as a neo-Luddite protest against the manifestations of the Fourth Industrial Revolution.

The search for a ban on outsourcing subsequently became violent. There were instances of vandalism involving activists, some of whom were apparently not students. This conflict became deep-rooted at various universities. It is contended that the outsourcing conflict is a wicked problem and entrapping. It might drag on for a long time to come. The students seem to have made a strategic negotiation error in allowing the terms of reference of the conflict to widen to include support to terminate the outsourcing of labour. It diluted and complicated their case, and could place them into conflict with the labour that they purported to support if large-scale retrenchments follow, as might well be the case. Those labour brokers who lose their contracts with the universities will all become alienated. The students have also limited their own flexibility by placing themselves into an alliance with the trade unions that do not share their worldview. These factors could consume their energy and undermine the gains that they have won. With respect to the protests against outsourcing, the students appear to have addressed a wicked problem as a tame problem, and are undoubtedly on the wrong side of the Fourth Industrial Revolution with respect to flexible labour contracts.

The disputes then morphed back, once again, into a protest against the scarcity of accommodation. It was conducted mostly as a normal conflict although there were occasions where the conflict became violent and deep-rooted, particularly at the University of Cape Town. After this, the conflict morphed once again. It switched to a call for the scrapping of Afrikaans as a medium of instruction in historically Afrikaans universities. Burton's[125] research indicates that the call to drop Afrikaans will probably, in due course, trigger violent deep-rooted conflict. There is much compelling international evidence showing that language conflicts, which revolve around the fundamental human needs of Identity, Freedom, Creation, Participation and Understanding together with Being, Having, Doing and Interacting are, by definition, deep-rooted. They often become violent and can convert into life-and-death struggles.

The conflict then mutated into a general protest against colonialism and its manifestations, and included the #RhodesMustFall campaign. Arson and the burning of a colonial art collection at the University of Cape Town, as well as other acts of violence accompanied these protests. The latter conflict was once again deep-rooted in its nature and concerned different narratives of South African history. The fundamental human needs that underlay these protests included Freedom, Identity, Creation, Participation and Understanding, and Interacting, Being, Having and Doing.

6.4.4 The Students Negotiated Independently of Advisers

The #FeesMustFall protest was different from any other undertaken in South Africa to date. It was arranged without the involvement of any political parties. Indeed, the students insisted that political parties and trade unionists were specifically excluded from leading the protests or being involved in their leadership. This was a wise decision. The guiding principles of the protest were obtained from South Africa's new democratic Constitution and it was conducted within the framework of constitutional sovereignty. The students were proud of the fact that the protest was conducted in accordance with the guarantees that are made in the Constitution and not in terms of political party affiliations.

The students demanded that the 10.5% increase that had been approved by the University of the Witwatersrand for 2016 should be cancelled. This demand was taken up across all the South African universities and led to nationwide protests involving virtually all universities across the country. On 23 October 2015 Mr Jacob Zuma announced that the intended 2016 fee increase would be scrapped.

The #FeesMustFall case is an excellent example of successful negotiations in the context of the Fourth Industrial Revolution and eschewed the stereotyped accusatory pattern that has come to characterise collective bargaining in South Africa. This conflict was particularly interesting because the students were not influenced, and did not use, or emulate the unsuccessful negotiation strategies that have been used by trade unions during the process of collective bargaining over the past two decades. It has been noted that the students eschewed any trade union involvement or professional assistance during the course of these negotiations, and therefore maintained strict control and responsibility over all aspects of their interaction. This was wise because had the students sought the assistance of the trade union movement and political leadership, they would have diluted their case. They would have permitted the mental models of the First and Second Industrial Revolutions to eclipse the worldview associated with the Fourth Industrial Revolution which would have meant that they would have chosen the wrong rules of engagement and compromised their strategic independence. This would have created argument dilution. Gains were achieved by a closely co-ordinated networking process with other universities and students across the land, the media and other key stakeholders under the ambit of these new technologies that are available in the Fourth Industrial Revolution.

It is interesting to note that Mr Zuma and Dr Nzimande engaged in a futile attempt to use the traditional positional collective bargaining negotiation approach of granting gradual concessions with the students in a search for a compromise. The students' decision to exclude political and trade union leaders from assisting them in their cause was particularly interesting because it signified a generational vote of no confidence in those persons' negotiation skills, thereby suggesting why collective bargaining, as it is currently conducted, is failing.

Montalto[126] expressed the view that, notwithstanding the fact that the conflict arose from the ANC's ineffective tertiary education policy, the ANC would indeed seek to hijack this process for themselves. The question is: Would this hijacking endeavour be successful or not? The students ran rings around the government because of their Fourth Industrial Revolution worldview which eclipsed the worldview of the traditionalists whose inspiration harks back to the First and Second Industrial Revolutions. The negotiation process that was selected by the students was conducted using subtle and variable rules of engagement. Cell phones, Twitter and Facebook enabled the students to continuously network on the most favourable strategies which included the use of YouTube and e-mails. This resulted in the leadership being informed by a virtual crowd, who could critique their negotiation approaches in real time, using electronic devices.

The traditional one-dimensional conflictive approach that is used with collective bargaining in South Africa was not pursued. The students adopted a much more subtle multi-dimensional negotiation process. They continuously and appropriately fluctuated the rules of engagement and disbanded the ritualistic and conflictive negotiation approach that has been followed by the trade unionists and management in South Africa over the past few decades. This negotiation process involved simultaneous nuanced approaches of co-operation, collaboration, competition and conflict, all of which were invoked when and where required. Their negotiation goals were clear on the #FeesMustFall campaign but became unclear in the other protests against out-sourcing in which they subsequently became inveigled. This meant that their aspiration goals were generally succinct insofar as the matter of fees was concerned, and were based on the principle that the higher the aspiration level, the more favourable the negotiation outcome would be. The students' aspiration level was anchored in their slogan #FeesMustFall. Their negotiation objectives were achieved remarkably quickly and without the use of threatening struggle rhetoric. There were many associated instances of violence and vandalism, but it is clear that the vast majority of students rejected this tactic. The communication differed from the posturing, inefficient, incremental, polarised, disrespectful and conflictive interaction that has unfortunately become the pattern in much of the collective bargaining processes in South Africa. They were successful in achieving their negotiation goals in a professional manner. Indeed, they provided an example to the trade union movement, business and government of how negotiations about identifying satisfiers of fundamental human needs might be professionally conducted. By rejecting the bombastic win-lose interaction ritual that has characterised collective bargaining and caused it to fail in South Africa, they provided an exemplar of successful negotiation conduct for the country.

6.4.5 Disruptive Innovation and Tertiary Education

The students' victory in achieving a zero increase in university fees for 2016 has highlighted awareness of the redundancy of the universities' already fragile business models. These business models will have to be dramatically changed if the universities are to remain financially viable.

The student protests arose from the fact that a range of their fundamental human needs have been ignored over a long period of time, and they now form part of a bigger set of service delivery and political conflicts. The students' challenge to the leadership of South Africa is that they have practically demonstrated and articulated a fresh and alternative approach as to how South Africans might effectively negotiate upon fundamental human needs. The #FeesMustFall movement is rooted in problems that exist in the labour market and include indebtedness, poverty, very low rates of labour market absorption into the economy, and unemployment. These concerns need to be addressed in a systematic and holistic way.

The Fourth Industrial Revolution has made it evident that many administrative and clerical jobs will become obsolete because of disruptive innovation. It is probable that large numbers of administrative and clerical employees will become redundant and that stringent cost-cutting exercises will be invoked at all universities in South Africa. There will be a trend where all university courses that can reasonably be offered on a part-time basis will in due course be presented in this format in order to open up the opportunity for students to be employed while they study. It is anticipated that a well-organised, nationwide tertiary education system will be created to offer high-quality and free MOOCs in a structured manner to the peoples of South Africa. This would enable the unemployed to gain a high-quality tertiary education free of charge. Should this become a predominant business, it will eclipse much of the need for universities as they are currently structured. Online courses (MOOCs) are already disrupting tertiary education and this disruption is expected to accelerate, changing the nature of class teaching in universities and schools. The best universities in the world are now offering superb online MOOC courses in a multiplicity of subjects free of charge. This means that traditional South African universities will experience inexorable downward pressure on student fees, with ever-increasing requirements for teaching excellence.

The students are South Africa's intelligentsia and future leadership. They have broken away from the tired traditions of collective bargaining and have offered a fresh alternative approach as to how South Africans might effectively negotiate on fundamental human needs. The #FeesMustFall movement is rooted in problems that exist in the labour market and include indebtedness, many different forms of poverty and cripplingly low rates of labour market absorption into the economy. These concerns, although seemingly overwhelming, need to be boldly addressed in a systematic and holistic way.

The #FeesMustFall negotiation approach mimicked the approach that was used to drive the Tunisian revolution, termed the Jasmine Revolution. This mimicking was neither intentional nor ideological; it was serendipitous as it arose almost inevitably from the confluence of new interactive and amplifying digital technologies that are now being used in protest movements across the world. The Jasmine Revolution provides indications of how crowd behaviour might change under the mantle of the Fourth Industrial Revolution. The Jasmine Revolution began on 18 January 2010 and was triggered by the self-immolation by fire of Mohamed Bouazizi, who protested against the regime of Zine El Abidine Ben Ali, who was then president of the country. It then morphed along similar lines, but obviously in a very different contextual situation, as happened with the #FeesMustFall campaign. This revolution underwent many different configurations but eventually resulted in the fall of the regime of Zine El Abine Ben Al. He entered exile in January 2011. The regime change was brought about by a system of interacting factors, including critically using the new and innovative ways of communicating that have been ushered in by the Fourth Industrial Revolution, and these fed into the activation, passion and discontent of the masses. They were, as was the case of the #FeesMustFall movement in South Africa, linked by cell phones, Twitter, e-mail and Facebook. The protesters were able to use YouTube to witness events happening in real time. Strikes, mass demonstrations, protest marches, occupations of buildings, symbolic protests and acts of violence all took place contiguously and were covered in real time by the major international news channels as well.

This change of regime in Tunisia was subsequently mirrored in the sustained and connected crowd behaviour of the January 25 Revolution in Egypt that saw President Hosni Mubarak removed from power in 2011. The violent and disastrous revolutions in Libya, Syria and Iraq saw similar crowd behaviour that was also based on the disruptive innovation arising from the Fourth Industrial Revolution. The latter cases show that social change that is invoked by the Fourth Industrial Revolution can also go disastrously wrong. These forms of conflict were subsequently echoed with varying degrees of intensity in Yemen, Bahrain, Jordan and Lebanon during the past few years. The Fourth Industrial Revolution has resulted in new and unimagined sources of power that may influence crowd behaviour. These are being used innovatively and with greater frequency and effectiveness to address perceived social wrongs.

The visible crowd is characterised by the traditional trade union town hall meeting. The invisible crowd includes the electronic crowd of support and the multiplicity of intense interaction that takes place over the World Wide Web. The invisible crowd of the Fourth Industrial Revolution is arguably much more conspicuous and influential today than the visible crowd of the First and Second Industrial Revolutions. The invisible crowd can now access crowd funding and vast numbers of influential networks, both locally and internationally, to bolster their influence.

The conduct of these visible and invisible crowds can be expected both to lead and to follow these amplifying disruptive innovations that are embodied in the Fourth Industrial Revolution. They will undoubtedly change the basic way that collective bargaining is conducted. Should South Africa continue to blindly follow its current mode of collective bargaining and continue to adhere to the principles of the First and Second Industrial Revolutions, it can almost be assured that it will not be able to meet its growth and development requirements contained in the National Development Plan. As a result the country will possibly be relegated to a prolonged junk bond status and potentially even an International Monetary Fund structural adjustment programme.

It is anticipated that in the future there will be serious contestation about the content and design of school, technical college and university curricula. This could perhaps even become a matter of public policy. The crucial issue is that the employability of the masses is a matter of national concern. Employability is to a significant extent correlated with the dedication and quality of teaching. It is thus foreseeable that the students will insist that their curricula are congruent with absorption into the labour market and the future of employment.

6.5 Interaction between the Employed, the Unemployed and the Tripartite Alliance, and the Notion of State Capture

The average age of a unionised employee is 43 years, while the average age of an unemployed youth is 27 years. The unemployed youth is filled with energy, intelligence and potential, but is typically uneducated, unskilled, and on the wrong side of the Fourth Industrial Revolution. He or she does not have the resources, support, structure and guidance to get trained, skilled and educated for gainful employment. It is no wonder that some of the most creative and brightest of youthful minds in South Africa resort to lives of crime, drugs and nihilism and currently reside in prison. Their fundamental human needs of Subsistence, Protection, Affection, Understanding, Participation, Creation, Identity and Freedom, in conjunction with Being, Having, Doing and Interacting are simply not being met. They are neither being addressed individually nor collectively. This personal and collective negligence and indifference is giving rise to deeply entrenched social pathologies that are manifested in polarisation, alienation and incessant patterns of deep-rooted conflict that are evident across South Africa. The 43-year-old unionised employee is also on the wrong side of the Fourth Industrial Revolution but probably is unaware of this truth. It is projected that a large number of those persons who are currently employed will become redundant because of computerisation and the new digital interactive technologies. The 43-year-old unionised employee needs to hope that his or her employer has the wisdom, resources and energy to invest the necessary money and time into re-skilling and re-training for this age of computerisation.

Hartley[127] contended that the unemployed youth in South Africa have been disempowered by a capture of the state. This capture of the state is, in his view, manifested in an administrative seizure of power undertaken by the trade unions, which have acted in concert with the government, combined with an acquiescent business community. This informal plutocratic social compact ensured that employers were guaranteed labour stability, the unions had membership stability and the government had a ready supply of compliant voters. Policy-making authority is vested in the hands of highly paid government bureaucrats, trade union leaders, party political loyalists and business. It is Hartley's[128] opinion that secretive caucuses, meetings, fora, commissions and structures were used to perpetuate what is effectively a trade union, government and business cabal. To achieve this cabal, the social partners needed to discard the voice of civil society and abstain from systematically seeking to discover satisfiers of the fundamental human needs of the unemployed youth. Hartley[129] asserted that the 'greater good' of the social compact has sadly started to reveal itself over time as a Faustian pact that is expedient to the business, trade union and government's leadership elite, but is increasingly revealing itself as narrowly self-serving, and excludes benefiting their constituencies, stakeholders and supporters. Chief Justice Mogoeng of the Constitutional Court of South Africa offered a current legal case of state capture by a plutocracy that was congruent with Hartley's assertion. The Nkandla Case (Cases CCT 14/15 and CCT 171/15) decided on 31 March 1916, is cited as the *Economic Freedom Fighters v Speaker of the National Assembly and Others; Democratic Alliance v Speaker of the National Assembly and Others (2016)* ZACC. This judgment concerned President Jacob Zuma's failure to uphold the Constitution of South Africa, and his misappropriation of state funds for his personal benefit with the objective of building a residence called Nkandla on the state's account. It decided on the unchecked use of state power by the politically powerful and financially influential people for personal gain. This is commonly referred to as 'state capture' in South Africa. Zuma used his power of presidential office to create a cabal with six ministers and they connived to act against the instructions of the Public Protector and the Public Protector Act to pay back the private component of monies owed. This judgment provides a clear example of plutocratic state capture. In paragraph 1, page 1 of this judgment, state capture is defined thus:

> [1] One of the crucial elements of our constitutional vision is to make a decisive break from the unchecked abuse of State power and resources that was virtually institutionalized during the apartheid era. To achieve this goal, we adopted accountability, the rule of law and the supremacy of the Constitution as values of our constitutional democracy. For this reason public office-bearers ignore their constitutional obligations at their peril. This is so because constitutionalism, accountability and the rule of law constitute the sharp and mighty sword that stands ready to chop the ugly head of impunity off its stiffened neck.

The judgment found that President Zuma inveigled various ministers to do his bidding in this act of malfeasance.

The president cannot claim that he did not know what the ministers were doing and is therefore unaccountable. Paragraph 30 on page 18 of the judgment reads:

> [3] I reiterate that this would mean that, any failure to fulfil shared constitutional obligations by any member of the Executive, would thus be attributable to the President as his own failure. After all he appoints them and they are answerable to him. Their infringement, coupled with reliance on section 83, would thus justify the exercise of exclusive jurisdiction by this Court. Such an unbridled elastication of the scope of the application of section 83 or 1674 (4) (e) would potentially marginalize the High Court and the Supreme Court of Appeal in all constitutional matters involving the President.

The SADTU 'Jobs for Sale Report' that was conducted by Professor John Volmink and his task team had a broadly similar remit to that which underpinned the Nkandla case. It was analagous in the sense that it sought to establish whether and, if so, to what extent Basic Education in South Africa had been captured by a trade union for the benefit of its members at the expense of the learners. It subsequently emerged that there was a prima facie case of 'state capture' of South Africa's political leadership for financial gain by the Gupta family. In this regard Deputy Finance Minister, Mcebi Jonas, claimed that the Gupta family had offered him the position of Minister of Finance upon the dismissal of the then Minister of Finance, Nhlanhla Nene. If this allegation is indeed proven, Mr Zuma will have once again failed to uphold the Constitution of South Africa. Similarly, the former ANC parliamentarian, Vytjie Mentor, claimed that the Gupta family had offered her the position of Minister of Public Enterprises if she would abide by their wishes with respect to a flight route to India. Collective bargaining will fail when the market and its regulatory framework are effectively captured by the state.

Sole, McKune and Brummer[130] conducted an investigation that substantiates Hartley's[131] assertions and found that Gupta-owned state enterprises revealed "an extraordinary network of contacts close to the influential family that dominates the boards of South Africa's two largest parastatals, Eskom and Transnet". Mkhwanazi[132] informed that the auditing firm KPMG had terminated their auditing contract with businesses that are owned by the Gupta family on the basis of the allegations that President Zuma aided and abetted corrupt business relations with them. Mkhwanazi[133] reflected that: "Any reputable firm of advisers, financiers and auditors would have to think twice about working with the Guptas." The reputational risk of being their auditors was deemed to be too great to continue with this relationship. The notion of state capture is, therefore, entirely at odds with any prospect of achieving a viable social compact and of having a balanced regulatory framework in which fair collective bargaining can be conducted.

South African youth are uneducated, have been left out of apprenticeship training, skills training, and education, and there has been minimal, if any, investment in their employability. No imaginative, large-scale, organised and significant effort has been made to seek to find satisfiers of their fundamental human needs in the form of skills training and education on the scale and quality necessary to address South Africa's critical unemployment problem. Their plight is reflected in the extraordinary levels of violent crime, drug addiction, membership of criminal gangs, service delivery protests, political conflicts and other social pathologies that are evident in South Africa. They are depressingly entrapped in a dangerous poverty cycle.

Hartley[134] describes the social compact between business, government and labour thus:

> The effect of the new education and labour regimes was Orwellian in its double-speak and bureaucratic rectitude. The labour law was trumpeted as the legal framework within which employment would flourish. Well, the experiment has been running for two decades, and the results are there for all to see. The wages of the unionized have risen, and the ranks of the unemployed have grown. Who has suffered most? The youth are far and away the most savage victims of the closed labour market. In June this year, Stats SA released figures on youth unemployment: of 19.7 million youth of working age, only 6.2 million were employed.

According to Statistics South Africa's Statistical Release P0211.4.2 (2015), youth unemployment increased sharply during the period between 2008 and 2015. The unemployment rate among youth is more than twice the unemployment rate of adults over the same period. Statistics South Africa defines 'youth' as those persons in the

15–34-year-old age group, and adults as those persons between the ages of 35 and 64 years. This age-based difference in employment could lead to intergenerational deep-rooted conflict.

On the face of it one could assert that union membership has protected an aging workforce from the wage competition that would ensue from the up-skilling and absorption into the labour market of the unemployed youth. Table 6.1 presents a self-evident comparison between youth and adult employment rates.

Table 6.1: Comparative Youth and Adult Unemployment Rates in South Africa, 2008-2015

	2008	2009	2010	2011	2012	2013	2014	2015
Youth	32.7	33.7	35.7	36.1	35.8	36.2	36.1	36.9
Adult	13.4	12.4	14.9	14.4	15.1	15.0	15.6	17.0

Statistics South Africa Statistical Release P0211.4.2 (2015:3)[135]

According to Oosthuizen and Cassim:[136]

> In 2013, the youth unemployment rate was 63 percent of the youth labour force (3.2 million individuals) according to the expanded definition of unemployment, which includes as unemployed those who are not actively looking for a job (i.e. the non-searching unemployed and/or discouraged work-seekers). Youth unemployment is high, even in comparison with South Africa's very high average unemployment rate of 34 percent ... Of the 10.2 million individuals aged between 15-24 years, one third are not in employment, education or training. Roughly 30 percent of male youth and 36 percent of female youth are not in employment or not in training, disconnected from the labour market and opportunities that promote future employability. Unemployed youth are characterised by their lack of employability resulting from a range of socio-economic factors. They often have low levels of education, have dropped out of school and invariably do not have the literacy, numeracy and communication skills needed in the labour market. They also have little work experience, which is a particularly undesirable characteristic for employers. These young people lack strong social networks or social capital that allow them to source job opportunities, and tend not to have sufficient financial resources to enable mobility to areas where there is demand for labour. Of those who do have resources available as a result of their family support or network, they often have unrealistically high reservation wages, thereby resulting in relatively long periods of unsuccessful searching. Persistently high unemployment suggests a lack of effective policy

interventions. To date, policies that have been implemented have largely been supply-side initiatives aimed at the structural causes of youth unemployment; these include targeting the formal education system, post-school training, public employment and deployment programmes. From the demand side, an employment subsidy has been recently proposed by the National Treasury to incentivize employers to hire young people.[iii]

The labour absorption rate pertains to the percentage of persons that are absorbed into the labour market. A study of Table 6.1 above shows that the labour absorption rate is almost two-thirds lower for youth than it is for adults. The ratio of labour market absorption over the period 2008-2015 has averaged at about one to two thirds (youth to adult). This is a serious economic and human problem and it is astonishing that government, trade unions and business appear to be addressing this matter of such profound seriousness with such apathy and indifference to a putative intergenerational conflict.

The unemployment rate among youth is more than twice that of adults, while the absorption rate of youth into the labour market is substantially lower than for adults. The education and skills sets that are provided by schools, apprenticeship facilities, technical colleges and tertiary educational institutions show that the curricula are poorly aligned with employment and market requirements. This problem of labour market absorption needs to be addressed with expertise and on a grand scale if it is to be rectified. This should be a matter of national priority, the subject of dedicated remedial action, and addressed as a vast human development project that is accorded the same status as that of large infrastructure projects.

It could easily explode into deep-rooted conflict. Universities, schools, apprenticeship facilities, technical colleges and all institutions need to develop curricula in conjunction with input from experts in business and from all sectors of society that will ensure employability in the Fourth Industrial Revolution.

Table 6.2: Labour Market Status of Working-age Population, 2008-2015

	2008	2009	2010	2011	2012	2013	2014	2015
Youth	35.5	34.2	31.1	30.3	30.8	30.3	30.8	31.7
Adult	59.8	60.6	56.7	56.5	56.5	57.0	57.8	57.3

Statistics South Africa Statistical Release P0211.4.2 (2015:3)[137]

iii The International Monetary Fund on 31 July 2013 estimated that youth unemployment in South Africa was 52.9 per cent. Statement by Mr Saho, Executive Director of the International Monetary Fund for South Africa

Insufficient thought has been devoted to addressing the poor alignment between curriculum design, labour market absorption, employment creation and employability in the new world of work. Demographic forces have resulted in adult employees being in a significantly more favourable position than youth employees insofar as eligibility for employment is concerned. It is not clear what the reasons for these intergenerational differences are. One could hypothesise that those adults who are fortunate enough to be employed are so grateful that they cling to their jobs. This might be a possible explanation for the differential age versus eligibility for employment profile. The mature worker might have entered into employment in more secure economic times and incrementally learned the required skills sets necessary for gainful employment.

At present, the youth are experiencing enormous difficulty in penetrating the barriers that allow access to gainful employment. Union protectionism of adult employees at the expense of the youth is another possible explanation of the low absorption rate of youth relative to adults into the labour market. The 15-year difference in average age of employment between youth and adults leads to the inexorable deduction that union protectionism might indeed be age based. If this logic were indeed correct, it would follow, therefore, that the students, unemployed youth and trade unions might, in due course, find themselves in a generational conflict with one another on the basis of age-based discrimination. It is true that entry into the labour market is spread over several years depending on training, education and opportunities, and that this assimilation takes time. But entry into the ranks of the unemployed is clearly the plight of the youth. The unemployment rate among youth rose from 32.7% in 2008 to 36.1% in 2011 and then remained relatively stable between 35.0%-37.0% up until 2015. Many young job seekers have simply given up on their quest for employment. Statistics South Africa (2015) explained that this increase in unemployment was a result of the global recession. If South Africa were to be accorded junk bond status by the credit ratings agencies, youth unemployment will increase because of employment freezes and the process of retrenchment that would inevitably follow such a declaration.

Robotics, computerisation, 3D printing and disruptive innovation are projected to significantly exacerbate the problem of unemployment for both the youth and adult groupings. Disruptive innovation will affect the adult component of the labour force harshly because re-skilling, re-training and re-education will have to be conducted on a massive scale. In theory, the youth should have less of a problem in learning and acquiring new knowledge and skills that are congruent with the new world of work. The argument against this assertion is that basic secondary and tertiary education in South Africa is simply not aligned to the world of work, making it considerably difficult for the youth to develop the requisite knowledge and skills sets for entering a world of work shaped by the Fourth Industrial Revolution. If the educational system in South Africa were of higher quality the youth could be expected to adapt more easily to technological innovation, having been brought up in the digital age. Maswanganyi[138] showed that there are 19.7 million working-age youth between 15 and 34 years of age in South Africa. Of this cohort, 6.2 million are employed and economically active while 9.8 million are not economically active. This is a very large number of people and could, if activated, place the very fabric of society at risk. They currently do not have the right type of education for labour market absorption, and it follows therefore that if this present inferior quality of education is perpetuated, they will remain excluded from the labour market as structurally unemployed.

The unemployed are currently badly organised as a stakeholder grouping. This state of disorganisation will not continue. Multimedia, SMS and computer applications will foreseeably result in the unemployed becoming much more strategically organised. Students, in combination with the unemployed, might catalyse this trend using multimedia. If the unemployed were to become organised they would dissipate trade union power. This would place extreme downward pressure on wage negotiations and collective bargaining. The Tripartite Alliance could perhaps disintegrate under the viciousness of the ensuing inter- and intra-stakeholder conflicts that would emerge were this scenario to become a reality.

6.5.1 Social Grants

Should the government be compelled for economic or other reasons to retract social grants to the unemployed, it is probable that profound civil unrest and deep-rooted conflict would engulf those components of South Africa society that would be affected. Social grants are a temporary palliative. They might create the transitory illusion that the recipients' fundamental human needs are being satisfied, but this is obviously not the case. Their fundamental human need for Subsistence might be partially met, but their other needs for Protection, Affection, Understanding, Participation, Creation, Identity and Freedom in conjunction with Being, Having, Doing and Interacting would simply not be met. The social grants are a political attempt to buy off the anger of this large stakeholder grouping and it must be conceded that it has thus far, for the most part, been politically successful. The recipients of social grants are unemployed, underemployed, structurally unemployed and often unemployable. They are typically uneducated, untrained and unskilled, and live from hand to mouth. The recipients of social grants are rent-seekers and do not contribute to the productivity of the economy other than by being quiescent. Their quiescence might be a worthwhile price for ensuring political and economic stability.

The Tripartite Alliance initiated South Africa's social grant policy to provide sustenance to the unemployed. The decision to make social grants available to the unemployed was reached strategically, with the intention of defusing the risk of deep-rooted conflict emerging from this stakeholder grouping. Ferreira[139] confirmed that:

"The number of social grant recipients in South Africa has increased exponentially over the past twenty years: from an estimated 4 million in 1994 to 16.3 million by 31 August 2014."

Ferreira's statistics translate into the fact that about 30% of South Africans are now living off social grants. The amount paid by the state is about R118 billion and represents approximately 3% of South Africa's Gross Domestic Product. Given the modest size of the South African economy, R118 billion rand is a significant allocation to the unemployed, the underemployed and the unemployable. Were the economy to creep into recession or depression, its capacity to continue providing social grants would obviously be compromised.

This could conceivably be triggered by the ratings agencies downgrading South Africa's economy to junk bond status, and the International Monetary Fund being called upon to implement a structural adjustment programme, for example. Under a severe recession, there could foreseeably be cuts in social grants, and it is predictable that the extent of any cuts will correlate with the intensity of the resultant protests. Conflict between the government, the employed and the unemployed can thus be expected to emerge from this impoverished stakeholder grouping.

This disruption would, in turn, resonate across the entire society. It would cause significant fragmentation of stakeholder groupings within South African society. The employed in South Africa, regardless of how poorly they are remunerated, therefore constitute an elite while the unemployed are, in Fanon's[140] words, *The Wretched of the Earth*.

The unemployed are 'the elephant in the room'. We know from the peasant revolt in the Western Cape that the unemployed acted in solidarity with the employed and that there was, at that time, no evidence of a rift between the unionised employed and the unemployed. There are scenarios where this collaboration between the employed and unemployed might shift into competition and conflict for scarce employment positions. Such conflict and competition could generate extreme downward pressure on wages. Recession, disruptive innovation, computerisation and robotics could be the triggers of such deep-rooted conflict. Under the scenario of disruptive innovation, Luddite protests and violence can be expected to emerge. The extent of unemployment in South Africa is directly correlated with the weakness and frequent irrelevance of academic, technical and vocational education and training in this country, and the lack of curricular connection to labour market absorption. Collective bargaining is failing in South Africa because the parties to the process are not insisting that continuous training, education and skills upgrading takes place. In general, qualifications that are accorded in South Africa need to satisfy the requirements for labour market absorption. This is an important tangible measure of the value of certification.

6.6 The Police

The police are called upon to maintain law and order and to offer a physical presence as a deterrent to criminality, violence, corruption, anti-social behaviour and vandalism when there is social conflict. The police presently do not have the necessary training, competence and skill to address the escalation of normal conflicts into deep-rooted conflicts, or to de-escalate deep-rooted conflicts into normal conflicts and developmental processes. The police are also operating in the absence of a coherent theory of fundamental human needs that are driving conflict, crime and positive human aspirations. Escalatory conflicts often occur when there are breakdowns in the collective bargaining process itself over the failure to discover satisfiers of fundamental human needs. When the police's intervention is incompetent, as it most certainly was in the case of the Marikana Massacre, all stakeholder relationships are negatively impacted and the breakdown of stakeholder relationships occurs. The Farlam Commission of Inquiry into the causes of the Marikana Massacre revealed a toxic collusion between the Ministry of Police, the Minister of Mining and Energy, and business.

There was, in addition, divisive inter-union rivalry and conflict between the NUM and the newly established Association of Mineworkers and Construction Workers Union (AMCU). It is common cause that the state and business designed a joint strategy with respect to the labour conflict that preceded the Marikana Massacre. This joint state–business strategy had catastrophic negative and escalatory consequences.

The strategy of business and government appeared to be that of criminalising the wage dispute by attacking its moral legitimacy. It would seem that violence was deemed by both the state and business to be preferable to negotiations to resolve this conflict. They displayed a rigid mechanistic worldview congruent with the First and Second Industrial Revolution where violence was deemed to be a more efficient way of bringing the matter to a close than negotiating to discover satisfiers of fundamental human needs via the process of collective bargaining. The Lonmin management effectively therefore promoted the police, on their behalf, into primary negotiators in their collective bargaining process. Needless to say, the police were entirely bereft of talent in this interactive role. In so doing, Lonmin management absolved themselves of their fundamental management responsibility which was to manage the mine. The state and business then sought to criminalise the wage dispute and to present the conflict as though it were an act of sedition on the part of the miners. The consequence of this collusion was that it destroyed trust between the police, the unions, business, the Tripartite Alliance, the communities who were involved in the conflict and many other stakeholders besides. The police are themselves torn between their loyalty towards their own leadership and the communities in which they live and operate.

The Marikana Massacre is a classic example of applying the wrong mental models and collective bargaining strategies to wicked problems that require the highest level of discretion, skill, knowledge and insight. The approach of the police and mine management was devoid of talent or skill. They used symptomatic single-loop learning to approach a complex wicked problem that required double-loop learning if its intricate contextual nuances and continuously changing configuration were to be understood and effectively addressed. The police did not have either the knowledge or skill to diagnose and discover solutions to deep-rooted conflict and addressed the conflict as though it were a normal conflict. Finally there was no knowledge or attempt to seek to find satisfiers of fundamental human needs that were driving the conflict and to address these in a constructive manner.

6.6.1 Unprotected Strikes, Vigilante Action, Xenophobic Attacks on Foreign Businesses and Nationals, and Zama Zamas

6.6.1.1 Unprotected Strikes

During the period prior to the Marikana Massacre there were numerous unprotected strikes on the platinum belt which involved workers by-passing their trade unions. Swart[141] reported that Labour Court Judge Anton Steenkamp had heard five urgent applications raised by major employers in the space of a week asking for wildcat strikes to be declared unprotected. These employers included AngloGold Ashanti and Goldfields. "What was unusual," said Steenkamp, "was that employers were not seeking relief against unions; the interdicts were being sought against individual striking workers ... The unions have been assisting the employers in getting workers back to work ... This is unheard of."

Swart[142] cited labour lawyer Michael Bagraim as judging that:

> ... this trend towards guerrilla bargaining is a dangerous one. Within the formal system, unions could face employers as equals. Informal groups attempting to negotiate undermined this relationship. It is the worst industrial relations nightmare that I have seen in 30 years of practising labour law. This loss of faith has been in the making for years. In the early 1980's and 1990's, unions saw political and bread and butter issues as part of the anti-apartheid struggle. But post-1994 improving living conditions outranked the political struggle in worker minds. With that, the unions lost their best leaders to politics and the new leaders did not have the same expertise and enjoyed much better perks.

Swart[143] reflected that the spokesperson for NUM, Lesiba Seshoka, responded to the allegation that the union had more interest in politics and self-enrichment saying:

"Unions involved in bread and butter issues are going to fail, because broader politics are shaped at political level. The NUM does not have shares in Lonmin or any mining, energy or construction companies, in or outside of South Africa. That would amount to a conflict of interest."

Unprotected strikes are illegal. They are not conducted according to the provisions of the Labour Relations Act. This means that an employee who chooses to engage in an unprotected strike can be summarily dismissed; this is provided that the employer conducts such dismissals in a substantively and procedurally fair manner. The four-week-long illegal strike by the City of Johannesburg's monopoly garbage collecting agency, Pikitup, can be interpreted as an industrial relations equivalent of vigilante action. It vividly identifies the dangers of guerrilla bargaining cited by Michael Bagraim mentioned above. Pikitup employees embarked upon an illegal strike to achieve an increase in wages and to have the managing director of the company, Amanda Nair, dismissed on the grounds of alleged malfeasance. Mkhize[144] reported that the rubbish was piled up so high in the central business district of Johannesburg that people working there had difficulty in walking across the filthy streets. This conflict has similar underlying public policy and constitutional issues to those that pertained to SADTU's refusal to conduct the annual school readiness tests in accordance with instructions from the Minister of Basic Education. These two conflicts form a pattern of unconscionable indifference to the greater good. They reveal the prevailing cynical worldviews that are causing collective bargaining to fail in South Africa. They are indifferent to the principle of constitutional supremacy and the Bill of Rights.

Had there been an outbreak of an infectious disease, say bubonic plague, typhus, dysentery, or say Ebola as an improbable example, and a case was proven that this disease was caused directly by the SAMWU members' refusal to remove this festering garbage from Johannesburg's central business district in pursuit of their illegal industrial action, they would have been open to claims of delictual and indeed criminal liability. SAMWU and SADTU also both displayed a singular disregard for their duty of care for the greater good to the stakeholders in the community whom they purported to serve. The needs of the citizens of Johannesburg which Pikitup ostensibly served were ignored, disrespected and violated. The fundamental needs of the residents, ratepayers and taxpayers were transgressed. The collective bargaining process failed to address the stakeholder needs for Subsistence, Protection, Identity, Freedom, Being, Having, Doing and Interacting. All of these fundamental human needs were violated by the illegal strike and guerrilla collective bargaining approach. Mabotja[145] informed that the City of Johannesburg sent out dismissal notices to the strikers who had engaged in this unprotected strike. Dludla[146] reported that the Pikitup workers who were affiliated to the South African Municipal Workers Union vowed to intensify this illegal strike and that SAMWU's regional deputy secretary,

Paul Tlhabeng, told a radio station that was covering the unprotected strike that its members would ignore these notices of dismissal. One of the driving forces behind this illegal strike was that Pikitup had a monopoly over garbage collection in Johannesburg. There was thus a possible case to take Pikitup before the Competition Commission and ascertain whether this monopoly should not be broken up into competitive units and companies for the greater good of the citizens of Johannesburg.

Mabotja[147] reported the deputy regional secretary of SAMWU as threatening: "If the ANC government wants to dismiss 4 000 employees, they will be committing political suicide. Be sure that we will be supporting our members until they get what they deserve." Mabotja[148] informed that on Tuesday, 15 March, striking Pikitup workers provocatively overturned rubbish bins, directly in front of, in the full view of metro police who had been monitoring the strike. The police passively witnessed the transgression and made no arrests for this illegal activity. The strikers were, according to the Pikitup spokesperson Jacky Mashapu, also using intimidation to pursue their objectives. Union members allegedly shot at two garbage truck drivers who had attempted to remove waste and break away from the strike. It was clear that the union was threatening to withhold votes for the ANC in the municipal election if the government dismissed any of those who had been striking illegally in pursuit of their salary and demands, and for the dismissal of Amanda Nair, the managing director of Pikitup. The behaviour of SAMWU indicated that it was completely unconcerned about the legality or illegality of the strike, and the health and aesthetic ramifications for the community. This is a two-edged sword because legality cannot be claimed and discarded as a point of convenience.

The SAMWU strike was illegal and its regional deputy secretary, Paul Tlhabeng, allegedly took the law into his own hands. This conflict had all the basic hallmarks of vigilante activity. The union appears to have used the accumulation of filth resulting from the illegal strike and the non-collection of garbage as a negotiation ploy to invoke the citizens of Johannesburg to place pressure on the City of Johannesburg and Pikitup to settle the dispute on terms that were favourable to SAMWU. SAMWU's conduct was unconscionable because the accumulation of filth created the danger of a serious public health hazard. It appears to have been delictually negligent in visiting this risk on the citizens in pursuit of the wages, salaries and conditions of service demands. It negotiated contrary to *bonos mores* because it was then attempting to blackmail the ANC government with the threat of withholding votes if it elected to act lawfully by dismissing those union members who had engaged in this unprotected strike. Another hallmark of this vigilante strike was the various acts of intimidation that allegedly included shots being fired at non-strikers. SAMWU, in the case of the Pikitup strike, therefore became a vigilante group that acted as a law unto itself.

6.6.1.2   Vigilante Action

The inability of the police and the criminal justice system to counteract illegality and criminality has given rise to vigilantism which involves taking the law into one's own hands. Patel (2015) explained that vigilantes are self-appointed law enforcement groups who are "skeptical of the police's ability to protect the community and preserve the law".

Haefele (2004) characterises vigilante activity as involving people who perceive that policing and the legal system have failed them, and that they therefore have the right to take the law into their own hands and mete out justice to 'perceived criminals' as they deem fit, without the authority of the state. They live in communities that do not trust or enjoy the protection of the police and use their own forms of violence to mete out their own arbitrary form of justice. Vigilantism exists because of fundamental breakdowns in policing, the judicial system, and society at large, which then creates the space for many people to take the law into their own hands. These are not isolated breakdowns, but are systemic and interconnected. The inclination towards the informal system represents a vote of no confidence in the formal system. Starvation and destitution caused by unemployment have resulted in the creation of illegal, desperate and criminal forms of employment in an entirely unregulated economy where the rules of the jungle apply.

The Constitutional Court case referred to as *Economic Freedom Fighters v Speaker of the National Assembly and Others; Democratic Alliance v Speaker of the National Assembly and Others [2016]* ZACC in paragraph [74] page 38 confirms that the Constitution is based on the rule of law. Therefore:

> No decision grounded on the Constitution or law may be disregarded without recourse to the rule of law. To do otherwise would amount to a licence to self-help. Whether the Public Protector's decisions amount to administrative action or not, the disregard for remedial action by those adversely affected by it amounts to taking the law into their own hands and is illegal. No binding or statutorily sourced decision may be disregarded willy-nilly. It has legal consequences and must be complied with or acted upon.

Unprotected strikes therefore amount to self-help which can, in turn, be described as vigilante action.

6.6.1.3   Xenophobic Attacks on Foreign Businesses and Foreign Nationals

Xenophobic attacks on foreign nationals and the looting of their businesses is a form of economic vigilantism. Xenophobic attacks, unprotected strikes, vigilantism and illegal Zama Zama mining all involve taking the law into one's own hands and a deliberate decision to disregard South Africa's constitutional framework. Similar root causes drive unprotected strikes, vigilante violence and Zama Zama mining in South Africa. The Report of the Special Reference Group on Migration and Community Integration in KwaZulu-Natal (2015:59-60) asserted that:

> The triple challenges of poverty, unemployment and socio-economic inequality were identified as the most salient and prevalent underlying conditions that contribute to heightened tensions between various communities, including South Africans and foreign nationals. These triple challenges produce economic-oriented pressures and frustration among different communities, and thereby heighten competition for scarce resources and opportunities. This competition, while also taking place among South African communities, has been highlighted as a cause of tensions between South Africans and foreign nationals because of perceptions that any economic success attained by foreign nationals detracts from those potential successes of South African citizens. It is also important to disclaim that while the dynamics provide the context for violence, such conditions do not determine when and where violence against certain communities might occur.

According to Saba and Harper[149] the latest xenophobic violence started at Jeena's Supermarket in Isipingo, KwaZulu-Natal, on 15 December 2014. The employees at this supermarket went on strike for higher wages and bonuses. The owner of the business, Mr Goolam Khan, claimed that he was compelled to hire 50 temporary staff and he denied that he contrived that foreign nationals would replace the local strikers. Whether Mr Khan's claim is factually true or not has not been proven. What is important is that the narrative that foreign nationals were hired to replace South Africans became the 'emotional truth' and the gateway to the national explosion of xenophobic attacks on foreign nationals and their businesses. Saba and Harper[150] reported that a striker, Mxolisi Jawuse, said on 30 March 2015 that while picketing outside the supermarket, community members joined them: "People who already had their own problems joined us and started the whole thing. If we had anything to do with this attack we would have started it in December. But another employee said, 'We are part of the community and they know our struggles. Shoppers had guns pointed at them and their shopping bags checked by foreigners. How would you feel if someone from outside was making you feel like a criminal in your own country?'" When the attacks began the supermarket closed its doors for two days. Protesters moved from there to the rest of Isipingo, where the streets are lined with foreign-owned shops, and the violence began.

The strike at Jeena's Supermarket was, in due course, supported not only by disgruntled employees, but also by an alienated community at large. The strike was therefore the gateway to the xenophobic wave of violence that engulfed South Africa during the course of 2015.

The conflict began as a normal conflict about wages and bonuses. It escalated into a deep-rooted conflict when foreign scab labour was perceived to be employed as replacement labour. The fundamental human needs that led to the escalation from normal into deep-rooted conflict in terms of Max-Neef et al.[151] would include: Subsistence, Protection, Identity, Participation, Understanding, Interacting, Having, Doing and Being. These fundamental human needs did not pertain to Jeena's Supermarket only. They resonated with the fundamental human needs and the insecurities of the entire society.

The strikers first set about threatening shoppers who entered the supermarket and then they started attacking other foreign-owned shops at Isipingo. The situation quickly escalated from a normal into an intractable deep-rooted conflict and spread across South Africa. The Report of the Special Reference Group on Migration and Community Integration in KwaZulu-Natal (2015:53-58) recorded that during the course of these attacks about 5 000 foreign nationals were compelled to flee their homes and hundreds of small business were looted, burnt down and destroyed. The countries of origin of foreign nationals who were attacked included: Somalia, Democratic Republic of the Congo, Mozambique, Ethiopia, Malawi, Zimbabwe, Burundi, Lesotho, Nigeria, West Africa, Pakistan, Bangladesh and India, to name but a few.

The Report of the Special Reference Group on Migration and Community Integration in KwaZulu-Natal (2015:8) established that:

> The violent attacks started in and around KwaZulu-Natal's township communities and the attacks disproportionately targeted African foreign nationals. A number of African foreign nationals have integrated into township communities and a subset of them have found success in the informal sector. Their economic success has fuelled competition between themselves and many local South Africans who continue to struggle for their day-to-day survival. A number of South Africans perceive African foreign nationals as direct competition for limited social resources and economic opportunities. Many foreign nationals are still not accepted within KZN's communities.

This perception of direct competition for limited resources and negotiation as a zero-sum game bedevils collective bargaining and is wrong. The foreign nationals benefit the locals by increasing access to resources, employment opportunities, goods, services and wealth. The xenophobic worldview is indicative of how collective bargaining and negotiation is understood and conducted in South Africa. It is regarded as a zero-sum contest with absolutist and win-lose outcomes. The fact that the foreign nationals provided the locals with employment and vitally important goods and services was not seen as justifying co-operation and collaboration with them. This was entirely counter-productive, biting the hand that fed them.

The Report of the Special Reference Group on Migration and Community Integration in KwaZulu-Natal (2015:8) reflects that:

> Both the underlying and proximate causes of the March-May violence are complex and multi-faceted. The underlying issues, including high levels of poverty and unemployment, intermittent service delivery, and inequitable access to basic resources are to some extent the unresolved challenges of the social engineering that defined apartheid in South Africa. Relative socio-economic deprivation, heightened competition for employment and social services, widespread perceptions of impunity for criminals and a systemic lack of dialogue have further impeded cohesive and constructive relationships. South Africans continue to struggle with unemployment and poverty, and are challenged by the influx of foreign nationals into their communities, which South Africans perceive to be at their expense. The dominant myths, stereotypes and negative perceptions held by both local and foreign national communities about one another are damaging to the promotion of greater social cohesion. The limited integration evident today, where people have reached a state of co-existence but not acceptance, affects all people who reside in the province, a problem experienced not only by foreign nationals but also by people born outside KwaZulu-Natal.

6.6.1.4 Patterns of Escalation of Xenophobic Conflict

According to the Report of the Special Reference Group on Migration and Community Integration in KwaZulu-Natal (2015:53), in January 2015 in Soweto, Gauteng, a Somali shop owner "shot and killed a 14-year-old schoolboy, Siphiwe Mahori, during an alleged robbery. Another victim, Lebogang Ncamala, 23, was shot three times in the arm at the scene of the robbery. The incident triggered a wave of attacks and looting of 120 foreign owned shops." The shooting of Siphiwe Mahori for the alleged theft was escalatory and changed the threshold into deep-rooted conflict. Regardless of whether Siphiwe Mahori was guilty or not, his violent death resulted in his being martyred, as was Hector Pieterson when he was shot dead and became emblematic of the Soweto riots of 1976. Similarly, Tarek al-Tayeb Mohamed Bouazizi's self-immolation became the driving image of martyrdom that was equated with the Tunisian revolution of January 2011. These images captured incidents that all fall into the category of deep-rooted conflict.

The Report of the Special Reference Group on Migration and Community Integration in KwaZulu-Natal (2015:53) concluded that the xenophobic violence quickly gained momentum, and on 13 March Noel Beya Dinshistia, who was a Congolese citizen and employed as a nightclub worker in Durban, was doused in a flammable substance and set on fire by locals. It is alleged that on 20 March 2015 the Zulu King, Goodwill Zwelithini, stated at a meeting that was hosted by the Ministry of Police that foreigners should go back to their home countries. The perception among locals was then that the xenophobic attacks on foreign nationals and their businesses had the official stamp of approval from the King and the police. This was a very dangerous situation. The Report of the Special Reference Group on Migration and Community Integration in KwaZulu-Natal (2015:53) continued by mentioning that on 25 March 2015, the locals attacked foreigners at Isipingo and approximately 400 people were displaced. Locals used social media and WhatsApp to send threatening messages to foreigners and on 5 April 2015, two Mozambicans were found murdered in the Lusaka informal settlement in Chatsworth. During the latter part of April 2015, an anti-xenophobic movement started to develop in South Africa. Demonstrations and protests started to be mobilised to bring an end to the reign of terror.

The Report of the Special Reference Group on Migration and Community Integration in KwaZulu-Natal (2015:54-56) informed that the Lawyers for Human Rights strongly criticised the conduct of the police and asserted that foreigners were not being given a platform to voice their concerns, insisting that this should be provided in order to expose the violence. The intervention of the Lawyers for Human Rights was very important and positive because they offered a legal and constitutional framework for dealing with vigilantism and 'self-help'. The deep-rooted conflict showed signs that it might escalate onto an international platform when on 15 April 2015, the South African Embassy in Lagos was summoned and issued with an ultimatum that there would be action against South African businesses in Nigeria if the South African government did not put a halt to xenophobic violence against Nigerians. It is contended that it was absolutely essential that the matter of xenophobic violence be escalated to international stakeholders because this placed extreme pressure on the national government to improve their conduct and act professionally. It raised the international political stakes. The Report of the Special Reference Group on Migration and Community Integration in KwaZulu-Natal (2015:56) said that the next day ambassadors and diplomats from African countries called for a meeting with International Relations Minister, Maite Nkoana-Mashabane, to seek solutions to the xenophobic attacks.

On 17 April 2015, Mozambican citizens took the law into their own hands and stoned South African trucks entering Mozambique in an act of tit-for-tat against the xenophobic violence that was visited upon Mozambique foreign nationals and their businesses in South Africa. On 17 April 2015, the Economic Community of West Africa condemned South Africa's handling of the xenophobic violence.

The Report of the Special Reference Group on Migration and Community Integration in KwaZulu-Natal (2015:57) mentioned that the African Union Summit was held in Pretoria during June 2015. Thirty-one Civil Society Organisations from across the African continent signed an open letter to the African Union enjoining them to ensure that South Africa provides a long-term security guarantee for refugees, migrants and asylum seeks who live in the country.

All this international pressure resulted in the creation of shelters and the xenophobic violence started to gradually abate. The roots of xenophobia, however, are alive and can flare up at any moment because of the failure to seek to discover satisfiers of fundamental human needs across the country.

It is significant that on 10 December 2014, the KwaZulu-Natal Somali Community Council sent a letter to the Mayor of Durban, the Public Protector and other officials to alert them to the tensions between the local community, and the vandalism and looting of Somali shops. They felt that there was a mendacious mood among the locals in the province that would precede xenophobic attacks. They therefore anticipated the foreseeable consequences of the subsequent attacks. It would have been commendable if this forewarning had been heeded.

6.6.1.5   Zama Zamas

Zama Zamas are illegal miners who are mostly foreign, and who work in an informal shadow economy on the dark side of the formal mining industry. They are a vigilante form of employment, operating under exceptionally violent and dangerous circumstances. Their violent and criminal modus operandi places them in direct conflict with the police, the trade unions, business leadership, the Chamber of Mines, the South African Revenue Service, the Ministry of Home Affairs, and the miners who are legally employed in the formal mining sector in South Africa. Motale[152] explained that the Zama Zamas consist of gangs of illegal miners who are typically armed with advanced weaponry including explosives and semi-automatic weapons that include AK 47s and other firearms. Motale[153] maintained that: "these Zama Zamas are effectively at war over the control of illegal mining operations in Gauteng, Free State and the Northern Cape". He cautioned that the position of Zama Zamas in the Gauteng province was particularly vexing as "the police appear to be unable to deal with the underground shootings as they fear for their lives – they have not been trained to deal with such situations".

The Zama Zamas usually work in armed groups. They mine in both disused and currently operating mine shafts for their precious metals. They also strip disused mines of their residual metals and infrastructure and sell these to illegal scrap metal dealers who export these metals to international markets. They have no social security whatsoever. They cannot seek protection from the police because of both their criminal activities and illegal residential status. They also operate in a world where labour relations are entirely unregulated (in a manner that is similar to blood diamond operations in Africa) and therefore act totally outside the ambit of collective bargaining. The Zama Zamas present an important case that illustrates the consequences that will arise if there is not a massive nationwide project to skill the unskilled and create viable forms of employment on a mass scale. If the Zama Zamas are left unchallenged, the foreseeable consequences will be that other forms of organised crime will sprout up that mimic their business model. Illegal mining and illegal business ventures will steadily proliferate in South Africa.

IRIN Humanitarian News and Analysis (2015) explained that there has been a proliferation of illegal mining in the Free State and Gauteng which is costing the South African economy about R5 billion per annum. They cite the then Mineral Resources Minister, Susan Shabangu, as confirming that: "Several thousand Zama Zamas are thought to work below ground at any one time, often mingling with legally employed mineworkers in order to gain access to abandoned sections of active mines and to smuggle food and supplies in and out."

It is projected that South Africa will slowly move towards operating in a dark hole of illegal business if there is not a serious endeavour to address the challenge of employment creation in the Fourth Industrial Revolution, thereby rendering Zama Zamas obsolete. For many unskilled employees, illegal forms of employment will be the only employment that is possible in South Africa under the digital revolution. The Zama Zamas present a business model that is conceived to operate completely outside of the law.

6.7 Loan Sharks as Predators on the Poor

Loan sharks seek to grant loans to gainfully employed and unionised workers. They use the mechanism of garnishee orders to gain legal authority to deduct interest from the payroll of companies in the name of the loan applicant when there is a default in repayment. They know then that the people who have taken out the loans have a reasonably assured income and are therefore low-risk clients, but they also know that they will default on their loans and these defaults form part of their business model. The default on loans works to the loan sharks' ultimate benefit because it entraps the debtor in a perpetual situation of financial bondage to stratospheric interest rates which are charged on these recycled loans. These garnishee orders are often obtained illegally and the interest charged is unconscionable. Loan sharks are therefore free riders on the collective bargaining process, functioning as parasites on their debtor-hosts at wage and salary increase time. Together, the loan sharks and their unionised clients form part of a greater and messier collective bargaining system in South Africa.

The relationship between loan sharks and their unionised clients has a major impact on all aspects of the collective bargaining process and the quality of life of poor people. Loan sharks have a vested interest in the unionised employees negotiating high wage settlements because they translate into assured deductions from the unionised employees' salaries and wages for these micro-lenders. Loan sharks have also been found in court to generally secure their garnishee orders against employees illegally.

An example of loan sharks' ruinous inveiglement in the lives of unskilled and semi-skilled employees is revealed in the case referred to as *The University of Stellenbosch Legal Aid Clinic v Micro-Lender Case (2015)*, Case no: 16703/14. The University of Stellenbosch's Legal Aid Clinic prosecuted micro-lenders for the criminally inflated interest rates that they charged to impoverished citizens and the illegal manner in which they had secured the garnishee orders on which these loans were predicated. Loans from micro-lenders led to appalling financial entrapment and the illegal garnishee orders were instruments of civil and criminal bullying that is conducted on an enormous scale. The Stellenbosch Legal Aid Clinic case was important because it clarified how loan sharks structure parasitic relationships with financially destitute employees. It revealed the disturbing nationwide extent of the indebtedness of people who are employed on the lowest rungs of South African society. There is a fundamental need for an ethical banking system for the poor in South Africa. That system has not yet been designed. If this challenge were met, it would be a major achievement of the Fourth Industrial Revolution.

Davis (2015) observed that the offices of 13 micro-lenders were conspicuously placed in the main street of Marikana at the time of the massacre. For him, it served as an indication of the centrality of loan sharks in the everyday lives of the miners. Zille[154] explained that the Western Cape farm workers' strike revealed a similar dynamic between labour and loan sharks. She said:

> The life of a seasonal farm labourer is a very difficult one. Thousands of poverty-stricken people come to the Western Cape from across Southern Africa for the fruit-picking season, desperately seeking work in one of the few

remaining sectors that still employs unskilled labour. Many of these migrants have remained in the province permanently, and have set up home in shack settlements, on the outskirts of rural towns. Unemployed for most of the year, they rely on the short fruit-picking season to earn some income, much of which disappears immediately into the coffers of loan sharks on whom they depend to keep their families alive.

The loan sharks are an informal and unregulated component of South Africa's banking system. They hold sway over millions of poor South Africans' financial lives and are the arbiters of misery. Loan sharks, vigilantism and Zama Zama miners are therefore all driven by the failure to discover creative satisfiers of fundamental human needs. It is the responsibility of business, government and the union movement to create a banking system that has a regulatory framework that enables those persons who are presently un-bankable to bank with security. *The University of Stellenbosch Legal Aid Clinic v Micro-Lender Case (2015)*, Case no: 16703/14 is an important case that might offer a framework for understanding what needs to be done to discover how to bank the un-bankable according to an enduring and fair regulatory framework.

6.8 The Incremental Erosion of the Social Compact in South Africa since 1994

During the early stages of South Africa's political transition into a non-racial democracy (circa 1994), the negotiation rules of engagement between business, trade unions and government became, temporarily, slightly less adversarial than they had been during the period of mass mobilisation in the 1980s. For a short period of time 'negotiation space' was created for more nuanced collaboration and co-operation between the stakeholders. There was a fragile social compact. This brief social compact was based on an assumption that government, labour and business would, in the event of serious problems, put their differences aside and act together for the greater good. During the first decade of democracy, strikes were often protected, although certainly not always conducted in a legal and procedural fashion. However, there was hardly ever a case of cynical industrial relations vigilantism as was described in the Pikitup case.

In subsequent years, historical antagonisms and intractable policy differences, both between and within the key stakeholder groupings, generated both mistrust and conflict. Strategic alignments among the stakeholders have therefore shifted, and the loyalty of former allies has become suspect. Community conflicts and social protests, including industrial conflicts, are ever more frequently conducted illegally in an unprotected and un-procedural manner as acts of vigilantism. This disregard for legality signifies a trend towards industrial relations vigilantism and is undermining collective bargaining at its very core. Trade unions that are affiliated to COSATU are regularly challenging its independence and the hegemony of the ANC government of which they are a part. This is incrementally eroding the social compact.

Paton[155] pointed out that in recent years: "Long and violent strikes have become an important part of South Africa's growth and investor story. The response by the government has been talk-shops and pact-making. Business has responded by appealing for more policing and security. These are passive responses that have had a limited effect, if any, on the dynamics of the labour market." From the perspective of government, it is clear that the talk-shops and pact-making process have constituted a simplistic, passive and ineffective approach to addressing the complex populist fall-out that arises from long and violent strikes predicated on a host of unaddressed fundamental human needs. These are mechanistic and single-loop learning responses to complex wicked problems, and deep-rooted conflicts that are fuelled by the failure to discover satisfiers of fundamental human needs. Talk-shops have failed abysmally to address the fundamental human needs, desires and governing values that are driving the deep-rooted conflict in the first place.

Levy, Hirsch and Woolard[156] have traced the gradual dissipation of social compacts in South Africa after the advent of constitutional democracy in 1994. They assert that: "A robust social compact has long been the 'holy grail' of South Africa's political economy. Tripartite co-operation between government, business and labour was pivotal in facilitating the transition to democracy. Since the dawn of South Africa's democracy, there have been repeated efforts to build on the early successes, and renew a robust 'corporatist' partnership [...] attempted social compacts in South Africa have generally been unsuccessful." They point out that NEDLAC was established in 1994 and had a promising beginning, but that the Labour Market Commission failed to implement the plans. The Growth, Employment and Redistribution strategy (GEAR) was implemented without the 'blessing' of COSATU. It therefore lacked crucial legitimacy from within the Tripartite Alliance itself. Over the years, the social compacts that have been designed to address challenges in the labour market have all floundered upon implementation.

Extraordinarily high levels of conflict of different types characterise the day-to-day lived experience of ordinary South Africans. There is a plethora of different forms of industrial and civil unrest as well as political and criminal conflict that combine into waves of protest, often having similar root causes. In South Africa, strikes are energised by the same dynamics that cause service delivery conflicts, political conflicts, student fee protests, Zama Zama conflicts, gang warfare and xenophobic violence. These other forms of social conflict are not discrete from strikes and have overlapping basic root causes, including the failure to discover satisfiers of fundamental human needs on which many and different forms of poverty manifest themselves.

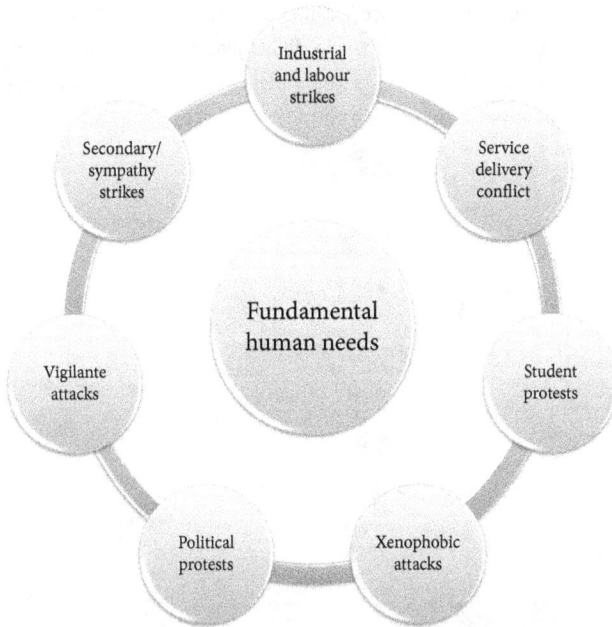

Figure 6.1: Failure of Collective Bargaining – Erosion of Social Compact

Figure 6.1 above offers a schematic depiction of the fragmentation of the social compact. The driving force that is causing collective bargaining to fail and that underlies service delivery conflicts, xenophobic violence, unprotected strikes, vigilante attacks, political violence, gang membership and warfare, and a host of other social pathologies that are placing South African society at risk, is the failure to seek to discover satisfiers of fundamental human needs. The failure of collective bargaining tends to morph into the other forms of social conflict, and similarly, the other forms of social conflict morph back into collective bargaining, resulting in the social compact becoming ever more precarious.

This common thread is the unwillingness, inability and lazy-mindedness of those vested with the responsibility of leading collective bargaining to seek to creatively discover abiding and scalable satisfiers of fundamental human needs. Labour strikes are therefore interlinked and interact with secondary and community conflicts. These secondary conflicts and sympathy actions may involve the engagement and mobilisation of entire communities because all are systemically interconnected. Employees, the unemployed, and the general community may participate in service delivery conflicts that have as their goal the redress of matters that are by custom and practice unsuitable for the collective bargaining agenda. Vigilante attacks are the communities' way of policing their property and protecting themselves from crime. Vigilante action has arisen because of the collapse of confidence in policing and the judicial system. Xenophobic violence is caused by envy, and the notion that strangers and foreigners have a better deal than locals. Unemployment and poverty inflame xenophobic attacks. Political protests and violence are caused by a perception that fundamental human needs do not warrant the effort of being satisfied.

7

Collective Bargaining on Dysfunctional Premises

The rationale that is provided for conducting collective bargaining at centralised level and extending these agreements to non-parties is that it enables terms and conditions of employment to be allocated with efficiency to the greatest number of people, ostensibly, for the greater good. In South Africa collective bargaining is not associated with improvements in productivity and economic growth. The role of bargaining councils is to resolve labour disputes, ensure that agreements on collective bargaining are implemented and to facilitate the creation of labour policies, laws and schemes. Trade unions, through the bargaining council system, have succeeded in raising minimum wages and improving their own working conditions. Centralised collective bargaining, as it is conducted in South Africa, is frequently insensitive to the requirements and reality of each business's unique business model, particularly insofar as small, medium and micro enterprises are concerned (SMMEs). They often have centralised agreements extended to them without their involvement or support. Unsustainable wage and conditions of employment increases have often been imposed upon marginal businesses by decree. This has forced them to either retrench employees or to go into liquidation. The South African Metals and Engineering Industries Bargaining Council is the largest bargaining council in South Africa. Steyn (2016) reported that the economic slowdown and declining price of steel in global markets, together with higher wages and terms and conditions of service negotiated at centralised level had, according to Gerhard Papenfus, the Director of the National Employers Association of South Africa, resulted in 90 000 jobs being lost since 2008. She cited Papenfus as claiming that: "The bargaining council has set in motion a devastating process of deindustrialization, a huge contributor to unemployment and consequently economic and social instability."

The SMME's critique of centralised collective bargaining is therefore that it creates an ever-diminishing vicious circle of fewer and fewer employees being the beneficiaries of the process. The assurance of improved wages and terms and conditions of employment can, in the long term, only be accorded to those persons who are fortunate enough to work in the more powerful companies that are innovative and whose productivity is improving. Their colleagues, who are employed in the fragile SMMEs, will have much less employment security and will be extremely vulnerable to retrenchment.

The trade unions will always vociferously oppose retrenchments, but once employees have been retrenched they lose their status as trade union members, and the problem of their unemployment is soon forgotten. All employers continuously search for alternatives to labour in the form of robotics and other technologies in order to reduce the cost of production. Collective bargaining is not guided by consideration of the unique business models which inform the conduct of each enterprise, whether it be small or large. In other words, it is conducted without a basic feedback loop to the value and growth propositions on which the business is based.

Collective bargaining is also failing at the Metals and Engineering Industrial Bargaining Council in South Africa because of financial incompetence. Steyn[157] pointed out that the council had repeatedly failed to submit audited financial statements to the Department of Labour, and that it was facing a R14 million deficit because of maladministration. The Metals and Engineering Industrial Bargaining Council in South Africa failed to secure an administrative levy from businesses that were becoming increasingly reluctant to finance a bargaining council whose interests were perceived to be fundamentally antagonistic of those of small, medium and micro enterprises.

Steyn[158] informed that the Metals and Engineering Industries Bargaining Council represented about 10 000 employers and 300 000 employees. Papenfus described the bargaining council as being hostile to the interests of SMMEs and as a platform on which big business, acting through the largest member of the council, the Steel and Engineering Industries Federation of South Africa (SEIFSA), could conclude deals with the trade unions, chiefly the National Union of Metalworkers of South Africa, that would favour what they believe could constitute stability and labour peace. The argument was therefore that the powerful trade union and powerful businesses had set up a business–labour monopoly arrangement. Should this logic be correct, it is projected that SEIFSA will begin to fracture the moment that the market for metals and engineering deteriorates for the larger and more powerful businesses because they will then find themselves in the same situation as the vulnerable SMMEs.

Johnson[159] observed that South Africa's unit labour costs escalated by 60% between 1994 and 2007. This was notwithstanding very significant decreases in productivity. He furthermore calculated that that labour productivity dropped 41.2% between 1994 and 2013. He maintained that the ANC "has presided over an unprecedented period of de-industrialization.[160] In 1994 manufacturing accounted for around 23-24 per cent of GDP. Twenty years later, this has fallen to 11.1 per cent." There are various reasons for this, but exceptionally high strike rates and the extension of centralised agreements to non-parties is an extreme disincentive for maintaining a manufacturing industry in South Africa. The strikes, conflicts, extension of industry-wide bargaining agreements to non-parties, and rigid labour market legislation have created an extremely hostile environment for foreign direct investment in South Africa. Khuzwayo[161] pointed out that the United Nations Conference on Trade and Development found, in February 2016, that foreign direct investment to South Africa had plummeted by 74% to US$1.5 billion. This decline in foreign direct investment can be understood as part of a long-term international withdrawal from manufacturing in South Africa.

Johnson[162] comments further:

> The suicidal combination of soaring wage levels with collapsing productivity is almost without international parallel. It can only be understood as a result of a strange combination of factors. First COSATU has since 1994 enjoyed a highly protected niche in which it has safeguarded the interests of a tiny labour aristocracy at the expense of the vast mass of the unemployed. Second, workers have exploited this new and favourable situation to get away with what they can. Third, the sight of elite level corruption and the general atmosphere engendered by the frantic rush towards black self-enrichment have created a great emulative wave.

Osterwalder and Pigneur[163] conducted excellent research on a very wide range of different business models that are available, and differentially applied, across different economic sectors, according to the merits of each business case. Each business model is unique, and therefore should be addressed on its own merits. Enterprises have different requirements for labour, and the other factors of production, and it is from this basic mix that they derive their value proposition. The failure to develop a viable business model means simply that the enterprise will fail. There are nine interactive vectors or components that comprise Osterwalder and Pigneur's[164] business model canvas. These vectors are: the value proposition that is being offered by the business to customers, and which justifies its existence; the unique ensuing customer relationships that the value proposition requires; customer segments which seek to understand the basic question of: who are the customers? and to understand how they should be treated; the channels that the customers require for the transaction which pertain to the unique paths that need to be followed to ensure that the goods or service reach its customers; the revenue streams that will arise from transacting the value proposition and that identify, and justify, the goods or service for which the customer is prepared to pay; the cost structure, on which the business is based, and the resultant price of the goods and services that are required; the key resources that are required to support the business value proposition, that enables the sale of goods and services; the key activities that will support the value proposition to achieve profitable revenue streams and distribution channels; and, the key partners and networks of people that will be required to achieve the value proposition and to conduct business.

The success or failure of these nine vectors of the business model to interact harmoniously will correlate directly with the success or failure of the business and will therefore be directly reflected in the balance sheet. The trade unions' requirement of collective bargaining is to negotiate a fair deal on wages and conditions of service, and to discover satisfiers of the fundamental human needs of its members. Business' requirement of collective bargaining is to achieve an agreement on wages and conditions of employment in a manner that is sustainable and satisfies the needs of the many stakeholders that are congruent with its business model. The state's requirement of collective bargaining is to create a policy and an enabling environment that will allow these objectives to be reconciled between business and trade unions for the greater good.

Figure 7.1 below depicts Osterwalder and Pigneur's[165] business model canvas.

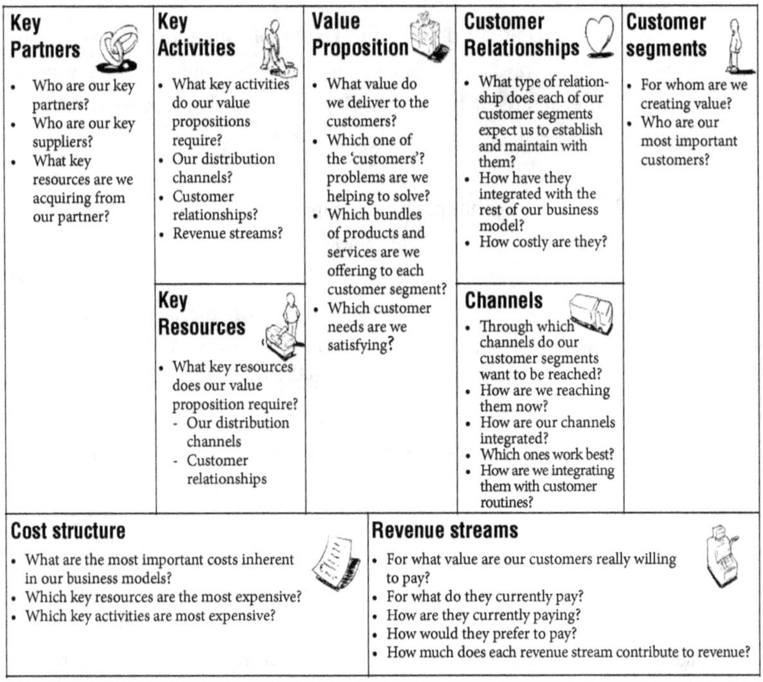

Figure 7.1: The business model canvas

Centralised collective bargaining is conducted by trade unions in a manner that is seemingly oblivious to the imperative to address all of those interacting elements of a business model that are specific to each business. Businesses conduct collective bargaining in a manner that is seemingly unconscious of the need to discover satisfiers of fundamental human needs. The state overseas collective bargaining by providing a regulatory framework that makes the achievement of these objectives very difficult. The massive waves of retrenchment that are taking place in the financial and mining sectors across the world are generally caused by the financial imperative to continuously revitalise business models in the face of disruptive innovation emanating mostly from computerisation.

The parties to the centralised collective bargaining process simply do not have the time, patience or competence to negotiate wages and conditions of employment in a manner that addresses the mass customisation of business models. Centralised collective bargaining is therefore an overly simplistic instrument for addressing the unique requirements of each company's business model. The manner in which collective bargaining is conducted in South Africa consequently precludes labour costs from being systemically linked to productivity, and this is an important structural imperative that is driving the search to create capital-based alternatives to labour as a factor of production. Amplifying interactive technologies are enabling the design of advanced digital applications that enable this search to design labour out of the system. On the basis of these disruptive innovations, employers will have an ever-greater choice of designing their business models to exclude an unsustainable dependency on labour.

Cokayne[166] reported that NUMSA was insistent on establishing a megabargaining council underpinned by a one-year agreement with the Retail Motor Industry Organisation (RMI). NUMSA envisaged that this negotiation council would consist of the automobile manufacturers, petroleum refineries and the retail motor trade. Jakkie Olivier, who was the Chief Executive of the RMI, said that NUMSA was intent on conducting collective bargaining on dysfunctional premises. His rationale for rejecting the megabargaining council was entirely congruent with Osterwalder and Pigneur's[167] business model canvas that is presented above. Olivier said that: "The RMI did not believe that a megabargaining council was a workable solution because the retail motor industry was comprised of small businesses that had a different business model and served a different client base ...." He continued: "As far as the RMI is concerned lumping us with a big business in a megabargaining council is not going to happen. It will put our members' survival under threat." Olivier's argument is essentially that a centralised megabargaining council is simply not economically or financially viable and is entirely incongruent with the multiplicity of fragile business models that characterise this sector of the South African economy.

Soko and Balchin[168] asserted:

> One of the most visible problems in the labour market is the crisis in collective bargaining. The dominance of centralised bargaining in South Africa – at odds with the move towards decentralised bargaining arrangements internationally – favours large employers, institutionalizes the power of trade unions and results

in greater incidents of fixed wages across sectors. The main problem with centralized bargaining is that it does not adequately recognise differences across enterprises, and stifles labour management at the enterprise level. There is a body of empirical evidence to suggest that centralised bargaining also restrains wages in certain sectors – with financially stronger employers only required to pay the modest wage increases that can be afforded by smaller or weaker enterprises, while the weaker enterprises face the prospect of being squeezed out because they cannot afford the increases in wages that the majority of enterprises in the sector are prepared to pay.

In addition, the practice of extending collective bargaining agreements across entire industries places small businesses and entrepreneurs at a disadvantage. The push by trade unions had also resulted in a quid pro quo, insisted on by employers, in the practice of setting actual wage increases rather than minima at the industry level, which means that employers are accommodated at the lowest levels of affordability. Furthermore, industry level bargaining precludes the option of linking wages to productivity. A productivity-linked wage system could address the problem of a combination of rising unit costs and falling productivity, which threatens job creation and undermines the competitiveness of the South African economy.

Collective bargaining should therefore be conducted at a centralised level only by those enterprises whose business models are suitable for this particular structure of negotiation. It should likewise be conducted at plant level for those enterprises whose business models are incongruent with centralised bargaining. Those organisations that wish to be party to both platforms of negotiation should be free to make this choice. The extension of collective bargaining agreements to non-parties is a high-risk practice and can cause – and has already caused – the demise of industries. It should be disallowed because it falsifies the notion of both trade union and employer representativeness.

The decline of South Africa's clothing, textile, leather, shoe and furniture industries are a few examples of cases where business models and rigid centralised bargaining structures have contributed to the decimation of those industries. It is interesting that trade unions and the big businesses that are dominant on the bargaining councils have generally addressed centralised bargaining as an organisational issue. They have tended to minimise the complaints that are expressed by smaller and more fragile businesses – claims about the economic impact of the extension of these centralised agreements to non-parties.

This dismissal of the concerns of small and fragile businesses about the lived experience of the impact of the extension of collective bargaining to non-parties is very risky. Industrial relations in the clothing industry showed that the more powerful players soon become an ever-smaller circle. The powerful businesses eventually also ultimately fall by the wayside in a systemic manner over a period of time until there is a total collapse.

Businesses that protest about the extension of these centralised agreements to non-parties have not yet explored the matter as an anti-competitive and monopoly-driven process. The more powerful businesses use the higher wage increases that are reached at the centralised level as a tacit monopoly agreement with the trade unions to prevent competition from entering these economic sectors. The extension of bargaining council agreements to non-parties is, effectively, a labour–business monopoly arrangement. It might be useful to assess the legality of these centralised collective bargaining arrangements in terms of a breach of the Competition Act.

For Johnson (2016:159), "The basic problem with South Africa's manufacturing industry has always been that while it could not compete with Europe on quality or productivity, its relatively high wages has made it uncompetitive with Asia. Unit costs are twice as high as in Indonesia, Malaysia, or Taiwan and they are even slightly higher than the USA." One indicator of the veracity of Johnson's argument is contained in the malaise of structural unemployment in South Africa. Foreign direct investment is attracted to Indonesia, Malaysia and Taiwan, in preference to South Africa, because the wage costs and unit costs are dramatically lower, and the quality of work and productivity are higher.

7.1 Collective Bargaining, Labour Broking and Employment Creation

Schwab and Samans[169] noted that there is a powerful international trend across all industries towards flexible work and atypical employment. COSATU rejects flexible work, atypical employment and labour brokers out of hand. COSATU has sought to achieve a complete ban on labour brokers because it encourages the process of atypical employment which, in its view, results in exploitation.[170]

During November 2015, COSATU passed a resolution at its annual conference, announcing a total ban on labour brokers. According to *COSATU Today*,[171] the rationale for its push for a ban on labour brokers "is that they act as go-betweens in the employment relationship, taking a fee from the party who should be the employer, for nothing! In this way the real employer dodges employment responsibility and the law, the labour broker gets rich through being a trader in labour, and the worker is exploited worse than ever."

During 2015, the Labour Relations Act and Basic Conditions of Employment Act were amended to provide additional security for temporary employees by legislating their permanency after a period of three months. These amendments to the Labour Relations Act were compliant with COSATU's search for a ban on labour broking and atypical employment. The purpose of the amendments was to both compel and impel employers to hire temporary employees and convert them into permanent employees after they have been employed by an enterprise for a period of three months, under the same terms and conditions of employment as those of permanent employees. This simplistic attempt to legislate employment permanency will almost certainly have the opposite effect from what was intended. It will violate the business models of many enterprises and encourage them to discontinue employing temporary employees. It will therefore contribute to structural unemployment by rendering temporary workers unemployable. Indeed, it will have a sustained and negative impact on employment creation in South Africa. The decision to legislate these amendments represents confusion at a policy level and a failure of the state, business and trade unions to reconcile their differences.

For the youth, temporary and casual work often is the path that leads towards permanent employment. It is almost analogous to an apprenticeship. Temporary employees are an important contributor to the South African economy. The prohibition on temporary employment will discourage employees from employing casual or temporary workers, leaving this category of potential employee in a state of permanent structural unemployment. Restaurants commonly employ staff on a temporary basis, and this ban will inhibit employers from employing temporary staff. This inhibition will apply across all economic sectors. Similar logic applies, to a lesser or greater extent, to the building industry, construction industry, security, day care, health care, agriculture, seasonal work, projects, situational contracts, the hotel trade, events management, the film industry, market research, retail and other sectors too many to mention. A significant proportion of the population purposefully seeks temporary employment because they benefit from the flexible hours and shifts. De Lange[172] regards these legislated restrictions on temporary employment as ill conceived. He projected that they will cull enormous numbers of potential and actual jobs. He asserted that employees who are employed by labour brokers constitute approximately 30% of total employment in South Africa. Furthermore he noted that permanent employment had grown at a mere 2% since 2008, while labour brokers had achieved a six-fold greater growth at 12%.

Papenfus[173] similarly claimed that labour broking is the fastest-growing sector of the South African economy. He stated that about one million people are presently employed in labour broking arrangements. This trend of employment creation by labour brokers matches those in Europe and the United States of America where atypical and flexible employment is becoming a significant feature of these economies. He pointed out that labour broking is a substantial R44 billion industry. Their employment security is threatened by COSATU's drive to achieve a complete ban on labour broking. It therefore seems inevitable that, in due course, COSATU will enter into conflict with the unemployed and those employed by labour brokers.

Papenfus[174] asserted that labour brokers initiate a substantial number of workers into their first experience of employment. This reveals that labour brokers are an important link between job seekers and employment, and labour market absorption. The Labour Department's own regulatory impact assessment conducted by Benjamin, Bhorat and van der Westhuizen[175] has shown that the banning of labour brokers would result in the loss of employment for about 850 000 persons who are currently gainfully employed. Papenfus[176] therefore concluded that "such a move would contribute to increased levels of unemployment and deprive households attached to these workers of a valuable source of income ... Labour brokers should be used as a tool for workers to gain industry knowledge and expertise."

The Fourth Industrial Revolution is such a powerful international force that no government or trade union movement anywhere in the world will be able to hold its cumulative power back with blindly restrictive legislation. The obvious solution is to ensure that labour brokers are placed under a regulatory framework that prevents abuse of their employees rather than their dismissal.

The Presidency and Department of Labour commissioned Benjamin, Bhorat and van der Westhuizen[177] to conduct an impact assessment on selected aspects of legislation that pertained to the termination of temporary employment and a clampdown on labour broking. At the time of its publication it was subjected to various criticisms, including questions as to the appropriateness of its research methodology. These researchers appear to have thus far vindicated themselves. The provisional data on retrenchment and redundancies that is emerging from the day-to-day activities of the CCMA indicates that these are running at an all-time high. Benjamin, Bhorat and van der Westhuizen (2012) were remarkably prescient insofar as their assessment of the emerging reality of these policies are concerned.

Barron[178] cited the director of the CCMA, Cameron Moranje, as reflecting that the foreseeable consequences of the amendments to the Labour Relations Act and Basic Conditions of Employment Act, which seek to severely constrain labour broking and compel employers to convert temporary employees into permanent staff, is already impelling employers to engage in massive waves of retrenchments. The CCMA is South Africa's statutory industrial relations dispute-resolution agency. In 2016, it was already processing 687 disputes about retrenchments per day. This number of daily retrenchments approximates about 250 000 retrenchments per annum.

This, according to Moranje, is an increase of 23% since 2011, which was, of course, prior to the enactment of the amendments to the legislation. Moranje expects these retrenchments to increase significantly on the basis of the possible downgrading of South Africa's economy to junk bond status. Benjamin, Bhorat and van der Westhuizen (2010) did not consider the matter of restrictions on labour brokers and temporary employees under a scenario of South Africa being accorded junk bond status.

These retrenchments that Cameron Moranje, director of the CCMA, rightly bemoans can be expected to increase exponentially on account of labour-saving disruptive innovation that will come in the wake of the Fourth Industrial Revolution.

Business models that were previously stable suddenly have an ever-decreasing half-life. The trade unions and the state presume a permanent, rigid and inflexible employment structure. Computerisation is driving the business models in a diametrically opposite direction according to the international trend of flexible work relationships, atypical employment and on-demand work.

Collective bargaining needs to be redesigned to ensure that space can be created to instil an ethic of trust, respect, co-operation and collaboration with one's negotiation counterpart. A path needs to be discovered that counteracts the mistrust, hostility, competition and conflict that characterises the collective bargaining process as it is currently conducted in South Africa. We are actually all in the same boat and collective bargaining needs to be empathic about the position of the other if it is to achieve social cohesion in a complex and ambiguous world of work.

South Africa's economic, social, scientific and political reality is based on a totally different platform from that which prevailed during the period of apartheid. It therefore requires the redesign of negotiation approaches that seek to satisfy fundamental human needs.

Collective bargaining therefore requires a complete makeover in the way that it is understood, conducted, written into law, and how it is taught in the practical world of work and in institutions of learning. In this regard the IMF[179] urgently called upon the government to increase "the flexibility of the wage bargaining mechanism, especially for small and medium sized enterprises (SMEs) and newly created business; increasing the flexibility of labour laws and regulations and reducing compliance costs to improve the business environment and increase employment opportunities and introducing well-designed active labour market reforms to encourage youth employment and providing working experience or on-the-job-training."

7.2   The Presumption of Inevitable Conflict Zero-sum Game Negotiation

The Labour Relations Act 66 of 1995 is predicated on the presumption of the emergence of inevitable conflict at the workplace. This legislated presumption of conflict creates a self-fulfilling prophecy of perpetual conflict. Building a growing and inclusive economy requires cooperation and collaboration, and not dissent. South African labour legislation provides a virtual guarantee that matters that should be addressed in a spirit of wise analytical problem solving will, all too often, be approached divisively in a climate of conflict. Collective bargaining is failing because bigger-picture thinking about discovering solutions to fundamental human needs is actually discouraged by the energy-sapping pre-eminence of inevitable conflict. In addition, these fundamental satisfiers of fundamental human needs are not being considered entrepreneurially in terms of their potential to form the basis for new and innovative business models and in terms of a potential framework for congruence with future business model sustainability. Business model sustainability and the discovery of satisfiers of fundamental human needs of labour (upon which the business model is based) are seen as separate and impermeable worlds.

Feedback is experienced as barbed criticism and defeat. Indefensible positions are slavishly, and often disingenuously, defended because of the pervasiveness of the conflict paradigm. This leads to an invidious process of groupthink, ritualistic conformity and ensures that learning during the collective bargaining process is circumscribed at best, and that fundamental problems are not addressed.

A basic unstated presumption of collective bargaining in South Africa is that it is a negotiation process designed to reach agreement on wages and on terms and conditions of employment which, when deadlocked, can be understood as leading to normal conflict. A normal conflict is not pathological in nature and can be resolved by engaging in behaviour that is substantively and procedurally fair. Its emotional character might be a tiff, a huff, transitory anger, a standoff, a cold shoulder, a rebuttal and so forth. The CCMA was designed to resolve normal conflicts. Many of the conflicts that take place in South Africa are of a deep-rooted nature and need to be addressed with different levels of knowledge and wisdom from those that are required to address normal conflict. The CCMA requires a differential diagnostic and prognostic arrangement to ensure that persons with the appropriate levels of wisdom, skill and knowledge are called upon to address normal and deep-rooted conflict respectively. A central question is therefore: 'How can deep-rooted conflict be converted into constructive processes of growth and development?'

Collective bargaining is, all too frequently, conducted as a zero-sum and win-lose negotiation process, even in circumstances where the negotiation counterparts would benefit significantly from the kind of collaboration and co-operation that would enable win-win outcomes. The authority for this proliferation of conflict derives from and is vested directly in the Labour Relations Act, and visited upon the stakeholders in the South African economy with regulatory. The Act subscribes to a First and Second Industrial Revolution worldview, whereas the international economy is currently immersed in the reality of the Fourth Industrial Revolution. The Labour Relations Act assumes that relationships between employers and trade unions are unceasingly conflictive, and that conflict provides the best yields for the greater social good in terms of both economic growth and human development. The parties to collective bargaining thus continue to act according to an unvarying conflictive negotiation paradigm because nothing more creative than this is required of them. Instead of seeking to create social cohesion and trust, the parties to collective bargaining have chosen to perpetuate conflict and exacerbate stakeholder fragmentation. This means that they do not have to take responsibility for success whilst, sadly, failure is all too often assured.

The default option of perpetual conflict allows the negotiators to become lazy because they do not have to generate positive and creative solutions. It encourages a default option of timidity dressed in the clothing of bravado, militancy and populism. The default worldview of collective bargaining in South Africa is that negotiation is a conflictive zero-sum interaction. The negotiation outcome will thus by definition be win-lose. Consequently, win-win negotiation alternatives are all too frequently ignored. This deeply conflictive approach towards collective bargaining has embedded itself into many other aspects of private, commercial and political negotiations in South Africa to the detriment of the greater good. This conflictive approach towards collective bargaining has sometimes been generalised, with disastrous consequences, into the commercial and political space.

Conflict can be healthy and lead to positive change and the discovery of creative solutions. There are times when a negotiation situation requires a conflictive approach because it is the essential ingredient that leads to an optimal solution. Equally, there are many occasions when the choice of conflict as a negotiation rule of engagement is entirely counter-productive and leads to a suboptimal malaise, where nothing is solved and everything gets progressively worse. There are times when the basic social fabric of our society is placed at risk because of the inappropriate surfacing of conflict. We become overwhelmed and social cohesion is destroyed.

We need to have modest expectations about the capacity of collective bargaining, as it is presently conducted in South Africa, to address the fundamental issues of massive and grinding poverty, and employment creation in a situation of catastrophic unemployment, and seek alternative and innovative approaches towards discovering solutions to these challenges.

7.3 Collective Bargaining in the Public Sector – Negotiating without Feedback Loops

Collective bargaining is failing in the public sector because the government seems to be unwilling to, or incapable of, rejecting the wage and salary demands that are posed to the state by the trade unions. Johnson[180] informed that about 3.07 million persons are employed in the public sector. This number constitutes approximately 22.6% of the approximately 13.6 million persons who are gainfully employed in South Africa.

He commented that collective bargaining with trade unions in the public sector has seen extraordinarily high salary and wage increases being granted to civil servants over many years. He cautioned that these wage and salary increases are now of such magnitude that the wage and salary payments are starting to freeze out expenditure on maintenance, building infrastructure and numerous other extraordinary expenses. Steyn[181] observed that the highest average wages in the public sector are in the electricity, gas and water sectors at R28 500 per month. These wages are far higher than the equivalent remuneration that is paid for similar work in the private sector. Public sector employees include school teachers, academics, administrative personnel, persons employed in the armaments industry, municipal employees, persons employed in parastatals, prisons, courts of law, government departments, transport, finance, the revenue services, communication and many more besides.

Johnson[182] vividly illustrated the exponential increases in public sector wage and salary settlements. He observes that by 2009, wages and salaries comprised approximately 40% of public spending. In the three-year period between 2009 and 2012 public spending on wages and salaries increased to approximately 54%. Thus, between 2009 and 2012 the amount expended on public sector wages and salaries grew at an average compound growth rate of 15.5% per annum, and had increased by 400% since 2000. This is an unprecedented escalation in expenditure. These increases in wages and salaries cannot be justified on a rational economic basis. They have not improved service delivery; indeed, service delivery has deteriorated chronically over the past two decades as is evidenced by the incessant and violent service delivery conflicts. One possible explanation is that droves of persons have been employed in the public sector in order to create a docile cadre of public sector political support. The wage and salary increases are not accompanied by increased productivity, enhanced service delivery, or a better-run public sector. Indeed, they are accompanied by the opposite effect.

Johnson[183] pointed out that by 2010, public sector wage and salary levels were 40% higher than the equivalent private sector remuneration for the same job. This is unheralded and unsustainable in the medium to longer term. Public sector employees are protected from economic cycles and enjoy much greater employment stability in comparison with their private sector counterparts. The international trend is therefore that public sector employees traditionally receive lower remuneration than their private sector counterparts to compensate for their relative job security. They receive lower remuneration because their work is less vulnerable to economic risk. The opposite is the case in South Africa. Johnson[184] recorded that in 2000 public sector wage and salary remuneration exceeded private sector wages by 12%. This inflated public sector remuneration trajectory escalated over the intervening decade and by 2010 wages and salaries were an average of 43.6% higher than the private sector earnings.

Paton[185] reflects on the consequences of conducting collective bargaining without sensitivity to budgets and prior deep financial and economic knowledge of the sector or enterprise in which the negotiations take place. Her findings generally corroborate those of Johnson.[186] She also reported that the trade unions that operated in the public sector achieved very large and economically unsustainable wage and salary increases on a year-on-year basis, with seemingly scant regard for the economic implications of these salary increases on the state's levels of indebtedness and credit ratings. Paton[187] commented thus:

> Trade unions that organize the 1.3 million people that the [South African] government employs have won great improvements for their members. Between 2008 and 2014, spending on wages of public servants in the departments that employ large numbers of people doubled. Last year, spending on wages consumed 40% of all government spending. Although the government planned to increase salaries by 7% last year, generous increases in housing allowances meant salaries rose 10%. This will compound in the years ahead.

South Africa entered into the collective bargaining process with public sector employees without conducting a deep prior strategic assessment of the foreseeable consequences of such escalatory increases and of the economic sustainability of such high settlements.

These public sector wages are granted by the government without a feedback loop that is linked into rigorous calculations of productivity and affordability. The wages and salaries are acceded to with very little concern being displayed for service delivery.

The preoccupation of employing civil servants at maximum wage and salary levels has resulted in municipalities and parastatals not being able to carry out their work because all the budgets are misappropriated to remuneration.

The IMF[188] called upon the South African government to improve on the "composition of its spending" on the public sector wage and salary bill. The "composition of its spending" refers to the imperative that they should exercise restraint and discretion in the selection and appointment of state employees so as to ensure service delivery and a sound foundation for real growth and employment creation. Additional public sector employees are required in specialised areas where there are skills shortages. The foreseeable consequence of leaving wages and salaries uncapped, and not heeding the advice to improve the "composition of spending", might in due course compel South Africa to go to the IMF, cap in hand, to participate in its own self-inflicted structural adjustment programme. Should this ignominy take place, the country will have effectively forfeited its independence, for which so many people sacrificed their lives. It is an ominous fact that at this juncture the state does not appear to have either the leadership or will to withstand the pressure from the public sector trade unions for delusory wage and salary increases.

Johnson[189] described those unionised persons who are employed in the public sectors as the *bureaucratic bourgeoisie*. The *bureaucratic bourgeoisie* have higher levels of education and enjoy better-quality lifestyles than their working-class compatriots who operate in the mining, manufacturing, service and retail industries. The reason why public sector trade unions have wielded such enormous influence within the state is that they constitute a financial and educational elite within the Tripartite Alliance. Public sector employees are demographically very similar to South Africa's political elite. This makes it difficult for the political elite to say 'no' and reject their wage and salary claims.

The wide-ranging service delivery conflicts reveal that these public sector employees are not productive and do not live up to their service mandate to communities in which they operate. The public sector is generally grossly overstaffed and overpaid in administrative and clerical positions that are easily replaceable. It is severely understaffed in crucial high-skilled occupations. The bureaucratic bourgeoisie form a new class of rent-seekers who have the capacity to have a major impact on the salary bill contained in the national budget. They lobby with the ANC to assert their financial and policy objectives, and the government has regularly conceded to wage and salary demands that are financially unsustainable over the longer term. The public sector trade unions have a significant influence on the ideological and policy direction that is followed by COSATU and the Tripartite Alliance as a whole.

Johnson[190] provided clear logic as to why collective bargaining is failing in South Africa. He argued that the notion that COSATU is predominantly a working-class trade union congress is no longer true. It is predominantly a public sector trade union federation for the *bureaucratic bourgeoisie*. This is a fundamental change in South African recent labour economic demographics. In the past the most influential membership grouping within COSATU was unquestionably the NUM. The Marikana Massacre was triggered by various driving forces including inter-union rivalry between NUM and AMCU. This inter-union rivalry signified the dissipation of NUM's hegemony. After the advent of democracy, NUM went into decline and has been eclipsed for the first time by public sector union membership. It has also lost a significant portion of its membership to AMCU. It follows that the most influential membership faction within COSATU are now the civil servants. For Johnson, COSATU is a middle-class trade union movement that utters the rhetoric of victimhood and capitalist exploitation using Marxist-Leninist vernacular. This is ironical and incongruous because the *bureaucratic bourgeoisie* appear to be oblivious to their own middle-class privilege. Those unionised workers who are employed outside of the public service and who are not members of the *bureaucratic bourgeoisie* are at the bottom of COSATU's new class-based hierarchy. They earn significantly less than their public sector counterparts. The gainfully employed working class, who include public sector and private sector employees, constitute a labour aristocracy. They are also a labour aristocracy in comparison with the desperate plight of the unemployed who can at best eke out an existence on social grants and have to live subsistence existences begging, engaging in crime and on the edge of the social system. Indeed SADTU represents an excellent example of a trade union whose membership is composed of the *bureaucratic bourgeoisie*.

There is a consequently a deep and growing schism between the trade union movement and the unemployed that could become a flashpoint of social and political conflict. The wage and salary differential between union members in the public sector and private, as well as the absence of income and destitution of the masses of unemployed, encapsulate this potential flashpoint. The new class schism can be seen as one between the relative privilege of the rent-seekers in the public sector versus workers who contribute to real economic growth versus the third tier of desperate unemployed. The third pillar of the struggle is therefore that both these aforementioned employed classes constitute a labour aristocracy against an invisible or barely visible third class who can be described as the seething mountain of the unemployed.

Johnson[191] pointed out that: "South Africa's bureaucratic bourgeoisie has several distinguishing features. First it is heavily unionised. Only two groups enjoy unionisation rates of over 70% – miners and public servants. Hence, public sector and white-collar workers have come to be predominant within COSATU, a feature further accentuated by the ongoing collapse of NUM, previously the largest union."

South Africa's Public Sector Wage/Salary Bill	Middle-income Peer Group Countries Comparison: Chile, Colombia, Russia, Israel, Poland, Thailand, Slovak Republic, Romania and Turkey	Case Examples of the Variance of South Africa's Wage and Salary Bill Relative to its Middle-income Peers
The South African Public Sector Wage Salary Bill as Share of GDP = 14%	Highest among all peers	Twice as high as Chile which has a 6% of GDP Wage and Salary Bill
The South African Public Sector Wage and Salary Bill as Share of Fiscal Revenue = 40%	Highest among all peers	Almost twice as high as Slovak Republic at 21%
The South African Public Sector Wage and Salary Bill as per cent of government spending= 38%	Second highest among peers	Twice as high as Slovak Republic at 18%
The South African Public Sector Wage and Salary Bill as a share of the work force = 22%	This is by far the highest among its peers	This statistic is four times as high as Colombia

Figure: 7.2: South Africa's Public Sector Wages and Salaries Compared to Middle-income Peers
Source: Figure adapted from Johnson[192]

Figure 7.2 is adapted from the work of Johnson.[193] It endeavours to depict South Africa's public sector wages and salaries and compares them with the wages that are paid in a selection of similar middle-income countries. South Africa's public sector wage and salary bill as a proportion of GDP is 14%, more than double that of Chile. Its wage and salary bill as a share of fiscal revenue is 40%, which is almost double that of the Slovak Republic. Its wage and salary bill as a proportion of government spending is 38% and is again almost double that of the Slovak Republic; and its wage and salary bill as a ratio of the share of the work force is 22%, which is nearly four times greater than Colombia's. These statistics, when presented to ratings agencies and the IMF, will inevitably trigger the questions: Is the state hiring employees in the public sector who will improve service delivery? Or is it hiring rent-seekers and potential allies for votes that cannot be justified on any productive measures?

In the event of a serious economic downturn or recession, those rent-seeker members of the *bureaucratic bourgeoisie* are intensely vulnerable to mass retrenchment. Their education and skills levels have placed them on the wrong side of the Fourth

Industrial Revolution and they could easily be displaced. Khuzwayo[194] illustrated this employee vulnerability by referring to a Standard Bank calculation that forecasted that the economy would contract to a 0.4% growth rate and over 200 000 jobs will be lost in the short term if the economy is downgraded to junk bond status by the ratings agencies. Indeed the IMF, the credit rating agencies and many private investors have all questioned whether the government really has the political will to stand up against the unrelenting pressures of the *bureaucratic bourgeoisie* – a position that is all the more difficult for the government to take because the government itself is part of that class.

7.4 Effective Feedback Loops – the German Approach towards Collective Bargaining

In Germany, collective bargaining is aligned with the country's industrial and economic policy. Collective bargaining is conducted where business and labour share comprehensive knowledge about the financial and strategic status of the enterprise long before negotiations even take place. The parties share consensus about the enterprise's business model. Threats and opportunities, employment prospects, prospective skills requirements, and challenges to the business model are well known. The German starting point for collective bargaining is therefore to seek to gain a shared, trusted and co-determined (between business and labour) strategic outlook for the enterprise or sector. Before there is any discussion about wages and conditions of service, the business and trade union leaders work together to achieve consensus on a credible appreciation of the strategic outlook for the business. This strategic outlook is therefore co-determined between employers and trade unions. It is not unilaterally imposed on the negotiation counterparts. This consensus understanding is accorded a high level of credibility by the parties to the negotiations. The business and trade union leaders actively seek to achieve consensus.

This strategic outlook is conducted *prior* to any discussions about wages and conditions of employment and sends out a clear message that salary increases are subordinate to the bigger picture of the sustainability of the economic and financial conditions in the enterprise. If the market position of the business is good, wages and conditions of service will be correspondingly rewarded, and if the opposite prevails, they will be bad. The wage and conditions of service agreements in Germany are conducted efficiently and constitute a ratification of the strategic outlook of the enterprise that is achieved prior to collective bargaining even taking place.

In South Africa, the strategic outlook for the sector, enterprise or business is presented *after* the receipt of the wage and conditions of service demands have been submitted by the trade union. We therefore follow the opposite negotiation sequence to that which is wisely chosen by the Germans. In South Africa, we start with the implicit presumption that wages and conditions of service are more important than the economic and financial conditions in the sector, enterprise or business. The business model that underpins the enterprise is all but ignored. The trade union's wish-list of demands is obviously not shared by the business, but they keep quiet about this for the moment because both parties have acquiesced to this collective bargaining process. The starting point for collective bargaining in South Africa is therefore that there is no consensus between business and labour on the strategic outlook for the enterprise, and that the wage demands and terms and conditions of employment requirements are spurious.

These basic and divergent presumptions about the process of collective bargaining almost inevitably result in conflict. Indeed, the collective bargaining negotiations in South Africa traditionally begin with the trade union presenting claims that are not linked to the business model or the economic and financial strategic outlook for sector, enterprise or business. When, during the course of collective bargaining, the hard reality of the actual constraints on the business model and economic and financial circumstances are finally realised by the workers as an inevitable truth, this realisation is often accompanied by deep disappointment, and the evaporation of hope among the workers. The hopes and expectations that are encapsulated in the initial demands that were presented without adequate financial context by the trade union negotiators are therefore dramatically curtailed. Individual disillusionment translates into collective anger, collective anger escalates into polarisation and alienation, and a cycle of pathological deep-rooted conflict is often set into motion. The business's rejection of the demands is framed as betrayal by the trade union, and negative stereotypes of the parties to negotiation are perpetuated. The root cause of the conflict is experienced as a betrayal, but it is not a betrayal. The breakdown in collective bargaining is a systems problem resulting from the ritualised sequence of activities and the manner in which collective bargaining is conducted in South Africa. The first step that should be carefully addressed at the outset of the collective bargaining process is to achieve a consensus understanding on the business model and the imperative to address wages and conditions of employment, and to seek to discover satisfiers of fundamental human needs in a wise manner. This consensus outlook should be accorded a high status.

Trade union leaders need to have a deep, systemic understanding of the status of the business model that guides the enterprise, and cannot rely on impressionistic insight.

In South Africa, the parties to collective bargaining rarely enter into pre-negotiation discussions that afford the counterparts the opportunity to gain an excellent factual, strategic understanding of the prospects for the sector, enterprise or business.

When businesses seek to do this, it is usually construed as a propagandistic attempt to undermine the wage and conditions of service demands that have been issued by the trade union. It is therefore met with cynicism and contempt, such are the levels of trust that emanate from the rule-making process for collective bargaining contained in the Labour Relations Act. It follows that collective bargaining all too often fails and it is unsurprising that vehemence and bombast are often regarded as an alternative to reason and understanding. Mr Cameron Moranje and his colleagues at the CCMA can therefore expect a great deal of work concerning retrenchments and redundancies in the public sector in years to come. It follows that: the Labour Relations Act, with its legislated bias towards the emergence of inevitable conflict between business and labour, tends to disallow a negotiation climate to be created that enables the counterparts to discover satisfiers of fundamental human needs and to understand the business model. This legislated bias towards conflict contained in the Labour Relations Act leads towards the self-fulfilling emergence of inevitable conflict which distracts the parties from discovering trusted and sustainable solutions to our human and socio-economic challenges.

The Labour Relations Act bias towards the inevitability of conflict leads to the creation of a fearful and defensive negotiation climate where the negotiation counterparts are reluctant to remove their guards. This prevents them from entering into wise problem-solving processes that are conducted in a climate of trust to solve the enormous and long-term challenges concerning the future of employment.

The Labour Relations Act needs to be rewritten afresh on the basis of its utility to regulate relationships, and terms and conditions of employment at the workplace, and grow and develop the economy in a manner that creates sustainable employment in the context of the Fourth Industrial Revolution.

8

Conclusions

8.1 Collective Bargaining, Employment Creation, and the Fourth Industrial Revolution

The Labour Relations Act (66) of 1995 needs to be assessed and rewritten in a manner that is congruent with the future of employment and the requirements of the South African economy in the midst of the Fourth Industrial Revolution.

Schwab and Samans[195] ask: "How should business, trade unions, governments and ordinary citizens address these challenges?" The worst-case scenario for South Africa would be exponentially accelerating technological change and disruptive innovation, based on mass retrenchments of current labour and ongoing unemployability of labour attempting to enter the labour market; accompanied by acute skilled labour scarcity and inequality in an already deeply unequal society. These authors submit that:

> ... re-skilling and up-skilling of today's workers will be critical. While much has been said about the need to reform basic education, it is not possible to weather the current technological revolution by waiting for the next generation's workforce to become better prepared. Instead it is critical that business take an active role in supporting their current workforces through re-training, that individuals take a proactive approach to their own lifelong learning and that governments create the enabling environment, rapidly and creatively, to assist these efforts. In particular, business collaboration within industries to create larger pools of skilled talent will become indispensable, as will multi-sector skilling partnerships that leverage the very same collaborative models that underpin many of the technology-driven business changes that are underway today.

What additional practical steps can be taken to ensure that all South Africans are appropriately placed to address the challenges of employment creation in the context of the disruptive innovation that is underpinning the Fourth Industrial Revolution?

Firstly, it needs to be acknowledged that the people who have the greatest knowledge about the future of employment are employers, entrepreneurs and persons who do business, on the one hand, and academics, technologists, scientists and persons who are actually on the cutting edge of creating the Fourth Industrial Revolution on the other. A high-quality trans-disciplinary stakeholder grouping that possesses deep knowledge about the future of employment needs to be appointed to create a national manpower steering committee to cover all the economic sectors of the economy. They need to present clear and detailed statements of the knowledge and skills requirements for sustainable employment across each of the economic sectors in the national economy for the next three decades. These experts should meet with schoolteachers, school principals, university vice chancellors, professors, artisans and apprenticeship experts, technical colleges and all educational and training institutions in the country, and offer constructive suggestions in curriculum design in order to ensure employability. They should explore what they understand the labour market requires in terms of curriculum design and subject choice that will lead to sustainable employment in the context of the Fourth Industrial Revolution. All teachers should be required to ensure that their curricula are strongly, but not dogmatically, aligned with employment creation.

Similarly, the businessmen and women who are knowledgeable about employment creation should be called upon to meet with university professors and teachers and provide detailed statements of the knowledge and skills requirements that are necessary for sustained employment in all academic disciplines that are on offer in South Africa and internationally. This process should be conducted with apprenticeships as well and indeed at all levels of training for gainful employment in South Africa.

The above processes should be initiated immediately. Simultaneously, it is recommended that a team of experts should be brought together to conduct a Commission of Enquiry into the Future of Employment in South Africa. Its remit should be to offer practical frameworks for creating sustainable employment and its suggestions should have statutory support. The Treasury and big business should also be of assistance.

Disruptive innovation will result in rapid business model redundancy, and therefore cause unemployment. It will simultaneously lead to employment creation for those whose skills are required. It is therefore both a deprivation and an opportunity. Curriculum design, education, business models and chosen career are presently not systemically connected. They remain in isolated silos. This needs to change completely. A feedback loop that informs curriculum design, education, business models, career choice, schools, apprenticeship colleges and technical colleges, and addresses the matter of labour market absorption, needs to be designed and acted upon as a national priority. The challenge is a national one, of ensuring that curricula at all levels of education and training are explicitly designed on the basis of excellent and relevant knowledge, and result in labour market absorption and employment creation. It is of no purpose to be educated and unemployable, or uneducated and unemployable.

South Africa has a vast challenge of changing its entire education system to become aligned with the knowledge and skill requirements of the Fourth Industrial Revolution. Business leaders, for example, need to be called upon to assist with curriculum design so that education leads to employment. Carefully structured, continuous, nationwide conversations and workshops about the future of employment, led by a cross section of experts from all economic sectors who are knowledgeable about this matter, should be conducted in South Africa as a matter of urgency. They need to identify national training and educational needs that are congruent with the requirements of the Fourth Industrial Revolution.

The challenge in South Africa is for the youth to place themselves, and to be assisted to place themselves, on the right side of the Fourth Industrial Revolution. They need to be educated, trained and skilled to be employable in areas that are congruent with these new areas of innovation and which will constitute the new world of work. There will, of course, be many stable areas of employment that will continue as usual and will be unaffected by the Fourth Industrial Revolution. Those persons who are presently employed in traditional forms of employment need to ensure that they are able to weather the storm of the Fourth Industrial Revolution and its associated disruptive innovation by constantly re-skilling and re-educating themselves for sustainable employability. Employees will need to adapt themselves to undertaking several different careers over the course of their lives. This is a matter that requires serious consideration. The transition process from one form of employment into another, new form of employment will introduce considerable insecurity that will require careful and wise career management.

The meaning of this Fourth Industrial Revolution and its holistic impact on the future of employment is not yet comprehensively understood. Unfortunately, it will first need to become part of lived experience before its ramifications are properly appreciated.

A wise next step would be for South African business to independently finance a captivating national marketing strategy on the future of employment in the Fourth Industrial Revolution that is designed to appeal to all the demographic groupings in the country. This marketing strategy would use television, press and multimedia to present the challenges that disruptive innovation and the Fourth Industrial Revolution hold for the future of education and employment in South Africa.

Disruptive innovation in the form of computerisation and applications, digitisation, robotics and 3D printing are going to revolutionise the world of work over the next several years, and affect and significantly change the entire structure of employment and all the underlying business models upon which collective bargaining is predicated, not only in South Africa, but across the world. Disruptive innovation is certainly going to shorten the 'life span' of a multiplicity of careers at all levels of skill and complexity. These matters should be explored systematically and carefully in order to discover timely solutions to the problem of mass job obsolescence, unemployment and redundancy. Curriculum design at schools, technical colleges, universities and indeed, all institutions and places of learning, should be devoted to addressing the problem of labour market absorption which has resulted in South Africa having a dangerously high youth unemployment rate.

The students' fee protest, entitled #FeesMustFall, indicated that all South African universities' business models are becoming ineffective, and therefore need to be redesigned. This has ramifications for the entire tertiary education project.

8.2 Collective Bargaining without Consideration of Fundamental Human Needs

There is a twofold flaw in the way that collective bargaining is understood and conducted in South Africa. These two basic flaws feed systemically into one another and create deep-rooted conflict. The first flaw is that collective bargaining is conducted without consideration of fundamental human needs. The second flaw is that collective bargaining is conducted without a systematic and detailed integration with the enterprises' business models. This means that collective bargaining is conducted without two vital feedback loops. The first concerns the meaning of the needs that are under negotiation and the second concerns the capacity of the business to finance these needs in a sustainable manner. The absence of these vital feedback loops is analogous to the absence of a cardiovascular healing process.

The failure by business, labour and government, and the many other associated stakeholder groupings, to respond to the fundamental human needs that are arising from the new world of work is setting South Africa back. The exponential increase in strikes, service delivery protests and socio-political conflict of a deep-rooted nature indicates that the way in which collective bargaining is currently conducted in South Africa has become an inefficient, time-consuming, expensive and archaic ritual with diminishing returns and beneficiaries. It is detached from the modern world of work and fails to understand that disruptive innovation is redefining the nature of employment and the world of work. It is, by the manner in which it is conducted, a dehumanising, disrespectful and retributive process, and it needs to be modernised and humanised in order for a restorative interactive process to emerge.

We presently engage in collective bargaining in the absence of a coherent theory of fundamental human needs. There is much talk about the transformation of the apartheid labour market and yet there is no clear articulation of what that transformation seeks to achieve. A clear and flexible theory of human needs would be of great assistance. Max-Neef et al's[196] matrix of satisfiers of fundamental human needs to be considered for inclusion into the collective bargaining agenda. This will assist all parties in creating a much more constructive agenda to address the contested matter of transformation in South Africa in a clearly defined and constructive manner. Transformation will then have a clear microeconomic purpose.

The wise entrepreneur uses this basic insight to create innovative business models and wealth.

8.3 Collective Bargaining without Consideration of a Guiding Business Model

Collective bargaining is conducted on dysfunctional premises in South Africa. The business model is neither accepted by the trade unions, nor used in the actual process as the guide for rational negotiation by the business. The reasons for this state of affairs are complex and locked into our master-servant apartheid history. During apartheid the manager presumed that he was 'all knowing' and understood the business, and therefore did not entertain any discussion and critique of the business model. This condescension has crept into the normative conduct of collective bargaining.

The negotiation sequence of collective bargaining is entirely wrong. It begins with wage demands that are not integrated into the business model. Fundamental human needs are ignored. The fires are stoked by a Labour Relations Act that validates conflict as the fundamental presumption of industrial relations. Amendments to the labour legislation have recently been promulgated that have already resulted in large-scale retrenchments and place many fragile businesses at extreme risk. Policy makers in South Africa are often unappreciative of the negative default consequences of the laws that they promulgate. Once faulty laws are implemented they gain a tenacious inertia, regardless of the damage that they cause to the greater good.

Collective bargaining in South Africa is conducted based on an erroneous general presumption about business models. It assumes mechanistically that all business models in the same industry and economic sector are similar and have the same requirements and impediments. Indeed, for all practical purposes, it assumes that they are identical. This is a very useful presumption for the powerful monopoly business that is able to determine the wage levels to preclude entry and competition. But it is a gross and reckless simplification. Osterwalder and Pigneur[197] show that the cost of the factors of production, which include land, labour, capital and entrepreneurship, are unique to each business because each business has a specific value proposition that is contained in its business model. Each business model is unique, and therefore should be addressed on its own merits. Enterprises have different requirements for labour, and the other factors of production, and it is from this basic mix that they derive their value proposition. It follows therefore that the extension of collective bargaining agreements that are reached at centralised level to non-parties often constitute an attack on the business model. When this is the case, the collective bargaining process leads to the collapse of the business and thus to unemployment.

The business model that is presented by an enterprise during the course of collective bargaining, is frequently neither accepted nor believed by the trade unions, nor is it understood. Thus the business model is all too often under-utilised as a rational guide to negotiations.

8.4 Business as an Agency for Change

There have been very few attempts by businesses and employees to create an employment relationship that satisfactorily addresses both wages and conditions of employment, and that also seeks to discover satisfiers of fundamental human needs. Business leaders have retained a narrow view of the employment relationship. They have tended to dismiss the socio-political reality of their employees' living conditions in impoverished communities and townships as falling outside of their managerial remit, thereby retaining many of the features of the apartheid economy.

Business leaders perceive that their managerial remit pertains strictly to the improvement of wages and working conditions. They have not sought to come to terms with the fundamental human needs of their employees that are driving these conflicts and to address them in a systematic and considered manner. Their employees, on the other hand, do not clearly express their fundamental human needs and these usually remain unarticulated and poorly defined during the collective bargaining process. This severely complicates understanding and creates blockages.

Business's ongoing avoidance of accepting co-responsibility for addressing employees' fundamental human needs during the collective bargaining process is unsustainable. It perpetuates poverty. Deep-rooted conflict frequently emerges because of this absence of congruence about the needs of both the employee and employer. This mistrust between the parties arises from an absence of consensus on the definition, meaning and purpose of collective bargaining.

The fundamental human needs tend to naturally emerge and become clear during the process of collective bargaining. When left unattended, they fester, and eventually surface with exceptional vehemence, sometimes escalating into violence. This failure to address fundamental human needs in an orderly and wise manner is perpetuating political conflict and significantly increasing the political risk of doing business in South Africa. It is obviously discouraging investment. Business's disengagement from the challenge to seek satisfiers of fundamental human needs leads almost inevitably to further polarisation, alienation and unrest that is, in due course, visited upon the entire community, including business itself. Collective bargaining conflicts, service delivery protests, student unrest, xenophobic violence, vigilante action and gang wars are but a few examples of conflicts that have the same root causes of a failure by their leadership to seek and discover satisfiers of fundamental human needs. All these deep-rooted conflicts are fuelled by the same root causes of various forms of poverty. The reluctance to engage in a process of discovering satisfiers of fundamental human needs is practically and morally untenable.

Business should, and could, be an important agency for addressing social change in South Africa. After the transition to democracy the parties to collective bargaining did not seek to change the manner in which the process of collective bargaining was conceived and conducted. The Labour Relations Act 66 of 1995 is predicated on the presumption of the emergence of inevitable conflict at the workplace. This legislated presumption of inevitable conflict creates a self-fulfilling prophecy of systemically reinforcing recurring conflict. Conflict is thus legislatively encouraged as the default option of collective bargaining. The Labour Relations Act (1995) needs to be placed under review in order to ensure that it is congruent with employment in the new world of work shaped by the Fourth Industrial Revolution. Collective bargaining has therefore remained a needlessly conflictive process that is deeply out of synch with the needs of the people and the needs of the economy.

This has undermined the creation of social cohesion in post-apartheid South Africa. These deep-rooted conflicts whose root causes have been left unaddressed by business, trade unions and government have started to corrode goodwill at a national level. Goodwill is being displaced by resentment, polarisation, alienation and antagonism and has led to unprecedented levels of violence and unrest in South Africa.

When strikes have been accompanied by violence and vandalism, business has typically appealed for more policing. Calls for more policing and security have all too often failed, as was illustrated when 44 miners were shot during the Marikana

Massacre. The call for more policing and security is a symptomatic response. It does not address the fundamental human needs that are not being satisfied and that are, indeed, driving the wave of industrial conflicts, including the associated crime. It is the duty of all stakeholders in South Africa to address this challenge and to dutifully discover satisfiers of these fundamental human needs. Calls for more policing and security do not address the basic questions of: Why and what are the governing values that are leading to the conflict? It does not pose probing questions of whether business, trade unions and government are actually part of the problem and how they could become a constructive part of the solution. If these questions are seriously addressed, then it might be possible to identify those factors that are generating deeprooted conflict in South Africa and to create the space for a systemic developmental and growth process that assists in dissolving their root causes. It may also result in the parties adopting a more constructive approach towards collective bargaining.

Simpson[198] stated that business has not chosen to be an agency for social change in South Africa. He reflected that:

> The vision of most employers has remained rather conservatively limited to futile attempts to insulate the workplace from encroaching violence, rather than engaging in any way with the origins of the problem beyond the factory gates. Furthermore, employer concerns over community violence have frequently been limited to concerns with productivity, and have more often than not been relegated to employee care programmes aimed at addressing victims within the workforce. The result is that in-house programmes have tended to address the symptoms rather than the causes of violence and, in so doing, have been inclined to individualize the problem, instead of engaging with its collective implications and its broader ramifications on industrial relations. Another consequence of this conservative approach has been to effectively draw a clear line of distinction between company insiders, and those members of the community who have no direct access to corporate care programmes. Perhaps this conservative view assumes that violence only affects workplace relations, through direct victimization or when industrial conflict is most extreme, such as in strike situations. I believe this traditional approach ignores the influence of both direct and indirect experiences of violence on workplace relationships, and ultimately constitutes the 'non-management' of the transition process on the part of employers and managers – despite frequent demands and pleas from worker representatives, and victimized communities for business organizations to get involved. The result is that the potential of the workplace as an agency for social change is severely underutilized and the narrowly conceived strategies to insulate industrial relations thus actively undermine the potential for relative peace that the workplace has.

Collective bargaining is conducted in a manner that is disengaged from the problems that exist beyond the immediate precincts of the factory gates, in the homes of employees. It is precisely these matters which are outside of the immediate purview of business that need to be grasped in order to prevent them from inflaming deep-rooted conflict and continuing to make business so difficult to conduct in South Africa. Attempts to insulate business from discovering satisfiers of fundamental human needs are futile because of the encroaching violence. Simpson observed that businesses have attempted to individualise the problem instead of addressing its collective implications. This has resulted in a failure to address the growing socio-pathological conflicts that are afflicting communities across South Africa. A mechanistic mental model has been employed in a futile attempt to insulate business from the reality of change and from being an effective agency for change. By choosing not to engage with the challenge of addressing the fundamental human needs of employees, an extremely volatile and fragile set of communities has developed across South Africa. These slums, squatter camps, townships and ghettos tend to lie beyond the Constitution and the rule of law, in a vigilante 'self-help world' where the law of the jungle applies. This business disengagement from addressing problems beyond the factory floor is creating a default social system that threatens the entire society. There is a basic failure on the part of business to come to grips with the fundamental needs of their employees and also of the trade unions and government to constructively assist in this regard.

When the requirement and expectation to satisfy fundamental human needs is not met during the collective bargaining process (which is indeed a frequent occurrence), the process itself breaks down. These breakdowns should be addressed as a social systems problem so that their interrelated risks can be mitigated to ensure that they are not repeated. The consequential strikes escalate into conflict in other areas, including service delivery conflicts, xenophobic violence and political conflict. Employees regularly and ritualistically risk 'their all' in the pursuit of wage and conditions of service demands that the business is quite obviously not able to afford. Employers, likewise, often do not understand that their employees' demands are not merely material demands, but intangible and symbolic of human dignity as well. Employers and employees engage in collective bargaining, and are guided by their basic differences in understanding as to the meaning and purpose of the process. The employer is guided by the worldview of an orderly constitutional society that is grappling with problems of growth and development. The employees' worldview is of a hostile hand-to-mouth existence where the Constitution is a piece of paper and the law of the jungle prevails.

8.5   The Manner in which Collective Bargaining is Conducted in South Africa

Business and trade unions need to carefully monitor how industrial relations are taught and the presumptions that underpin curriculum design. Are the presumptions of the inevitability and preponderance of conflict of the Labour Relation Act (66) of 1995 themselves generating conflict? The notion that collective bargaining is inevitably conflictive is wrong and there are numerous conspicuous examples of collaborative collective bargaining, including industrial relations in Germany, Holland, Norway, Sweden and Finland that all have high levels of trust and low levels of conflict between the parties. Industrial relations needs to be taught in a manner that explores the bigger picture, including the economic state of the country and the future of employment; negotiation should be taught as a core skill, as should active listening. The negotiation rules of engagement should have a balanced emphasis on co-operation, collaboration and competition, and reject the fixation with conflict. The purpose of negotiation is to create value and wealth for all. This is singularly forgotten when it comes to collective bargaining in South Africa.

The mental models, mythologies and techniques that inform collective bargaining in South Africa need to be challenged to their core. Space needs to be made for the development of new narratives that are congruent with the current world of work. Collective bargaining needs to be conducted with a focus on the bigger picture of the industry and economy. It should move away from the obsession with personal self-interest.

There is a deficit of professional knowledge and skill about how to address normal and deep-rooted conflict among the parties to collective bargaining in South Africa. This knowledge is essential for understanding how normal conflicts might escalate into deep-rooted conflict, and how to de-escalate a deep-rooted conflict into a normal conflict, and convert it into a development process. Unskilled, incompetent and unqualified persons are frequently appointed to engage in the collective bargaining process, with extremely negative human consequences. Different levels of skill, credibility, knowledge, wisdom and experience are required to address deep-rooted conflicts, from the attributes that are appropriate for dealing with normal conflicts. A body of experts who are competent at resolving deep-rooted conflicts needs to be readily available to address these matters, and could possibly form part of a specialised arm of the CCMA. The universities therefore need to redesign the way that industrial relations is taught. This would include, inter alia, negotiation to discover satisfiers of fundamental human needs; collective bargaining and the business model; multimedia and negotiation; the escalation and de-escalation of deep-rooted conflict; collective bargaining and negotiation, as appropriate. An analysis of normal conflict and deep-rooted conflict provides a caution against the pervasive tendency of offering simplistic solutions to intensely complex human problems. Simplistic thinking and mental models have characterised many failed collective bargaining processes in South Africa over the years. Collective bargaining should be addressed with mental models that are congruent with the levels of complexity of the negotiations that it presupposes. There is a deficit of professional knowledge and skill about how to address normal and deep-rooted conflict among the parties to collective bargaining in South Africa.

Collective bargaining is all too frequently conducted as a zero-sum negotiation process. The parties to collective bargaining continue to implement a conflict-ridden negotiation paradigm. Instead of seeking to create trust, the parties have elected to perpetuate conflict. They have rigidly held onto a pre-information age mindset which is inappropriate for the requirements of the current world of work. There has been no attempt by the parties to collective bargaining to discover new, innovative and appropriate modes of negotiating. Perpetual conflict and an archaic Cold War mindset characterise negotiation at the industrial relations interface. What is required is a far more subtle and nuanced negotiation approach that accepts the normative imperative of negotiation rules of engagement, including co-operation, competition, collaboration and conflict, and understands that they need to be flexible in adapting to the changing context. In this regard, the police need to urgently be trained to act effectively in the face of mass protests and strikes. The police do not at present have the training, competence and skill to address the escalation of normal conflict into deep-rooted conflicts or to address mass protests, strikes and crowds.

There are parallel systems of policing and mining in South Africa. The one is formal and legal, and the other is informal, vigilante and illegal. The illegal system of Zama Zama mining exists because of a breakdown in the legal system of mining, and the inability to gain legal sources of employment. Vigilantism exists because of fundamental breakdowns in both policing and the judicial system, which then creates the space for many people to take the law into their own hands. Xenophobic violence, unprotected strikes and illegal loan sharks are all forms of vigilantism.

The micro-lenders, colloquially referred to as loan sharks in South Africa, are an informal and unregulated component of South Africa's banking system. They hold sway over millions of poor South Africans' financial lives and are the arbiters of financial misery. The loan sharks are, in fact, financial vigilantes. It is the responsibility of business, government and the union movement to create a banking system that has a regulatory framework that enables those persons who are presently un-bankable to bank with security.

8.6 Collective Bargaining on Dysfunctional Premises

8.6.1 Centralised Bargaining and the Extension of Agreements to Non-parties

The rationale that is provided for conducting collective bargaining at centralised level and extending these agreements to non-parties is that that it ostensibly enables terms and conditions of employment to be allocated with efficiency to the greatest number of people, for the greater good. In South Africa, collective bargaining is not associated with improvements in productivity and economic growth. The role of bargaining councils is to resolve labour disputes, ensure that agreements on collective bargaining are implemented and to facilitate making labour policies, laws and schemes. Trade unions, through the bargaining council system, have succeeded in raising minimum wages and improving their own working conditions. Centralised collective bargaining, as it is conducted in South Africa, is frequently insensitive to the requirements and reality of each business's unique business model, particularly insofar as SMMEs are concerned. They often have centralised agreements extended to them without their involvement or support. Unsustainable wage and conditions of employment increases have often been imposed upon marginal businesses by decree. This has forced them to confront the choice of either retrenching employees or facing liquidation.

The South African Metals and Engineering Industries Bargaining Council is the largest bargaining council in South Africa. Steyn (2016) reported that the economic slowdown and declining price of steel in global markets together with higher wages and terms and conditions of service negotiated at centralised level had, according to Gerhard Papenfus, the Director of the National Employers Association of South Africa, resulted in 90 000 jobs being lost since 2008. Steyn (2016) cited Papenfus as claiming that: "The bargaining council has set in motion a devastating process of deindustrialization, a huge contributor to unemployment and consequently economic and social instability." The SMME's critique of centralised collective bargaining is therefore that it creates an ever-diminishing vicious circle of fewer and fewer employees being the beneficiaries of the process. The assurance of improved wages and terms and conditions of employment can, in the long term, only be accorded to those persons who are fortunate enough to work in the more powerful companies that are innovative and whose productivity is improving. Their colleagues, who are employed in the fragile SMMEs, will have much less employment security and will be extremely vulnerable to retrenchment. The monopolistic extension of centralised collective bargaining agreements to non-parties should be challenged by redress to the Competitions Act.

The trade unions will always vociferously oppose retrenchments, but once the employee has been retrenched they lose their status as trade union members, and the excruciating problem of their unemployment is soon forgotten. All employers continuously search for alternatives to labour in the form of robotics and other technologies in order to reduce the cost of production. Collective bargaining is not guided by consideration of the unique business models which inform the conduct of each enterprise, whether they be small or large.

The Fourth Industrial Revolution involves the integration of mass production with mass customisation. Mass customisation involves a quantum satisfaction of individual human needs, which was entirely absent from the age of mass production. Mass customisation and the satisfaction of individual business needs are absent from collective bargaining as it is currently conducted. Collective bargaining is conducted in South Africa premised on a fundamental logical flaw. The stakeholders to the collective bargaining process assume the straitjacketed notion that all business models in the same industry and sectors are identical. They presume that the cost of labour, the skills required and the nature of employment are the same for all businesses. This is a wrong and indeed, dangerous presumption, because if collective bargaining is conducted without sensitivity to the requirements of the individual enterprise's business model, the foreseeable consequence is that the business will fail and the workers will be left unemployed. The truth is that the manner in which collective bargaining is conducted at centralised level in South Africa is not clearly predicated on business models that are based on productivity, growth and value creation. The employees therefore learn very little about business during the collective bargaining process as it is not grounded in reality.

8.6.2 Collective Bargaining in the Public Sector

It is questionable whether the government has the will to challenge the material aspirations of the *bureaucratic bourgeoisie* that are presented as wages, salaries and conditions of service demands during the collective bargaining process. The stream of qualified audits that have been levelled against public sector financial malfeasance by the Auditor General's office over the years is an ingrained pattern that shows no signs of abating. There seems to be little concern for a qualified audit. Uneconomic wages, salaries and conditions of employment are an established ritual, and will continue to be granted until such time as those public enterprises enter into economic and financial crisis. It is then that the bubble will burst. Those parastatals that indeed can be subjected to business rescue will probably be rescued by privatisation. Those parastatals that are incapable of undergoing rescue will see mass retrenchments that will be exacerbated by redundancy arising from having skills that are on the wrong side of the Fourth Industrial Revolution. Lobbying and advocacy with the relevant political leadership has proven to be an efficient and effective way of securing wage, salary and conditions of employment for the *bureaucratic bourgeoisie* who are employed in the public sector. Lobbying and advocacy with compliant political leadership has achieved far better terms and conditions of employment than would ever have been possible by collective bargaining. Public sector employees have 'successfully' achieved uneconomic wage and salary settlements over two decades. The settlements that have been reached over the years have regularly defied congruency with sound economics, including the market value of the job, contributions to productivity and service delivery, quality of and scarcity of skills, and principles of wise and frugal budgeting. This annual cost-plus cycle of conferring higher than inflation salary increases for non-service delivery is obviously unsustainable. These public sector entities will in due course be unable to pay their salary bills and this will result in retrenchments and conflict. In this regard, Johnson[199] observed that public sector wages, payments on social grants and interest payments on the remuneration bill have grown to consume 60% of the budget and the situation is becoming very difficult to control.

The uneconomic and inordinately high public sector wages and salaries have an inflationary impact on wages and salaries in the private sector. They systemically fuel unrealistic wage and salary expectations in the private sector, which in turn trigger industrial unrest, strikes and retribution. In the private sector though, the market rapidly punishes any uneconomic activities, but nevertheless the sword of Damocles of high and delusory expectations is ever present and is a disincentive for foreign direct investment in South Africa. Indeed the IMF, the credit rating agencies as well as many private investors have all questioned whether the government really has the political will to stand up to the unrelenting pressures of the *bureaucratic bourgeoisie*. This duty is all the more difficult because the government itself is part of the *bureaucratic bourgeoisie*.

Endnotes

1   Bhorat and Tseng, 2014.
2   De Visser & Powell, 2012.
3   Frey and Osborne, 2013; Schwab & Samans World Economic Report, 2016; Huws & Joyce, 2016; Toohey, Sottos, Lewis, Moore & White, 2007.
4   Max-Neef et al., 1989:26.
5   John Burton, 1989.
6   De Visser & Powell, 2012.
7   Schwab & Samans, 2016.
8   Laborsta Data Base, 2013:1
9   Bell, 2012.
10 Bell, 2012.
11 Du Preez, 2014; Patel, 2013.
12 Gordon, Roberts and Struwig, 2013:1.
13 Gordon et al., 2013:2.
14 Johnson, 2015: 158-159.
15 Osterwalder & Pigneur, 2010.
16 Schwab and Samans, 2016.
17 Congress of South African Trade Unions (COSATU), 2012.
18 Barron, 2016.
19 The International Monetary Fund (IMF), 2013:6.
20 Johnson, 2015.
21 Soko and Balchin, 2014:2.
22 Underhill, 2012.
23 Underhill, 2012.
24 Underhill, 2012.
25 Max-Neef et al., 1989.
26 Max-Neef et al., 1989:26.
27 Max-Neef et al., 1989: 20-21.
28 Max-Neef et al., 1989: 20-21.
29 Max-Neef et al., 1989: 20-21.
30 Max-Neef et al., 1989:20-21.
31 Max-Neef, Hopenhyn, Herrera, Zemelman, Jataba, & Weinstein, 1989.
32 Max-Neef et al., 1989: 20-21.
33 Paulo Freire, 1993:25.
34 Burton, 1987: 3-4.
35 Burton, 1987: 4.
36 Max-Neef et al., 1989.
37 Kraybill, 1990: 52-53.
38 Heald, 2006.
39 Burton, 1987.
40 Kraybill, 1990: 52-53.
41 Max-Neef et al., 1989: 35.
42 Max-Neef et al., 1989:35.
43 Max-Neef et al., 1989.
44 Max-Neef et al., 1989: 32.
45 Argyris, 1990: 92-94.
46 Max-Neef et al., 1987.
47 Horst Rittel and Melvin Webber, 1973.
48 Rittel and Webber, 1973.
49 Rittel & Webber, 1973:161-167.
50 Rittel & Webber, 1977.

51 De Visser & Powell, 2012.
52 Max-Neef et al., 1989.
53 De Visser and Powell, 2012.
54 De Visser and Powell, 2012.
55 Max-Neef et al., 1989.
56 Schwab & Samans, 2016.
57 Frey & Osborne, 2013:44.
58 Frey & Osborne, 2013.
59 Rifkin, 2011.
60 Stiglitz, 1993: 1021.
61 Faku, 2016.
62 Seekings, 2000.
63 Gharejadaghi & Ackoff, 1984:290.
64 Gharejadaghi & Ackoff, 1984:293.
65 Max-Neef et al., 1989:22.
66 Schwab & Samans, 2016.
67 Huws & Joyce, 2016.
68 Schwab & Samans, 2016.
69 Huws & Joyce, 2016.
70 Toohey, Sottos, Lewis, Moore & White, 2007.
71 Toohey, Sottos, Lewis, Moore & White, 2007.
72 Frey & Osborne, 2013.
73 Schwab & Samans, 2016.
74 Frey & Osborne, 2013.
75 Laborsta Data Base, 2013:1.
76 Laborsta Data Base, 2013:1.
77 De Visser & Powell, 2012.
78 Wilderman, 2014:9.
79 Bhorat & Tseng, 2014.
80 Bell, 2012.
81 Bell, 2012.
82 Bell, 2012.
83 Stoddard, 2014.
84 Lindeque, 2015.
85 Lindeque, 2015.
86 Lindeque, 2015.
87 Zille, 2013.
88 Du Preez, 2014.
89 Du Preez, 2014.
90 Patel, 2013.
91 Patel, 2013.
92 Max-Neef et al., 1989 & De Visser and Powell, 2012.
93 Max-Neef et al., 1989:21.
94 Max-Neef et al., 1989:26.
95 Whittles, 2014.
96 Whittles, 2014.
97 Ndzamela, 2013.
98 Vecchiatto, 2012.
99 Vecchiatto, 2012.
100 Musgrave, 2015.
101 Ndaba, 2015.
102 Maphumulo, 2015.
103 Pillay, 2014.

104   Maphumulo, 2015.
105   Pillay, 2014.
106   Meyer, 2015.
107   Evans, 2015.
108   Paton, 2013.
109   Harper & Masondo, 2014.
110   Schwab & Sala-i-Martin, 2016: 327.
111   Nkosi, 2015.
112   Nkosi, 2015.
113   Masondo, 2016.
114   Masondo, 2016.
115   Gordon, Roberts & Struwig, 2013:1.
116   Gordon et al., 2013.
117   Gordon et al., 2013:2.
118   Gordon et al., 2013:2.
119   Mngoma, 2010.
120   Masondo, 2016a.
121   Mantouvalou 2010:3.
122   Kahn, 2016.
123   Kahn, 2016.
124   Ngoepe, Quintal and Wakefield, 2015.
125   Burton, 1987.
126   Montalto, 2015.
127   Hartley, 2015.
128   Hartley, 2015.
129   Hartley, 2015.
130   Sole, McKune and Brummer, 2016.
131   Hartley, 2015.
132   Mkhwanazi, 2016.
133   Mkhwanazi, 2016.
134   Hartley, 2015.
135   Statistics South Africa Statistical Release P0211.4.2, 2015:3.
136   Oosthuizen and Cassim, 2014.
137   Statistics South Africa Statistical Release P0211.4.2, 2015:3.
138   Maswanganyi, 2015.
139   Ferreira, 2015.
140   Fanon, 1961.
141   Swart, 2012.
142   Swart, 2012.
143   Swart, 2012.
144   Mkhize, 2016.
145   Mabotja, 2016.
146   Dludla, 2016.
147   Mabotja, 2016.
148   Mabotja, 2016.
149   Saba and Harper, 2015.
150   Saba and Harper, 2015.
151   Max-Neef et al., 1989.
152   Motale, 2015.
153   Motale, 2015.
154   Zille, 2013.
155   Paton, 2014.
156   Levy, Hirsch & Woolard, 2015: 33-34.

157 Steyn, 2016.
158 Steyn, 2016.
159 Johnson, 2015: 158-160.
160 Johnson, 2015:158.
161 Khuzwayo, 2016.
162 Johnson, 2015:159.
163 Osterwalder & Pigneur, 2010.
164 Osterwalder & Pigneur, 2010.
165 Osterwalder & Pigneur, 2010.
166 Cokayane, 2016.
167 Osterwalder & Pigneur, 2010.
168 Soko and Balchin, 2014:2.
169 Schwab and Samans, 2016.
170 COSATU, 2012.
171 COSATU Today, 2012.
172 De Lange, 2012.
173 Papenfus, 2012.
174 Papenfus, 2012.
175 Benjamin, Bhorat & van der Westhuizen, 2010.
176 Papenfus, 2012.
177 Bhorat & van der Westhuizen, 2012.
178 Barron, 2016.
179 IMF, 2013: 6.
180 Johnson, 2015:114-115.
181 Steyn, 2014.
182 Johnson, 2015:114-115.
183 Johnson, 2015.
184 Johnson, 2015:176.
185 Paton, 2016.
186 Johnson, 2015.
187 Paton, 2016.
188 IMF, 2013:6.
189 Johnson, 2015: 106.
190 Johnson, 2015:107.
191 Johnson, 2015: 107-108.
192 Johnson, 2015:176.
193 Johnson, 2015:176.
194 Khuzwayo, 2016.
195 Schwab & Samans, 2016.
196 Max-Neef et al., 1989.
197 Osterwalder & Pigneur, 2010.
198 Simpson, 1994:2.
199 Johnson, 2015: 23-125.

References

Argyris, C., 1990, *Overcoming Organizational Defences*, Prentice–Hall Inc, Upper Saddle River.

Barron, C., 2016, 'Diplomacy so Quiet if Often Seems Inaudible', *Business Times*, 24 January 2016.

Barron, C., 2016, 'Layoffs and New Law are Perfect Storm for the CCMA', 20 March 2016.

Bell, T., Brown, A., Feinstein, A., Steinberg, J. & Tesfay, N., 2012, *The Marikana Massacre*: Conference Chaired by Richard Dowden, Director of the Royal Africa Club, streamed at The Frontline Club in London, England.

Benjamin, P., Bhorat, H., & van der Westhuizen, C., 2010, *Regulatory Impact Assessment of Selected Provisions of the: Labour Relations Amendment Bill 2010, Basic Conditions of Employment Amendment Bill 2010, Employment Equity Bill 2010, Employment Services Bill 2010*, Prepared for the Department of Labour and the Presidency, Development Policy Research Unit, University of Cape Town, 9 September 2010.

Bevan, S., 2007, 'Power Line Theft Leaves South Africa in the Dark', *The Telegraph*. [Online]. Available: http://www.telegraph.co.uk/news/worldnews/1555530/power-line-theft-leaves-south-africa-in-the-dark [Accessed 20 June 2016].

Bhorat, H., & Tseng, D., 2014, South Africa's Strike Data Revisited, *Brookings, Africa in focus*, 2 April 2014.

Brookings. Africa in focus. [Online]. Available: http://www.brookings.edu/blogs/africa-in-focus/posts [Accessed 20 June 2016].

Brookings. Africa in focus. [Online]. Available: http://www.brookings.edu/blogs/africa-in-focus/posts/2014/08/15-unemployment-south-africa-oosthuizen [Accessed 20 June 2016].

Burton, J., 1987, *Resolving Deep-Rooted Conflict*, University Press of America, New York.

CNN, 2015, 'South Africa's Zama Zamas: Is this the World's Worst Job?' [Online]. Available: http://www.edition.cnn.com/2015/08/Africa/south-africa-illegal-mining [Accessed 20 June 2016].

Cokayne, R., 2016, 'NUMSA Driving Automotive Industry Towards Tough Talks', *The Star*, 20 June 2016.

Congress of South African Trade Unions, 2012, *Concept Paper: Towards New Collective Bargaining, Wage and Social Protection Strategies*: Input to COSATU's Central Executive Committee, 28 May 2012, COSATU House, Johannesburg. COSATU, 2013, *Draft for Discussion Summary of Critique of the National Development Plan, March 2013* – (This is not an official View of COSATU), COSATU House, Johannesburg, South Africa.

Cox, A., & Chernick, I., 2015, '12 Hours of Mayhem', 9 September 2015, *The Star*, Johannesburg, South Africa.

Davis, R., 2015, 'The Debt-Hole that Fuelled the Fire', *Daily Maverick*, 3 September 2015. [Online]. Available: http.www.dailymaverick.co.za/article/2012-10-12-marikana [Accessed 20 June 2016].

De Lange, D., 2012, 'Labour Law Changes will Destroy Jobs', *Independent Newspapers*, 25 July 2012.

De Visser, J., & Powell, D., 2012, *Service Delivery Protest Barometer 2007-2012*, Cape Town, Multi-Level Government Initiative, Community Law Centre: Charles Stewart Mott Foundation, the National Research Foundation and the Ford Foundation.

Dludla, S., 2016, 'Pikitup Strike Far From Over', *Independent Newspapers*, Johannesburg, 23 March 2016.

du Preez, M. 2014, 'Our Protest Culture is Far from Dead', *Pretoria News*, Pretoria, 11 February 2014.

Durr v ABSA Bank Ltd and Another [1997] 3 All SA 1 (A).

Economic Freedom Fighters v Speaker of the National Assembly and Others; Democratic Alliance v Speaker of the National Assembly and Others [2016] ZACC, Cases CCT 143/15 and CCT 171/15 decided on in Constitutional Court of South Africa on 31 March 2016.

Ekines, P., & Max-Neef, M., 1992, *Real Life Economics*, Routledge, London.

Ensor, L., 2016, 'SARS Leaks Test Gordhan's Authority', *Business Day,* Johannesburg, 25 January 2016.

Evans, S., 2015, 'Public Sector Unions on Carousel', *Mail & Guardian,* 4 September 2015.

Expanded version is available at www.max-neef.cl/download/Max-neef_Human_scale_development.pdf.

Faku, D., 2016, 'New Labour Federation Good for Country Maintain Experts', *The Star Business Report,* 13 April 2016.

Fanon, F., 1961, *The Wretched of the Earth – A Negro Psychoanalyst's Study of the Problems of Racism and Colonialism in the World Today,* Grove Press, New York.

Ferreira, L., 2015, 'Factsheet: Social Grants in South Africa – Separating Myth from Reality', *Africa Check.*

Freire, P., 1993, *Pedagogy of the Oppressed,* Penguin Books, Strand, London.

Frey, C., & Osborne, M., 2013, *The Future of Employment: How Susceptible are Jobs to Computerization?* Oxford Martin School, Programme on the Impacts of Future Technology, University of Oxford, Oxford, United Kingdom.

Gharajedaghi, J., & Ackoff, R., 1984, 'Mechanisms, Organisms and Social Systems', *Strategic Management Journal,* 5, 289-300.

Gharajedaghi, J., 1999, *Systems Thinking, Managing Chaos and Complexity,* Butterworth Heinemann, Boston.

Gordon, S., Roberts, B., & Struwig, J., 2013, 'The State of the Union? Attitudes to South African Trade Unions', In *South African Social Attitudes Survey (SASAS),* Human Sciences Research Council, Pretoria.

Haefele, B., 2004, 'Vigilantism in the Western Cape', Department of Community Safety, Provincial Government of the Western Cape.

Hamel, G., & Breen, B., 2007, *The Future of Management,* Harvard Business School Press, Boston, Mass.

Harper, P., & Masondo, S., 2014 'How SADTU Sells Posts', *City Press,* 27 April 2014.

Harper, P., 2015, 'Cows for Jobs Scandal: SADTU wants City Press Boycott After Exposé, *City Press,* 19 May 2015.

Hartley, R., 2015, 'How Nelson Mandela's Brave New Country Became an Anti-Youth Machine', *Sunday Times,* 25 October 2015.

Heald, G., 2006. *Learning Amongst Enemies – A Phenomenological Study of South African Constitutional Negotiations from 1985-1998,* A Doctor of Philosophy Thesis Submitted to the University of the Witwatersrand, Johannesburg, South Africa.

Huws, U., & Joyce, S., 2016, 'Size of the UK's "Gig" Economy Revealed for the First Time', *Crowd Working Survey,* University of Hertfordshire, Foundation for European Progressive Studies and Europa Global Union, February 2016.

International Monetary Fund, 2013, International Monetary Fund Staff Report for South Africa, Article IV, Consultation Debt Sustainability Analysis.

IRIN Humanitarian News and Analysis, 2015, 'Lesotho: Illegal Migrant Miners Risk Lives for Riches', 2 September 2015.

IRIN, 2012, 'Illegal migrant miners risk lives for riches', 16 July 2012. [Online]. Available: http://www.irinnews.org/report/95875/lesotho-illegal-migrant-miners-risk-lives-riches [Accessed 20 June 2016].

Jansen, L., Villette, F., & Fredericks, I., 2015, 'Unions Muscle in on ANAs: Pupil Assessment Put Off Till Next Year', *The Star,* Johannesburg, 14 September 2015.

Johnson, L., 2011, 'What if the Secret of Success is Failure?' *Financial Times,* 21 September 2011.

Johnson, R.W., 2015, *How Long Will South Africa Survive? The Looming Crisis,* Jonathan Ball Publishers, Johannesburg & Cape Town.

Kahn, M., 2016, 'Union Capture: Would the Real Elephant in the Room Blink', *Daily Maverick,* 31 May 2016.

Kapp, L., 2013, *The Responses of Trade Unions to the Effects of Neoliberalism in South Africa: The Case of COSATU and its Affiliated Trade Unions,* Submitted in Accordance with the Requirements for the Degree of Master of Arts in the Subject of Sociology at the University of South Africa, Pretoria.

Khan, N., & Bernickow, R., 2013, 'Scars Remain in Aftermath of Farm Workers' Strike', *Business Day,* 5 March 2013.

Khuzwayo, W., (2016), 'GDP Revised Down Amid Jobs Alert – South Africa Still Missing from Top 25 Nations', *FDI Confidence Index Business Report,* 24 May 2016.

Kraybill, J., 1990, 'Negotiating Deep-Rooted Conflicts', *Industrial Relations Journal of South Africa,* 10(3).

Laborsta, 2013, *Labour Statistics Data Base,* International Labour Office Geneva, Switzerland.

Levy, B., Hirsch, A., & Woolard, I., 2015, *Governance and Inequality: Benchmarking and Interpreting South Africa's Evolving Political Settlement: Effective States and Inclusive Development,* Research Centre (ESID) School of Environment and Development, The University of Manchester.

Lindeque, M., 2015, 'Mine Retrenchments a Deliberate Attack on ANC-led Government' *Eyewitness News,* Johannesburg 28 September 2015. http://co.za/2015/09/28/Mine-retrenchments-deliberate-attack-on-aNC-led-government.

Mabotja, K., 2016, 'Pikitup Workers Deserve Decent Pay', *Independent Newspapers,* Johannesburg, 16 March.

Magwanganyi, N., 2015, 'Youth Unemployment has Worsened Since 2008: Stats SA Report Shows', *Business Day,* 29 June.

Mahlakoana, T., 2015, 'Union Cries Foul Over its Investments – Alleges Bribery and a Refusal to Release the Money', *The Star,* Johannesburg, 17 October.

Mantouvalou, V., 2010, 'Is There a Human Right Not to Be a Trade Union Member? Labour Rights Under the European Convention on Human Rights', London School of Economics, Working Papers. Paper is forthcoming in the book *Human Rights and Perspectives on the Law and Regulation,* Novitz, T., & Fenwick C., (eds), Onati International Series on Law and Society (Oxford: Hart, 2010).

Maphumulo, S., 2015, 'SAMWU Officials Held Over Missing R178M', *The Sunday Independent,* 18 October.

Masondo, S., 2016 (a) 'Motshekga is Colluding with Right Wingers' to Destroy Us – SADTU', *City Press,* 17 February 2016.

Masondo, S., 2016, 'Break SADTU's Power', *City Press,* 15 May 2015.

Max-Neef, M, 1992, Development and Human Needs in Ekins, Paul & Max-Neef, Manfred (ed) *Understanding Wealth Creation,* Routledge, London:197-213.

Max-Neef, M, Elizalde, A., Hopenhyn, M., 1989, 'Human Scale Development: An Option for the Future', *Development Dialogue,* 1.

Mitroff, I., 1983, *Stakeholders of the Organizational Mind,* Jossey–Bass Management Series, San Francisco.

Mkhize, V., 2016, 'Rubbish Plagues Johannesburg Streets as Pikitup Strike Continues', *Eyewitness News,* Johannesburg, 23 March.

Mkhwanazi 2016, 'Top Auditing Firm Dumps the Guptas', *Saturday Star,* 2 April.

Mngoma, S., 2010 'Aggressive Pickets Drive Teachers from Schools', *News 24, The Witness,* 19 August 2010.

Montalto, P. A., 2015, '#FeesMustFall Protest Must be Closely Watched', *The Star Business Report,* 23 October.

Motale, P., 2015, 'Illegal Gold Rush Turns Deadly', *Independent Online Business Report* 28 June. [Online]. Available: http://www.iol.co.za/business/news/illegal-gold-rush-turns-deadly [Accessed 20 June 2016].

Musgrave, A., 2015, 'COSATU Edgy as SACCAWU Misses Deadline', *The Star,* 10 March.

Ndaba, B., 2015, 'Struggling SACCAWU Apologises for Failing to Pay Salaries on Time', *Sunday Independent,* 4 October.

Ndzamela, P., 2013, 'PIC Given Money Misappropriated from Trade Union's Retirement Fund', 13 May.

Ngoepe, K., Quintal, G., & Wakefield, A., 2015, 'Violence Mars Union Building Protests', *Times Live*, 23 October.

Nkosi, B., 2015, 'SADTU Boycott National Assessment of Schools', 2 September 2015.

Oosthuizen, M., & Cassim, A., 2014, 'The State of Youth Unemployment in South Africa', *Brooking Africa Growth Initiative* based at the University of Cape Town's Development Policy Research Institute, 15 August 2014.

Osterwalder, A., & Pigneur, Y., 2010, *Business Model Generation*, John Wiley & Sons, New York.

Papenfus, G., 2012, *A Fine Line to Maintain with Regard to Labour Brokers*, National Employers Association of South Africa [Online]. Available: http://www.driversinc.co.za/index.php/latest-news/11-interesting-articles-regarding-labour-brokers.html [Accessed 20 June 2-16].

Patel, K., 2013, 'Public Protests: Gauteng's Pressure Cooker', *Daily Maverick*, Johannesburg, 16 May.

Paton, C. 2013, 'SA workers "losing faith" in strife-torn trade unions'. *Business Day Live*. [Online]. Available: http://www.bdlive.co.za/national/labour/2013/04/09/sa-workers-losing-faith-in-strife-torn-trade-unions [Accessed 20 June 2016].

Paton, C., 2013, 'South African Workers "Losing Faith" in Strife-Torn Trade Unions', *Business Day*, 9 April.

Paton, C., 2014, 'Effective Action can be Taken to Reduce Long, Violent Strikes', *Business Day*, 13 February.

Paton, C., 2016, 'Gordhan's Medicine Will Not Go Down Well', *Sunday Times*, 21 February.

Phaliso, S., 2015, 'The Business of Illegal Electricity', *Independent On-Line News*, 28 May. [Online]. Available: http://www.iol.co.za/news/south-africa/western-cape/the-business-of-illegal-electricity [Accessed 20 June 2-16].

Pillay, V., 2014, 'Top Man's World Cup Junket', *Mail and Guardian*, 18 July.

Pourdehnad, J., & Bharathy, G. 2004, 'Systems Thinking and its Implications on Organizational Transformation'. In the *Proceedings for the Third Annual Conference on Systems Thinking in Management*, May 2004, University of Pennsylvania, Philadelphia.

Rampedi, P., & Wa Afrika, M., 2016, 'Tax Boss Moves to Block Pravin', *Sunday Times*, 24 January.

Report of the Ministerial Task Team Appointed by Minister Angie Motshekga to investigate the Selling of Posts of Educators by Members of Teachers Unions and Departmental Officials in Provincial Education Departments, 2016.

Report of the Special Reference Group on Migration and Community Integration in KwaZulu-Natal, 2015, commissioned by the Provincial Government of KwaZulu-Natal, chaired by Judge Navi Pillay, Durban, 31 October 2015.

Rifkin, J., 2011, *The Third Industrial Revolution*, Palgrave MacMillan, London.

Rittel, H., & Webber, M., 1973, Dilemmas in a General Theory of Planning, *Policy Sciences* 4, 155-169.

Rutledge, C. 2015. 'Mining communities are ready to explode, say activists', 1 July 2015. [Online]. Available: http://www.groundup.org.za/article/mining-communities-are-ready-to-explode-say-activists_3083/ [Accessed 20 June 2016].

Rutledge, C., 2015, *Mining Communities are Ready to Explode say Activists*.

Saba, A., Harper, P., 2015, 'Xenophobic Violence: Where did it Begin?' *City Press*, Johannesburg, 19 April.

Schwab, K., & Sala-i-Martin., 2016, 'The Global Competitiveness Report 2015-2016', World Economic Forum, Geneva, Switzerland.

Schwab, K., & Samans, R., 2016, 'The Future of Jobs Employment, Skills and Workforce Strategy for the Fourth Industrial Revolution', January 2016, http:www.WEF_Future_of_Jobs

Schwab, K., 2016, 'The Fourth Industrial Revolution What it Means and How to Respond', 16 January. [Online]. Available: http://www.weforum.org/agenda/2016/01/the-fourth-industrial-revolution-what-it-means-and-how-to-respond [Accessed 20 June 2016.]

Scientific American Editorial Review, 2014, 'Will Automation Take our Jobs?' *Scientific American*, 311(2), The Science Agenda, http://www.scientificamerican.com/article/will-automation-take-our-jobs.

Seekings, J., 2000, *The UDF: A History of the United Democratic Front in South Africa 1983-1991*, David Philip Publishers, Cape Town.

Simpson, G., 1994, 'Violence and Industrial Relations', *Employment Law*, 10 (3).

Soko, M., & Balchin, N., 2014, 'Breaking the Deadlock: Tackling the South African Labour Market Crisis', *GSB Review* 2 (Summer).

Sole, S., McKune, C., & Brummer, S., 2016, 'The "Gupta-Owned" State Enterprises', *Mail & Guardian* March 24 to 31.

South Africa's Democratic Teachers' Union (SADTU) v Minister of Education and Others (J5396/00) [2001] ZALC 144 (12 September 2001).

Statistics South Africa Statistical Release P0211.4.2 (2015) 'National and Provincial Labour Market Youth Quarter 1 2008 – Quarter 1 2015', The Department, Pretoria.

Steyn, L., 2014, 'The Downward Spiral of South African Trade Unions', *Mail & Guardian*, 14 November 2014.

Steyn, L., 2016, 'Bargaining council elicits no sympathy', *Mail & Guardian Business*, April 22-28.

Stiglitz, J., 1993, *Economics*, WW Norton & Company, New York.

Stoddard, E., 2014, 'South Africa Miners Return to Work after Longest Platinum Strike', *Reuters*, Johannesburg, 25 June. [Online]. Available: http://www.reuters.com.com/article/2014/06/25/u-safrica-mining [Accessed 20 June 2016].

Tau, S., 2015, 'Country Burning Protests a Ticking Time-Bomb – Expert', *The Citizen*, 21 October.

The University of Stellenbosch Legal Aid Clinic; Vusumzi George Xekthwana; Monia Lydia Adams; Angeline Arrison; Lisinda Dorell Bailey; Fundiswa Virginia Bikitsha; Merle Bruintjies; Johannes Petrus de Klerk; Shirley Fortuin; Jeffrey Haarhoof; Johannes Hendricks; Doreen Elaine Jonker; Bulelani Mahlomakhulu; Siphokazi Siwayi; Ntombozuko Toneyal; Dawid van Wyk v The Minister of Justice and Correctional Services; The Minister of Trade and Industry; The National Credit Regulator; Mavava Trading 279; Onecor (Pty) Ltd; Amplisol (Pty) Ltd; Triple Advanced Investments 40; Bridge Debt; Las Manos Investments; Polkadots Properties 172; Money Box Investments 232; Maravedi Credit Solutions (Pty) Ltd; Icom (Pty) Ltd; Villa de Roses; Money Box Investments 251; Triple Advanced Investments 99; Flemix & Associated Incorporated Attorneys; Association of Debt Recovery Agents and South African Human Rights Commission: In the High Court of South Africa (Western Cape Division Cape Town): Case no: 16703/14: Wednesday 8 July 2015: Judge Desai.

Thompson, R., 2014, 'Zama Zama, 'Illegal' Artisanal Miners, Misrepresented by the South African Press and Government', *The Extractive Industry and Society*, 1(2), 127-129.

Toohey, K., Sottos, N., Lewis, J., Moore, J., White, S., 2007, 'Self-healing Materials with Microvascular Networks', *Nature Material*, 6.

Underhill, G., 2012, 'Wine Workers Enjoying the Fruits of their Labour', *Mail & Guardian*, 7 December.

van Driel, M., 2008, *A Sociological Analysis of Social Grants in Post-Apartheid South Africa: A Case Study of Bophelong Township, Johannesburg*; Department of Sociology, University of the Witwatersrand Johannesburg.

Vecchiatto, P., 2012, 'DA Targets Ebrahim Patel Over Canyon Springs Scandal', *Mail & Guardian*, 24 January.

Webster, E., 2015, 'Labour Cracks', A University of the Witwatersrand Foundation Essay, 22 September.

Whittles, G., 2014, *Eyewitness News*, 11 November.

Wilderman, J., 2014, *Farm Worker Uprising in the Western Cape A Case of Protest, Organising and Collective Action*. Submitted as a Master of Arts Degree in Labour, Policy, and Globalization at the University of the Witwatersrand, Johannesburg, South Africa.

Zille, H., 2013, 'Real Story Behind Farm Strikes', *Cape Times*, 19 March.

Index

A

absence, 12–13, 17, 27, 68, 93, 124, 132–135
  derelict, 17
  fundamental, 51
absorption, 65, 84, 88
absorption rate, 89
  low, 90
abuse, 4–5, 59, 74, 117
  unchecked, 86
accorded professional status, 74
accountability, 86
  adopted, 86
acquiescent business community, 85
action
  administrative, 97
  non-representative, 31
acts, 16–17, 57, 60, 62, 65, 74, 77, 79, 83,
    85–86, 93, 96, 101–103, 105, 120
adaptability, 9–10
addiction, 12
  drug, 87
address mass protests, 139
address wages, 127
ad hoc negotiation forum, 13
administrative personnel, 121
administrative positions, 29
adult employment rates, 88
Adult Unemployment Rates, 88
advisers, 79, 87
  financial, 57–58, 61–62
  pension fund, 58
  trusted, 59
advocacy, 16, 141–142
affection, 7, 9, 16, 19–20, 25–26, 39, 56, 84,
    91
affiliations, 70
  political party, 80
African National Congress (ANC), 3, 34–35,
    50–51, 66, 72, 81, 96, 110, 123
  caucus leader, 51
  councillors, 50
  parliamentarian, 86
  relationship, 66
  stratagem, 51
  strategy, 51
African Union, 102
African Union Summit, 102
Afrikaans universities, 79
agreements, 1–2, 5, 70, 109, 112–113, 119,
    140
  bargaining council, 115

centralised, 109–110, 114–115, 140
  centralised bargaining, 3
  collective, 70, 74
  industry-wide bargaining, 110
  tacit monopoly, 115
agricultural community, 4
agricultural kibbutz, 6
agriculture, 41, 116
alcoholism, 5, 11
  pathological, 4
algorithms, 40
  complex, 30
  incorporating, 30
alienation, 22, 26, 34, 52, 84, 127, 135
allegations, 63–64, 66, 68, 86–87, 94
Allied Workers Union, 61
Amalgamated Mineworkers and
    Construction Union, 34
amendments, 116–118, 133
  labour law, 3
analysis
  content, 24, 57, 61
  qualitative, 48
analytical problem solving, 119
ANC Government, 62, 96, 106
  post-apartheid, 35
anger, 16, 26, 91
  collective, 127
AngloGold Ashanti, 94
Annual National Assessments, 66–67
Annual National Assessments on school
    readiness for children, 62
anti-social behaviour, 93
apartheid, 1, 6, 17, 27, 32, 35, 52, 118, 133
  defined, 100
  downfall of, 13, 32, 52
apartheid apparatchiks, 73
apartheid economy, 134
apartheid era, 86
apartheid government, 52
apartheid labour market, 133
applications, 32, 86, 94, 132
  advanced digital, 113
  innovative electronic, 43
apprenticeships, 6, 9, 116, 130
approach
  aggressive, 69
  conservative, 136
  constructive, 136
  differentiated conflict intervention, 48

union protectionism, 90
unions, 12, 40, 57–58, 60–62, 64, 66, 68–70, 72, 85, 93–96
  adversarial trade, 71
  affiliated, 60
  affiliated trade, 62
  basic trade, 68
  digital freelance, 41
  large public sector trade, 63
  largest, 124
  largest affiliated trade, 35
  middle-class trade, 73
  new trade, 61
  occupational, 68
  powerful trade, 110
  public sector trade, 63, 123
  registered trade, 60
  second trade, 61
  supported trade, 67
  traditional, 31
  trusted trade, 67
union security arrangements, 74
United Democratic Front (UDF), 35
United Front, 34–35
  putative, 35
universities, 9, 32, 78–80, 82, 89, 132, 138
  best, 82
  traditional South African, 82
university authorities, 76
university courses, 82
university hungry, 75
University of Cape Town, 5, 76, 79
University of Fort Hare, 76
University of Johannesburg, 76
University of KwaZulu-Natal, 76
University of Limpopo, 76
University of Pretoria, 76
University of Stellenbosch Legal Aid Clinic, 104–105
University of Stellenbosch's Legal Aid Clinic, 104
University of Western Cape, 76
University Student Protests, 57, 75
unprecedented levels, 135
unprecedented period, 110
unprotected strikes, 20, 57, 94–98, 107, 139
unrealistic expectations, 12
unrealistic expectations of collective bargaining, 12
unregulated component, 105, 139
unrelenting pressures, 126, 142
unresolved challenges, 100
unrest, 45, 135
  civil, 91, 106

  industrial, 27, 48, 55, 142
unrest incidents, 50
unscholarly admission, extraordinary, 69
unsustainable dependency, 113
unsustainable wage and conditions of employment, 109, 140
updated labour market regulation, 41
up-skilling, 88, 129

V

value creation, 141
value proposition, 111–112, 134
vandalism, 77–78, 81, 93, 102, 135
Variance of South Africa's Wage, 125
verbal interchange, 31
vested interest, 104
vicarious liability, 62
viciousness, 91
victimhood, 69, 124
victimization, direct, 136
victim role, exploited, 73
vigilante action, 22, 53, 57, 94–95, 97, 107, 135
vigilante activity, 96–97
vigilantes, 20, 97, 137, 139
  financial, 139
vigilante strike, 96
vigilante violence, 98
vigilantism, 97–98, 101, 105, 139
  economic, 98
violators, 18–20
violence, 4, 14, 17, 26, 42, 68–70, 77, 79, 81, 83, 92–93, 97–99, 101, 108, 135–136
violent, 18, 53, 78–79, 83, 102
violent attacks, 99
violent crime, 87
violent death, 100
violent picketing, 74
violent service delivery conflicts, 121
violent strikes, 106
violent threats, 61
violent uprising, 17
virtual crowd, 31, 81
  influential, 31
virtual teams, 41
visions, 56, 73, 136
  constitutional, 86
voters, 66
  alienate, 50
votes, 38, 72, 97, 125
  generational, 80

[Created with **TExtract** / www.Texyz.com]

www.ingramcontent.com/pod-product-compliance
Lightning Source LLC
Chambersburg PA
CBHW070913270326
41927CB00011B/2551